Southern Sin

True Stories of the Sultry South
and Women Behaving Badly

Edited by **Lee Gutkind & Beth Ann Fennelly**

Introduction by **Dorothy Allison**

InFACT
BOOKS
Pittsburgh

Requests for permission to reproduce material from this work should be sent to:
  Rights and Permissions
  In Fact Books
  c/o Creative Nonfiction Foundation
  5501 Walnut Street, Suite 202
  Pittsburgh, PA 15232

Cover design by Heidi Whitcomb
Text design by Tristen Jackman

ISBN: 978-1-937163-10-5

Printed in the United States of America

Table of Contents

Introduction   6
Sin
DOROTHY ALLISON

Editor's Note   10
Running from the Lord
BETH ANN FENNELLY

Editor's Note   14
Unforgettable True Stories about Bad
(and Sometimes Bizarre) Behavior
LEE GUTKIND

Acknowledgements   18

_____

What Was Left   20
MOLLY LANGMUIR

White Noise   28
SARAH CHESHIRE

The Renters   36
CHELSEA RATHBURN

Circles of Light   48
SHEILA RAESCHILD

Love in the Worst Way   56
AARON GWYN

Fat   68
SARAH EINSTEIN

Mad Love: The Ballad of Fred & Allie   80
SONJA LIVINGSTON

No Other Gods   94
SARAH GILBERT

In-Training   102
ELLEN HAGAN

The On-Ramp   108
AMY THIGPEN

Out of the Woods   118
GAIL GRIFFIN

Rum-Running Queen   130
LOUELLA BRYANT

Sportfucking in the South   140
SUZANNE ROBERTS

A Lesson in Merging   148
RACHAEL PECKHAM

Tongues, Lust, and a Man from Indiana   160
ADRIANA PARAMO

Trouble   172
ELYSE MOODY

Matinee   180
MENDY KNOTT

Do I?   190
C. W. KELLY

Nude Study   200
RIVER JORDAN

A Country Where You Once Lived   208
SHERYL ST. GERMAIN

Porn Star   220
ELANE JOHNSON

The Search for the Perfect Sidecar   224
KENDRA HAMILTON

Rahab's Thread   238
KATIE BURGESS

About the Contributors   248

Credits   254

Sin

Dorothy Allison

When I was a girl one of the many games my cousins and I played was one I called "worthless sinner." The competition centered on who among us was the biggest, and therefore most worthless, sinner.

"I stole change out of Mama's pocket book."

"I drank off half the whiskey in the bottle Uncle Jack keeps in that paper bag in his glove compartment."

"I trampled Aunt Dot's tomato plants!"

"I watched cousin Bobbie having sex with her boyfriend on the couch in the middle of the night!"

"I let Billie play with my nipples until he wet himself!"

I suppose the thing was a variation on "poor-mouthing"—competing with statements like "we're so poor, we can't afford insoles: we go 'round with our feet in the dirt, but they're so black they look like the bottoms of shoes."

Who was poorest, who was baddest, who was going to hell without even a glimpse of the pearly gates? Who, after all, was the most damned?

Oh, my cousins and I were pretty sure we were all going to hell. Sanctity was beyond us; sin altogether too tempting—the taste of liquor, the smell of sweat on flushed skin, the giddy exhilaration of shouting "Goddamn!" loud enough for the deacons to hear.

We were Baptists after all, hardshell and stubborn. We knew everybody sinned and fell short of the demands of God. But our religion contributed to our thinking ourselves oddly special. Did Yankees think like that? Did Catholics or Jews?

The preacher shouted our names and raised his Bible in the air to denounce our falling away from righteousness, our mealy-mouthed, warm-spit indulgence in the acts we had been told would darken our souls and lead us up Satan's dirt road. Dancing, we had been told, was a stratagem of the Devil; rock & roll, the gateway to perdition. But oh, it felt so good to stomp and spin and break a sweat in time to a drumbeat or a steel-string guitar. We rocked on our heels and grinned at each other, teeth gleaming with Sugar-Daddy spit and arrogant ambition. Oh yes, we were going to hell, but hell looked to be a party.

Oh Sin! Oh, the possibilities! If things you might enjoy or things that might make you laugh out loud were all equally outlawed, then what were you to do when the blood pumping through your veins sang wild enough to make you want to jump and shout? You can't save all that up for Sunday morning. Sometimes it just has to come out. And then where are you? On your knees at the front of the church with your daddy's hand heavy on your shoulder and your mother's tears watering the hymnal she is waving in your direction.

There was a kind of glory in that—to feel oneself Jerry Lee Lewis outrageous. To have the whole community look at you with a gimlet eye and a flat, angry mouth.

"You're going right to hell."

"Uh huh, I probably am."

We were ashamed of ourselves, but not too much so. Behind the shame was pride. Look what a stone-cold sinner I am, or was, or still am. Was that honesty, or bombast?

And we were conditioned to admit our sins, to stand up and witness our worst and most humiliating deeds. To look at our neighbors and see them looking back. There was something about acknowledging one's sins, saying, "I swear I'll not do that again" or perversely, "Yes, I will, but I won't call it sin."

In the modern world, sin has less resonance. A good therapist can trigger insights that tell you why you sneak into people's bedrooms and go through their dresser drawers. If it's a neurosis or an obsession, maybe it's not a sin at all. Maybe with the right medication or mantra, you might achieve a new, non-sinful present. It could be possible— redemption accomplished by self-examination and exorcism.

———•·•———

And stories? Stories allow for the most profound exploration of sin: how we come to it, justify it, revel in it, or mourn our abandonment to its implications. You can have your sin and your righteousness. Testify. Preach. Say what happened, or might have happened, or should have happened.

Did I tell you how I got this scar on my left calf? It's a sin what I can't bring myself to say, though with a little encouragement, maybe I will. Maybe.

The most dangerous stories are the true ones, the ones we hesitate to tell, the adventures laden with fear or shame or the relentless pull of regret. Some of those are about things that we are secretly deeply proud to have done.

"Yes, I put sugar in her gas tank! Do you know what she did to me?"

"Yes, I set fire to their garden shed!"

"Yes, I slept with her. I slept with her every time I could, and when she let me, I took pictures of her lying there post-orgasmic, limp, and sweaty."

We tell the story and we wait for the frisson that follows on our audience's open-mouthed awe. We recount acts of self-exaltation or indulgence for which we must invent a justification. We say, "This is what I did. Oh god forgive me, this is what I did." Then we sweat or grin or stare back fiercely at the audience.

It's all story.

———•·•———

So what is specifically Southern about sin? Do we do it better, with greater abandon? What crime of region or language marks us unique and original? What can we tell that has not been rendered passive by psychologists or social analysts?

That, you will have to judge from the stories you will find here. I have to say, for a Southern anthology, this one is a little light on Gluttony. But all the other biblical reference points are applied. Wrath in its many incarnations sticks out its knotty fists. Lust looms—not just desire, but longing that redefines what the soul reaches for most wildly, carnal pleasure taken without regard to custom or law. And there is Pride, that sense of superiority in the midst of a conviction of one's pitiful nature. What St. Augustine called "the love of one's own excellence" is definitely a Southern affectation. You'll find it here whenever the voices turn sly. Then there is Vanity, which is never as confident as it pretends, not in the really interesting characters. War has been characterized as the offspring of Pride and Greed—the war between the sexes, the classes, the regions. There's plenty of that here.

Finally there is Envy and Sloth. Envy loves a good story, the story of how that one got what we should have had. But Sloth follows right behind and is too lazy to say how it all happened. Envy is pain at the good fortune of others, Aristotle is supposed to have said. Sloth comes along and pretends to no such impulse, but truly all Sloth has to boast about is never acting on Envy or Rage or Lust or much of anything. Not much Sloth here.

This is the thing.

Sin smells. Sin smells of sex and sweat and the tang of fruit buried too long in the ground—peaches or muscadines, winey and sharp, drawing flies or yellow jackets. Sin sings. Sin sings like a blues harp or a slide guitar, the notes sharp enough to make your ears burn. Sin dances. Sin dances words across the page, telling all those lies that sound like truths, and disguising terrible truths in a language we want desperately to believe.

Take a deep breath and see if you don't know what I am talking about.

Running from the Lord

Beth Ann Fennelly

I f you'd told me twenty years ago that I'd be co-editing an anthology of essays about Southern sin, I'd have called you a liar. First, I wasn't a Southerner—twenty years ago, I was a twenty-one-year-old from the suburbs of Chicago. And second, I wasn't a sinner; I was an English major at the University of Notre Dame, a timid honors student, a virgin, a devout Catholic.

Then I turned twenty-two. Dumped my boyfriend, went abroad, cut off my waist-length locks, left the church, got a lizard tattooed on my lower back, showed it off. Some—maybe most—of this behavior was silly. Now I look back on that girl with bemused chagrin. But that silly badness was also a necessary rupturing of boundaries that allowed me to explore who I could be, who—if I really had the courage to figure it out—I was already, somewhere inside.

One of the problems with American female coming-of-age stories is that we have no model in which maturity appears an asset. How rarely we see a movie portraying a woman who is 50, single, and successful. Or a woman who goes "bad"—whether that means leaving her culture, religion, husband, or all three—and isn't punished. Which is a pity, because such badness is good when it's necessary to maintain the integrity of the soul.

Of course, there are plenty of sane, well-adjusted women who never needed to mess up to figure out what they wanted from this world. Good for them. I mean that. Hey, some of my best friends are sane, well-adjusted women.

But for me, and for others, the straight and narrow is the road not taken. William Blake wrote that "The road to excess leads to the palace of wisdom . . . for we never know what is enough until we know what is more than enough."

Some of us have to hitchhike a while down Blake's road of excess, stick out a thumb and a hip. Once when my husband and I were walking past a Baptist church as the service let out, I heard one man ask another how his daughter was. "Still running from the Lord," he replied with a sad shake of his head. That daughter was traveling the road I'm speaking of. And I don't know that our sojourns and our detours should be uniformly regretted if we've arrived at that palace of wisdom. And they sure make for good stories now, as these 23 writers prove.

This volume contains stories of women who commit transgressions that change their lives. Many of these changes are painful (aren't all changes painful?), but the women speaking to us from the far side of the process are schooled.

I've always believed that through reading we educate our emotional intelligence. Just as our dreams provide a space for us to psychically rehearse our day's anxieties, reading allows us to test alternate conclusions. We inhabit other characters and experience their choices as our own, through the exercise of empathy. By reading the memoirs collected here, we imaginatively re-experience the choices these "bad" women made. We can be cheaters and lawbreakers, liars and avengers, deviants and plotters. We can get away with murder. Will reading these tales prevent us from sinning? Not likely. But it's enlightening, as well as entertaining, to consider the wages of sin. It's possible our future decisions will be better informed.

I suppose I should address the question of why we editors narrowed our focus to Southern sin. Or, said another way, what is it about

Southern sin that demands its own volume? For Lee and I could have filled several books, not just one, with such tales.

Perhaps Southerners write about sinners for the same reason Flannery O'Connor said Southerners write about freaks: "because we are still able to recognize one." We recognize sinners here because there's so much emphasis on not becoming one. Of course, as we all know, the stronger the taboo, the stronger the compulsion to break the taboo—and when it *is* broken, sin splashes violently against this religious landscape. A recent Gallup poll indicates the states with the highest proportion of "very religious" people—those who say religion is an important part of daily life and who attend religious services every week—are in the South. The poll says that's 59% of the population in Mississippi, where I live. Compare this to, say, Vermont, with 23%, and you might agree again with good old Flannery, who observed in *The Habit of Being* that, "By and large, people in the South still conceive of humanity in theological terms. While the South is hardly Christ-centered, it is most certainly Christ-haunted."

As for me, I'm a Christ-haunted Southerner now. The year after My Year of Sinning found me in Arkansas, where I met the Alabama sinner I'd marry, and now Mississippi has been my home long enough that when I go back to Chicago and people hear me talk, they ask where I'm from. The most excellent word "y'all" is firmly lodged in my lexicon. My three children have drawls, and, for that matter, smocked bibs on their Sunday clothes. I'm no longer surprised when I meet someone new and the first question I'm asked is not what I do for a living, but where I go to church. I'm no longer surprised that I have a ready answer.

That scared twenty-one-year-old seems pretty distant now. And that's okay. Although I'd never have imagined the detours that brought me here, I'm happy growing as a transplant in this full-sun, Christ-haunted soil. I don't mourn my choices and I don't pine for my youth; I wouldn't *want* a time machine to whisk me back to twenty-one. Not unless I could use it to hand myself a copy of this book, and then zoom back into the future, where I'd be waiting, the wiser for having read it.

Improbable True Stories about Bad and Sometimes Bizarre Behavior

that the true stories in this book are about actual real
human beings are even stranger. . . .

Unforgettable True Stories about Bad (and Sometimes Bizarre) Behavior

Lee Gutkind

*A*ll of the true stories in this book are about women (and most of them are written by women) and how, why, and under what circumstances they behave badly.

"Badly" is, of course, a totally subjective judgment. What's usually considered to be "bad" behavior by women, speaking from a man's point of view, can seem good. I mean *really* good—tantalizing or downright enticing, like Amy Thigpen's "The On-Ramp." The story starts as Thigpen steps off a plane on a little weekend vacation. She wants to have fun—and she does, flirting her way across New Orleans and seeking romance . . . and much more, as it turns out. And then there's Adriana Paramo ("Tongues, Lust, and a Man from Indiana"), who goes to a concert by one of her favorite singers and finds herself seated next to a handsome, charismatic, almost irresistible Spanish-speaking stranger.

And wait until you meet River Jordan ("Nude Study"), who spends a long night driving cross-country in a hot car. Topless. Talk about exciting, and, OK, maybe a little bizarre—but there's nothing wrong with that. Or take Sheila Raeschild's wild and wonderful story, "Circles of Light." Visiting her retired parents in Miami Beach, Raeschild meets a man on the beach who compares her to Venus. Later that evening, she finds him sprawled on a blanket, wearing a wifebeater and an unbuttoned flower-print shirt, and—well, Raeschild doesn't spend much time with her elderly parents on that trip. (After reading this story, I'm considering investing in a flower-print shirt of my own, though I'm not sure I can quite pull off the *Miami Vice* look.)

If you didn't catch it, most of these stories have a steamy, sexy element, though I don't want you to think they're all stories of women having vacation flings. Many of these stories are far more complicated. Take, for example, Chelsea Rathburn's "The Renters": financially strapped after her divorce, Rathburn decides to take in a roommate, but she's in no hurry to give up her solitude. So she searches instead for a part-timer—a traveling salesman, maybe, or a long-distance commuter with a life somewhere else. No luck, until she sees a Craigslist posting that seems like the perfect solution:

Mature Couple Having an Affair: $400: We will rarely, if ever, be present overnight or for longer than four hours. Ideal situation if you need help with expenses but do not want a full-time roommate.

Does the arrangement work out? Would you open your home to an adulterous couple? Let's just say Rathburn gets a bit more than she bargained for. That sometimes happens with Craigslist, doesn't it?

But wait: I don't want you to think that all of these stories are about having sex. What about Sheryl St. Germain, who in "A Country Where You Once Lived" writes about *not* having sex? In middle age and a comfortable marriage, St. Germain finds that although she had once proudly proclaimed she would be "an old woman who still has sex," her reality is more complicated. Meanwhile, her husband, whom she loves and wants to live with happily ever after, is becoming increasingly desirous. It's quite a dilemma.

Sex. It makes people a little crazy. Sometimes it even drives people to kill. Elyse Moody ("Trouble") delves into her family history to try to better understand a jealousy-fueled murder. And in "Mad Love: The Ballad of Fred & Allie," Sonja Livingston vividly re-creates a story of highly forbidden desire that ends tragically.

And, of course, these stories all take place in the South. Does that mean that women in other parts of the country are more inhibited, conservative . . . uptight, so to speak? I don't think so. But something about the South inspires a spontaneity that is contagious. Maybe it's the heat and humidity, or the lilt with which Southerners speak, or the alluring grit of Memphis and the moaning trombones of New Orleans, or the mist that rises at night above the Mississippi River Delta, or the sweet intoxication of Kentucky bourbon, or the topless beaches of Miami—or maybe it is all of these and much more that make the South so sultry.

It's hard to say what the reason is, but in these true stories, at least—for women and for men, for the South's visitors and its residents—sin is as plentiful and wild as kudzu. You could, of course, behave badly yourself. Or as a safe and satisfying alternative, you can read the true stories in this book. You will learn all about women, sin, and bad behavior—and see what you are missing.

ACKNOWLEDGEMENTS

This anthology grew out of a special "Southern Sin" issue of *Creative Nonfiction* magazine, which was generously supported by Neil White and the Oxford Creative Nonfiction Writers Conference. Most of the pieces included here were among the nearly six hundred essays submitted for that issue, and the editors are grateful to all the writers who sent their work for consideration.

Any book is the work of many people. The editors would like to thank Victoria Blake and Sarah Rosenberg for their wise counsel; Robyn Jodlowski, Kristina Marusic, and Chad Vogler for their attentive fact-checking; Matt Spindler for his perseverance; Hattie Fletcher for her astute editorial skill and dedication to the project; and the entire staff at *Creative Nonfiction* and In Fact Books.

What Was Left

Molly Langmuir

The plan, which we came up with by the side of a highway somewhere in South Carolina, was to ditch our station wagon at a friend's house in Atlanta, take the bus to New Orleans, and then hitchhike back to the car. It wasn't such a good plan, and even at the time I wasn't sure we'd go through with it. But Nancy and I had played a similar game of chicken lots of times before and by the end we'd often done just that thing I didn't believe we'd actually do.

We were 19 and 20, and such suckers for the rush danger brings that usually we ignored any misgivings. So when, a few days after we'd arrived in New Orleans, a guy came up to us in a coffee shop and said he'd pay us each $100 if we'd let him take some pictures of us naked, we said sure. We figured this way we could take a train back to the car instead of hitchhiking. He showed us his portfolio, and it was filled with black-and-whites of naked women who came off as both demure and dirty, like in old nudie pics I'd seen in antique shops.

We had bodies similar to the women in those pictures—instead of the sharp, concave lines we wanted, ours had soft curves at the edges. I assumed this was why he'd picked us. Nancy had red hair and freckles everywhere, I had cheeks that stayed pink all the time, and we both had the pale white skin women used to have back when they protected themselves from the sun with parasols. We could have easily come across as wholesome. To avoid this we wore skirts so short we were sometimes mistaken for prostitutes.

As long as Nancy and I were together, I assumed we'd manage. We'd known each other since we were children, and our parents had known each other since long before that. We felt like family, in other words, and in high school, when we started seeking out all the trouble the New York City suburbs had to offer—shoplifting cheap bras at the mall; doing opium with the guy who worked at Dunkin Donuts; hanging out in the suburban projects with the coke dealers, Poppy and Big Al—she soon came to feel like the only family that mattered.

Besides, whatever physical dangers we could find weren't nearly as frightening as the feelings we carried around inside of us. The summer I was 15, I came home to find my mom in the living room with the shades drawn, flatly explaining that her marriage with my dad was falling apart. Nancy walked me around the neighborhood afterward. I was barefoot, the soles of my feet burning on the hot cement, and for the first time I understood that pain can be something you lean into. Soon my dad was coming home as little as possible, and my mom and I were fighting. One time I slapped her in the face; another time I kicked in my bedroom door and threw all the plants off the deck. I didn't come home for days, got as high as I could on whatever I could find, and made friends with the kids dropping ten hits of acid three nights a week at raves. I thought my parents might do something, try to stop me, I guess, but they never did, and eventually I understood they never would—a realization which was both liberating and horrifying.

Whatever I was dealing with felt juvenile compared to Nancy's problems. By the time I started having sleepovers with her in middle school, her father had become increasingly reclusive. I never knew where he was in the house or when he'd appear, drunk off vodka. He drank every day, with dogged determination. He was charismatic, mercurial, and cruel, capable of ripping Nancy to shreds with a few sharply aimed words, casually, across the kitchen table. Eventually her mom kicked him out and he moved to California, where he holed himself up in an apartment and drank himself to death.

At times it seemed like my friendship with Nancy boiled down to a series of alternating rescues, and with each one, we braided ourselves together more tightly. When she called me up her senior year of high school telling me she wanted to die, talking about the pills in the medicine cabinet downstairs, all I knew to do was keep her on the phone until it was late enough at night that she decided to just go to sleep. I was desperate, and not only for her, but for myself.

After we graduated, I went to a liberal arts college, and Nancy moved in with her sister in California and started waitressing. The night before she left we slept holding on to each other like lovers. But by the time we took the road trip, two years later, we were living very different lives, and the seams between us were starting to tear. The idea was that the trip would help us reconnect.

We took off in June in my mom's Subaru station wagon, sleeping in it most nights in hotel parking lots. It was a hot and heavy summer. Gas slipped below $1 a gallon, and we kept heading south.

Sometimes we stopped to look at road signs, and once we went to a petting zoo where a llama sucked on our hands, a strangely pleasant experience ("No wonder guys like sex," Nancy said, with this surprised look on her face). But sneaking into a few hotel pools to clean off was the closest we got to having any real fun.

Finally, I pulled the car over by the side of the highway in South Carolina and fell out onto the grass. In retrospect, the reasons the trip wasn't going well seem obvious. My parents' divorce was in full swing, and I was a few weeks into a bout of anorexia. Nancy wasn't eating either. She had recently started taking an antidepressant, and whatever it did to her mood, it killed her appetite.

But as we lay there by the highway in South Carolina we didn't discuss any of this. Instead, we decided the problem had to be the car. It was too insular, too filled with my mom's tinted sunglasses and automatic pencils. Two days later we were in New Orleans, staying at a ramshackle hostel with mini alligators in a pool in the back.

We wandered aimlessly around the city, through the aboveground cemeteries, past the old drunks, until the afternoon we ended up at the coffee shop. A wiry, skinny guy with hair that made it look like he'd stuck his finger in an electric socket stared at us from across the room. This was Rudolph, the photographer. He was obviously nuts. That was part of the appeal.

The next morning, as arranged, we met Rudolph at the coffee shop. On the walk to his house, he talked way too fast about aliens, and about alien and human sex, and somewhere along the way I smelled his breath and realized he was drunk.

He lived on the second floor of a rundown mansion on a wide street lined with stately trees. The bottom floor of his house was abandoned, so we climbed up the fire escape. Inside, the ceilings were high, and every inch of every wall was filled with art. There were framed still lifes of apples and flowers, and portraits of reclining naked women, and paintings of abstract colored shapes from the '70s.

In the room Rudolph used as his photography studio, white sheets covered the tall windows and old photography equipment was scattered among random props—a canvas parasol, an American flag. Everything smelled vaguely of cat. While he went to get the first of a series of beers, I took off my clothes.

He started by asking me to hold magnolias up to my breasts, handing me the flowers and telling me how to pose. Somewhere around the third beer, he started touching me—moving my leg then leaving his hand on my thigh, moving my arm and brushing his hand against my breast.

Nancy watched me, steady, as he took his pictures. We were at our best in moments like this, the two of us. If one of us had to take herself away from a situation, retreating into a far corner of the mind and leaving the body behind, she entrusted the most precious parts of herself to the other, for safekeeping.

After me, he took pictures of Nancy, then of the two of us together. He wanted to cover us in flour, but I said no. I didn't want to walk out of there with anything that would remind me of that place except $100.

By then I had realized getting the money was a long shot, especially after Nancy asked Rudolph what time it was—we'd only agreed to an hour—and he ignored her before finally saying there were no clocks in the house. Eventually, we decided to just start getting dressed, and in response he ran out of the house and locked the door behind him, telling us he had to buy cat food. I got this horrible feeling in my stomach then, like maybe all that itching for danger had taken me farther out than I could get back from.

He did pay us, though. Once he got back from the store, in the midst of rummaging frantically for a pen—there were these model release forms he wanted us to sign—he gave us the money, one crisp bill each.

We left right away, walking fast and faster through the neighborhood, back to the part of town where the houses weren't falling down. We hardly spoke on the walk, but we both understood the trip was over. All we wanted was to get as far away from that place as quickly as possible. The next morning we were on a train back to the car in Atlanta, and a few days later we were at Nancy's mom's house in upstate New York. That dead feeling in my stomach didn't leave for weeks.

———•———

I occasionally wondered if someone might be living with a naked picture of me on the wall, magnolias sprouting from my breasts, but I figured it was far more likely that those photos had ended up in a scattered pile in Rudolph's house, under some bills and a discarded can of cat food. Still, Nancy and I made a few attempts to find the pictures. One time when we both happened to be in New Orleans we even went to the gallery Rudolph had told us sometimes sold his work, but the woman working there said she hadn't heard from him in months. After Hurricane Katrina I assumed the photos must have been destroyed. For some reason, I also assumed Rudolph was dead.

Three years after the hurricane, though, I got an email from Nancy. I was surprised to hear from her. The previous summer we had had a terrible fight, a screaming blowout that ended with me crying as she stormed off down the street.

The problem, basically, was that our friendship couldn't accommodate distance; during the years that had passed since our road trip we had gradually become very different people. I had a badly paid magazine job and lived with my boyfriend in a converted barn in Massachusetts with a pellet stove for heat. Nancy worked in advertising and went through men like quicksand, men who offered her summer houses in the Hamptons and flew her to Europe for the weekend. But I also finished college and graduate school without debt, whereas Nancy's mom wouldn't even pay for her college applications, and as difficult as things were in my family, my dad had never called me a bitch over breakfast.

We hadn't handled any of this gracefully. Instead, like the worst kind of sisters, we had alternated between jealousy and judgment. The blowout had been a long time coming, and I thought that was probably it for us.

The email contained only a link, and when I saw that it took me to a literary website that had recently released an issue about New Orleans, I knew what was coming. A few clicks later, I arrived at a slideshow of Rudolph's photos. Among black-and-whites of heavily tattooed waitresses, an obese lady, and a woman draped in the American flag, there we were, kneeling with our arms resting on the sides of our heads, looking down at the space between us, mirror images of one another.

It was a nice photo, sort of charming, even, but it made me sad, this visual representation of the risks I used to be willing to take with myself. I tried to face everything with such bravado back then, but looking at that picture from the vantage point of my late twenties all I saw was the crumbly, miserable girl who would have been revealed without it. I had grown up, or at least was trying to, slowly working on climbing out of the dark place that as a teenager I was so determined to climb into, and it no longer seemed exhilarating to do things exclusively because they were dangerous. Instead it just looked like an old habit I'd mostly broken, one I'd acquired at a time when I couldn't feel much, and feeling fear was better than feeling nothing. Rudolph no longer seemed like the predatory creep I'd remembered, either. He struck me as an eccentric, somewhat unstable alcoholic, whom we might have been better off avoiding, but who probably meant us no harm.

Not being in touch with Nancy had already felt like something my mind couldn't quite comprehend. During the year we didn't speak, I thought about her all the time. There was no natural way for us to fit together anymore, but not talking made her into a phantom limb in my life, a presence I couldn't shake. Finally, after seeing the picture, I called her and left a message. When she called back we spoke without rancor, for the first time in years.

Later that month, my mom and I went to Nancy's mother's house for Thanksgiving, a long-standing tradition that I'd been assuming we'd forgo that year. I was holding a huge vat of stuffing when Nancy opened the door, and as she reached to take it from me there was a moment where both of us were holding onto it just looking at each other, more sisters than friends, smiling at the silliness of having gone so long without talking.

We spent the whole weekend together, and with Nancy's new boy-friend, a macho Bosnian guy with a gruff sexiness. I knew what she saw in him. He was similar to her dad in the way the men she likes always are—charismatic, egotistical, and a little dangerous. I watched Nancy, steady, as she pouted and said things like, "Is that all I'm worth to you?" when he looked for a ring for her on a jewelry auction website, as he mixed sharp dismissals with unexpected bursts of tenderness, as he drove us around suburbia in his humongous Rolls-Royce, blasting European techno and bragging about his connections to celebrities and Russian mobsters, and as Nancy took a muscle relaxant and passed out on his couch at the end of the night. Nancy and I were gentle with each other, softly probing the unfamiliar outlines of the other per-son's life. I remembered, then, about the parts of each other we had both been saving all this time, for safekeeping, protecting them even from ourselves.

White Noise

Sarah Cheshire

For every Southern belle who has never orgasmed

I t is 11:43 P.M. on the night before I am supposed to fly back to college for the start of my sophomore year, and I am drunk and barefoot in the middle of the ballroom of the North Raleigh Hilton, swaddled in yards of frill. The Lynyrd Skynyrd cover band is about six minutes into "Free Bird." All around me girls in white are drifting past. They look like lost parachutes, their slender arms draped loosely, almost limply, around the necks of their dates, whose eyes they struggle to meet. These girls will never look you right in the eye; they are always off target by an inch or two. It kind of cracks me up. Like, they will be talking to you about . . . I don't know . . . what brand of mascara you use because *my goodness* it so beautifully brings out the blue of your irises, and the whole time they won't even be looking at your irises; they'll be looking off into space, somewhere between your hairline and your shoulder and the ceiling.

I realize, too late, that I am gaping at this one girl. Her date looks like he has been sedated; his drooping, army-shaved head has landed in the groove of her clavicle. She looks at my chest like, "What the fuck." (I think she is aiming for my eyes.) I look away, flustered. I survey the room. I am dizzy and slightly nauseous and ready to leave. I need to find my date—my first cousin, whom I last saw creeping out the back with some blonde with pin-straight hair and enough rhinestones on her bodice to sink a small ship. I need to find my shoes. I retrace my steps in my head. *Where have we been?* I remember drinking Budweiser and Jack Daniel's in the room of three frat boys with matching camouflage hats. *What were their names? One began with a C and had one syllable. Cliff? Clyde? Clint? Clit? Clit. . . . hee-hee.* I burp up a little bit of puke, then swallow it.

They all had girlfriends with them. Their girlfriends had nice legs. I remember that. Their legs looked like they belonged on mahogany tables—all shiny and long and bronzed from long August afternoons spent frying on towels on the shores of the Outer Banks. I hate girls like that. I want to throw volleyballs at the symmetrical dimples in their lower backs, or pluck them up with one hand and throw them into the ocean, making sure the salt water washes away the reservoirs of styling gel barricading their hair from gusts of sea breeze. But dang, I wish I had those legs.

My legs are super pale. Like, white-sheet-over-the-corpse-of-a-dead-dictator pale. Under fluorescent lights you can see webs of blue veins underneath the skin. They are also kind of jiggly. Whenever I play beach volleyball and shuffle from side to side, my thighs are like jellyfish prodded with miniature-golf clubs. I have learned that this is a beach bro's favorite hobby; splitting jellyfish open with putters and then pouring Budweiser into the cracks to see if the purple and red and blue streaks dissolve. I wish all the Budweiser in my body right now would make the blue streaks in my legs dissolve. My grandma tried (and failed) to put me on a summer diet so I could have skinny mahogany legs for this weekend. Every time I'd reached across the table for a second helping it was, "If you eat one more sweet potato biscuit, you're not gonna fit into your debutante gown, young lady!"

I think this should be our state motto. North Carolina: *If You Eat One More Sweet Potato Biscuit, You're Not Gonna Fit into Your Debutante Gown.*

Young lady.

Our actual state motto is *Esse quam videri*, which means "To be, rather than to seem." I learned that in history class in eighth grade, I think. If I ever rebelled and got a tattoo, that's what it would say: *Esse quam videri*, in bold Lucida Grande font across my lower back (in between the muffin tops). I like it because sometimes I get this strange sensation that I don't really exist. It's like I am sitting behind a big glass window in a wicker lawn chair or something, watching everything play out in front of me as if life were a crappy soap opera or sitcom.

Today, for instance, the announcer at the cotillion ballroom adjusted the bowtie on his seersucker suit and called my name in his molasses-thick drawl, "Now presenting Ms. Sarah Cheshire of Durham. Daughter of Sprague Cheshire of Raleigh. She is escorted by her father." My father put down the giant white stool that the Terpsichorean Club gave him to carry around backstage in case his daughter got tired and had to rest her brittle, beautiful legs. We linked arms as they had taught us in rehearsal, and I pulled up the hem of my ivory gown as we stepped out into the jungle of fake orchids, girls with earrings the same shade of white as their shoes, and aging ladies who peered out from the audience with thick-rimmed spectacles, then leaned toward their husbands, whispering with either a slight nod or a shake of the head ("My word, Raymond, will you look at what *she* has on!") before tapping their hands together in applause light as the flapping of hummingbird wings. And from the moment I stepped out onto the stage, I was no longer standing there in a girdle and a glossy white gown. I was somewhere in the rafters, looking down and chuckling softly and thinking, *My, aren't they quaint?*

I need to find my shoes. I really need to find my shoes. The band has switched genres, from Lynyrd Skynyrd to Katy Perry. "California Gurls"—only, the girls are squealing and reciting the lyrics with "Carolina" instead of "California." I need to get out of here. I need to find my shoes. If I lost them, my grandma's gonna be pissed. Where could I have left them? I remember taking them off in the room of the frat boys and putting them . . . under the armchair? Beside the bathroom sink? I stumble out of the ballroom and down the hallway. What room number was it? 203? It could have been 204. Maybe 205. No, I'm pretty sure it was 203. I knock on the door.

A woman in a sheer black slip opens the door and collapses against the threshold. "Yeah?" Her bright red hair is tousled and there are little black half moons under her eyes where her mascara has smudged. She is beautiful. The fat on her inner thighs jiggles when she shifts her weight. The strap of the slip has fallen down, and I can see two-thirds of her left breast.

Giggling, I ask her, "Are you a debutante?"

"No, honey. Are *you* a debutante?"

I nod. I am still giggling, a little. She leans back and shouts into the room in an exaggerated accent, "Glory be—I've found us a debutante!"

"Why don't you tell her to come in?" a low voice shouts back. She opens the door wider.

The man sitting on the bed is wearing a white, faux-leather suit and shoes so shiny I can see miniature, distorted versions of the door and the armchair and the TV and myself reflected in them. I follow the reflection inside and sit down on the twin bed across from his. He has a gold crucifix around his neck and a knuckle-sized, cubic-zirconia stud in his left ear. *Suave.* She plops down next to him and drapes her smooth, slightly jiggly legs over his lap. Picks up a Dixie cup from the bedside table. Takes a sip and shudders, then looks up at me.

"Tell me, what's with the dress?"

I look down at the sea of ruffles unfurling underneath me and then up at her translucent slip. And the breast. My cheeks feel hot.

"It's a requirement. It symbolizes purity, I think."

The man lets out a sharp, guttural laugh and slides his hand up her leg.

"I can't say I know a lot about purity," she says. She closes her eyes for a second, and I can't tell if she is taking a deep breath or wincing.

"Are y'all married?" My voice comes out an octave too high.

"Is that a polite way of asking me if I'm a whore?"

"Ha ha, what?" I laugh again, then realize she isn't laughing with me and stop abruptly. "Are you?"

"Yes."

"Oh."

I look at him, cup my hand over my mouth, and stage-whisper, *"Does he know that?"*

"I sure hope so." She grabs his crotch. "You know I don't give this out for free, don't you?"

Watching them makes me feel jittery in the bottom of my stomach, like someone is tickling me, gently, just below my belly button. Right where the corset under my dress cuts off. I look at the tiles in the ceiling. They are made of interlocked white fibers and look kind of like giant biscuits of shredded wheat coated with confectioners' sugar. Or flattened bird nests. Crushed bird nests covered in snow. It makes me a little claustrophobic—the flatness. And the whiteness. The vastness of the whiteness. Claustrophobic, but also a little . . . cozy.

"Yeahhh," he sighs, and I come down from the ceiling. Shiver.

"Oh, dear, I think we're making her uncomfortable," she whispers into his ear, then turns to me. "Are we making you uncomfortable?"

Yeah, but it's okay, I think.

"No," I say. She raises her eyebrows, skeptical.

"Tell me . . . What's your name?"

"Sarah."

"Tell me, Sarah, have you ever been loved by anyone?"

I think about this. Love, or whatever. It brings me back to the familiar sensation, the feeling that I don't actually exist. I think about the first time I got close to a boy, how it didn't really feel like I was close to him at all. It was as if I was looking in through the window, watching two peoples' bodies converge on a stranger's bed while I thought about how the whole thing resembled a generic party hookup scene from the movies. A cliché: beer cans scattered all over the floor; hip-hop music reverberating from outside the door, the bass making the bedside table tremble; her dress falling off her shoulder; him pressing his face into hers, fumbling, not knowing where to put his hands; her eyes focused somewhere over his shoulder. Focused at the window. Or at the ceiling. Or something like that.

No, I think. *I haven't.*

"Sure," I say. "My family loves me."

I know this isn't what she means. I don't even know if it's entirely true. Or what I mean when I say it. But it's what they want to hear. It makes them laugh. Not in a "Dang, this girl should perform on *Saturday Night Live*" kind of way, but more in a "My, isn't she quaint?" kind of way. I like that, I think. Or maybe I resent it. I'm too tipsy to tell.

The digits on the alarm clock beside their bed flicker. Midnight. Shit. My flight back to college leaves in eight hours and seventeen minutes. Shit. I need to find my shoes. I need to find my cousin. Shit. I get up off the bed.

"I beg your pardon, I really need to find my cousin."

"Your cousin?"

"Yes ma'am. He's my date. I can't get home without him."

"Damn, you people really are caricatures," she says, shaking her head. I don't stop to think about what this means. I dart out the door. I can hear them chuckling behind me as I totter down the hall. Down the hall and back into the lobby. There is someone sitting on one of the lobby lounge chairs, playing with his phone. Legs spread wide. Camouflage hat flipped backward. He looks familiar. I move closer. It is the frat boy from earlier. Clit, or whatever.

"Hiiii," I scamper up to him. "Hi, have you seen my cousin?"

"Who's your cousin?" He stands up.

"Joe."

"Joe? Naw, haven't see him."

"*Jesus Christ!*" I exclaim in exasperation, then put my hand over my mouth. "I'm sorry, I don't mean to be so offensive."

"You're not offending me," he says, looking at my chest. "I don't believe in Jesus."

"Oh? Why not?"

"My faith has been shaken."

"Oh? By what?"

"The death of my mother." He looks at my eyes. I look at his necktie, which has little trout floating on it. I really want to know how his mother died, but I think that asking might be rude. I wonder if it was something sudden and unexpected. Like a car crash or a gang fight. Or something long and drawn out. Like breast cancer.

"I'm really sorry," I say, while at the same time he says, "You know what? I think I might have seen your cousin in the bathroom."

"Oh, really? How long ago?"

"Not too long. How 'bout we go check?"

I follow him across the lobby and into the girls' bathroom. The tiles feel cold and hard against my bare feet. He holds the door open for me.

"JOE!" He calls to the vacant stalls. "Joe! Are you in here, buddy?"

He turns to me and shrugs. "Gee, I guess he's not here."

"Oh no!" I lean against the sink. My dress is tight around my waist. I try to take a deep breath but feel like I am gasping for air.

"What*ever* should we do? I can't leave you here unsupervised, now, can I?" He is whispering now. I can barely hear him.

"What?! I can't hear you!" I shout.

"I guess that means I'm gonna have to move closer, then."

He moves closer. He smells sour and earthy. Kind of like pine straw . . . dipped in gasoline. And then lit afire. Or something like that. *Hot.* He takes off his camouflage hat and throws it to the floor.

I mean to say "You dropped your hat," but instead I say, "Oh."

Then, the little trout on his necktie are plunging toward me. Rapidly, as if being swept by some giant current. His mouth is slimy against mine. Like seaweed. Or algae. Or something like that. I close my eyes. I am underwater. I am drowning. Or swimming. Or something like that.

"*Esse quam videri,*" I whisper into the stubble on his upper lip.

The Renters

Chelsea Rathburn

The spring my marriage ended I couldn't afford my house payments on my own, so I did what any reasonable person might do: I looked for a roommate. But as someone leaving a long relationship and in no hurry to share close quarters with another human, as someone prone to crying jags and soul-searching and emergency calls to the therapist, I was uneasy with the thought of a traditional housemate. I searched instead for a part-timer—a traveling salesman, an engaged young Baptist forced to hide cohabitation, or a long-distance commuter with a life somewhere else. Faced with slim pickings and mounting bills, I did what no reasonable person should do: I took in a pair of adulterers.

Mature Couple Having an Affair: $400: *We will rarely, if ever, be present overnight or for longer than four hours. Ideal situation if you need help with expenses but do not want a full-time roommate.*

It was perfect. I had a room and needed the cash; they had money but didn't want a paper trail. They were "stable," "discreet," a "long-term couple." They would rarely, if ever, be present overnight.

The first time I saw the ad on (where else?) Craigslist, just as my husband and I were contemplating separation, I mentioned it to our marriage counselor. "Yes, the money would help," she said, "but do you really want to be complicit in adultery?" *They'd be together with or without my help*, I thought, but the posting was gone the next time I looked, and I put it out of my mind. It reappeared a few months later, after my husband had moved out and I was charging the electric bill and groceries to my credit cards. I decided not to mention it in therapy again.

It may seem strange, but the idea of opening my home to a couple of cheaters didn't bother me. My feelings toward marriage as an institution could be described as hostile at best. My own marriage looked something like this: three counselors over ten years; a shelf of self-help books with titles like *The Passionate Marriage*, *Getting the Love You Want*, and *How One of You Can Change the Two of You*; a husband who went out without me five nights a week, who refused to see a doctor for sexual dysfunction, and who admitted to rushing through sex to "get it over with"; tens of thousands of dollars of debt; hundreds of empty bottles (mostly his); countless flirtations and emotional entanglements (as far as I know, all mine).

Despite our problems, my husband did not want a divorce. He signed a six-month lease on an apartment and insisted on referring to our split as a "trial separation"—this was, in fact, the only way he agreed to move out. Even after we'd made the decision to file, he looked across the table in the notary's office, his pen poised above the signature line of the settlement agreement, and asked, "Are you sure we're doing the right thing?"

My family did not want a divorce, either. My parents had been together since they were eighteen and twenty-two, and they believed firmly in making sacrifices for the sake of the marriage. They assumed that any problems were my fault.

"You know what your problem is?" they'd ask, without waiting for an answer. "You want too much."

Since then, I've seen other people's families rally around divorcing relatives, but it was obvious that if my parents had to take a side, it wouldn't be mine. They continued to send my ex-husband Christmas cards and birthday checks. I heard, ad nauseam, that he was the nicest person anyone had ever met. And I'll admit he *was* nice, especially to other people.

So the idea of taking in the adulterers intrigued me. My family already disapproved of everything I did, anyway, and I thought it would probably offend my husband, so squeamish about all things sexual. Plus, to be honest, the idea made me feel oddly glamorous. I was thirty-one years old and ready for my life to begin. This could be the start of the new post-divorce me, the me who could have fancy-free affairs where no one got hurt. Perhaps not the person I was, but the person I could be.

I replied to the ad and received an email the same day from Tall_Man69. Yes, they were still looking for a room. He would send his girlfriend over to see if their furniture would fit.

My house sat just inside the Perimeter, the interstate dividing Atlanta from its outlying suburbs. A large split-level built in the '60s, it was entirely too much house for one person and more than enough for two. My husband and I had needed abundant space in order to live together. The downstairs rec room, his former music practice space, was now empty, as was the large guest bedroom—which was, perhaps, not large enough for whatever Tall_Man69 had in mind.

The girlfriend arrived in a budget SUV and never got off her cell phone. Apparently she approved of the place because a few minutes later, a Mercedes pulled into the driveway. The man who climbed out was indeed tall, unusually so, with a weak chin and a nervous energy. His girlfriend was short, about thirty pounds overweight, and shy. I noticed he wore a wedding ring, and she, painfully, predictably, did not.

After looking the house over, Tall_Man69 asked about my marriage. Was I certain it was over? He didn't want to move in only to be kicked out in a few months. He wasn't crazy about having to use the downstairs bathroom, either—their previous arrangement had had an en suite bath—but he supposed they could put up with a little inconvenience. He had one last question: Were any of my friends attorneys? He didn't want to run into anyone he knew while he was in his bathrobe.

As they walked out together, Tall_Man69 told me they'd move in on the first of the month and that their names were Melinda and Don. They were careful not to give last names.

———•———

I told my friend Johanna about my renters a few days later. Johanna was in the midst of treatment for breast cancer, and between her bouts of chemo, we got together for lunches at our usual restaurant, Manuel's, ordering our usual meals—grilled chicken salad for her, a crabcake sandwich for me—and iced teas. We sat at our usual table, a two-top against the window, joked with our usual waiter, and dissected our love lives, trying to ignore the possibility that Johanna's condition was serious. She had a policy of not asking her doctors for a prognosis, and if I asked how she was feeling, she'd try to be upbeat. That afternoon, her face was thinner but as lovely as ever, and she widened her eyes in mock horror at my arrangement.

"At least someone's going to be having sex there!" She teased me about having my very own den of iniquity; then her voice turned serious. "Won't it freak you out to hear them . . . you know?"

"How bad can it be? I mean, I had roommates in college, and none of them were exactly nuns. It's not like I'm going to be there in the room with them, right?"

"I guess. What do they look like?"

"Like people you don't want to picture having sex. Trust me. But really, it will be fine."

The day Melinda and Don moved in, I came home from work expecting to find them unpacking. The movers had been scheduled for 4:30, and it was barely 5:15. I called up hello and was greeted by high-decibel moans. An hour later, they slipped downstairs to shower, leaning into my office on their way out.

"I hope we didn't bother you," Don said, grinning. "Unless we hot-and-bothered you."

What in God's name had I done?

———•———

The next time I saw them, Don asked, "Do you like what we did with the room?"

"I haven't seen it," I said. This wasn't a complete lie. The night they moved in, I'd peeked in to see why they'd been so concerned about the furniture fitting. In the half darkness, I'd spotted a king-sized bed, an enormous dresser, and a mirror, then felt guilty and shut the door.

"Oh, you can look any time," Don said. "Just don't mind the paddles. We like a little discipline."

As soon as they left, I took a closer look. The room was covered in Elvis memorabilia: an Elvis bedspread, a velvet Elvis painting, and a ceramic bust that wore a pair of black plastic sunglasses. On the dresser was a framed photo of Melinda posing with an Elvis impersonator on the Vegas Strip. The only other decorations were a small black whip and four black leather paddles painted with the symbols of the suits of cards: a white club, a red diamond, a white spade, and a red heart.

In retrospect, things might have turned out differently if I had been a long-distance commuter rather than a person with a messy life. Even if I had worked a regular nine-to-five job, I might have rarely known they were there.

But I worked four days a week—one of them from home—for an ad agency outside Atlanta, in a county that prided itself on preserving its small town squares and bucolic way of life despite its proximity to the city. The owner of the ad agency, a self-proclaimed good ol' boy, specialized in serving wealthy family-run businesses in the county's outlying towns—businesses that had the money for large marketing campaigns but distrusted large advertising agencies. He believed, despite all evidence to the contrary, that the way to market to county residents was to drop not only consonants but also random vowels, so that *playing at the old swimming hole* would become "play'n' at the ol' swimm'n' hole." Not that there were any old swimming holes around.

The creative team's running joke was that any good headline needed to be countrified before we submitted it to the boss.

Thus I spent my workdays writing ads about how living in the county's newest live-work-play development meant time for swing'n' on porches while drink'n' sweet t'. I spent my Fridays off, my work-at-home Wednesdays, and occasional Saturdays or Sundays listening to the gymnastics of Melinda and Don, who would end one orgiastic frenzy only to begin another.

My house was close to Don's home and law firm; originally this had concerned him, but it had made longer, more frequent sessions possible. Despite the claims of his Craigslist posting, they were often over for longer than four hours. And despite the assurances I'd given myself and Johanna, it did seem like I was right there in the room. Don and Melinda went beyond the standard muffled moans and creaking bedsprings. They, or rather Melinda, sounded like a parody of porn or someone mimicking how she thought sex should sound. Her *oh, OH, oh God, OH GOD*s thundered from one end of the house to the other—exaggerated, self-conscious, and, I imagined, not very much fun.

------·•·------

A typical meeting took place one July afternoon. It was a Wednesday, the day I worked from home. Refilling my coffee, I looked out the window to see Melinda's coppery SUV parked under a tree in my cul-de-sac. A moment later, Don pulled up in his Mercedes, and as they walked together up my driveway, I ducked downstairs and grabbed my earplugs. I was under deadline on an ad, and I knew that what would follow was three hours of moaning, grunting, and screaming, punctuated by the smacks of leather on flesh.

Their routine was to have as much sex as they could squeeze into an afternoon, then shower together before Don returned to his law practice or his family. Melinda always stayed to dry and hairspray her hair. (My downstairs smelled like White Rain on the days they visited.) She lived in the same outlying county where I worked, so if heading home threatened to put her in rush-hour traffic, she'd read upstairs or nurse a beer. Sometimes she'd come down to my office for a chat. Unlike Don, whose only interest was joking about sex, Melinda liked to talk about books, movies, relationships. She insisted her arrangement with Don was ideal; she'd been married briefly and didn't want to be again. Don, meanwhile, claimed to be in a deeply unhappy marriage with a woman who emasculated him; he stayed, according to Melinda, for the sake of the kids and, according to Don, because he didn't want that bitch to get any of his money.

Those short chats with Melinda felt almost like having a real room-mate. I discovered she worked in a book distribution warehouse and had been a single mother until her disabled son had died. She'd met Don soon after. He gave her an outlet, she said, for her grief.

That afternoon in July, Melinda announced matter-of-factly, "Don has a little sexual obsession with you." This didn't seem to bother her, particularly.

It was true that, with increasing frequency, Don had been joking about inviting me to join their trysts—or, at least, I chose to act as though he were joking.

"We'll be upstairs. Come on in if you're feeling wild," he'd said the previous week. "Heck, we'll even give you some cash."

"Sorry," I said. "I don't mix business with pleasure."

A few days later, I'd received an email: *We may have another couple joining us tomorrow. Of course we'd rather have you. You're welcome any time.*

And another: *You're a cutie pie. Can you be bought?*

During another of our post-coital chats, Melinda revealed why their previous rental hadn't worked out. Don wanted Melinda to experience sex with two men, so he invited the guy whose apartment they were sharing. Not only had the man turned them down, but he'd cited Melinda's weight as his reason.

"He could have just said he wasn't into that sort of thing," she mumbled.

I studied Melinda: the long, baggy T-shirt that hung over her leggings; her sad face doughy beneath dyed-red hair. She looked like someone who didn't want to be seen, who was trying to obliterate her-self. I understood the impulse, though for me it worked in reverse.

I could feel myself disappearing, losing touch with everything and everyone I had known in my marriage. Some nights, all I ate was refrigerated cookie dough, digging my spoon into the plastic tube because the sweetness was all my stomach could handle and because I knew I needed calories, any calories, to keep from wasting away.

After Don and Melinda invited another couple over, I confided in Johanna. "What do my neighbors think? These strange cars come and go whether I'm home or not. What if someone asks me who they are?"

She suggested I tell people they worked in sales and needed a home base. "Everyone knows traveling salespeople are all a little crazy."

As it turned out, one of my neighbors did ask someone about the strange cars, but she didn't ask me. She asked Don's wife. And then Don emailed me.

Do you by any chance know Elizabeth Roman? She's one of your neighbors. She saw my car in front of your house, and she told my wife. I'm getting grilled about it.

Don decided that our story would be that I was helping him write a book from the raw material of his diary. Though I worried about a confrontation or a P.I. stakeout of my house, his wife's suspicions never came up again. Just in case, though, Don delivered a chapter of his five-hundred-page manuscript, which detailed his escapades at his first law job. I couldn't read more than a few pages, but it did suggest that Don's narcissism was bigger than I thought and that philandering was his lifetime career.

One morning, as I carried a basket of laundry downstairs, I jumped to see a man sitting in the rec room, covered head to toe in leather. Peeking around the corner, I realized the gimp suit was actually empty, its owner asleep on the couch. This was Bob, a friend of a friend, who was giving the renters a run for their money. A few months after Don and Melinda had moved in, Bob had contacted me, asking if he could crash at my house occasionally. He'd supply a couch for my still-empty rec room and toss in a couple hundred dollars a month. He also needed to store a chest—this, he added, I was welcome to explore.

And so my den of iniquity grew. I knew that Bob, like the friend who'd introduced us, was big in the national BDSM community—what I'd grown up hearing referred to as S&M, or Whips & Chains. Bob attended conventions and published fetish fiction under a pseudonym. A former federal employee, he told funny stories about BDSM contraptions intercepted by quizzical customs agents, and he knew which high-ranking government officials were secretly into extreme bondage.

I liked Bob. He was the real deal, while I'd long suspected that Melinda and Don were make-believe deviants. Sure, they hung leather paddles on the wall and waxed enthusiastic about their predilections (especially Don, who mentioned that he was a "dom" in almost every conversation)—but they protested too much, methought.

I mentioned to Bob that he and the upstairs renters might get along, and he offered to share the contents of his mysterious chest, which turned out to contain mostly videos and books. The next time Don and Melinda came to the house, they stopped by the door of my office.

"We looked through the box your friend has and watched one of the videos," Don said. He seemed more nervous than usual. "That guy is into some weird shit."

———

Over time, I came to realize that I *was* part of a threesome, even if it wasn't physical. Melinda confided in me when she and Don were having problems. When her work schedule changed, making it temporarily difficult to schedule meetings, she worried that Don would leave her. And a few days later, Don emailed me: *We won't be around much this month because Melinda has a new schedule. This may destabilize the relationship. We'll see.*

Then there was the time Don arranged for another woman to join them—I still wasn't available—and Melinda got stuck in traffic. She arrived half an hour late to find that the party had started without her, something she had not signed on for. I began to suspect that Don was a garden-variety schoolyard bully rather than the exotic sexual dominant he fancied himself.

In the meantime, I was still clinging to my image as a carefree libertine. When I told friends about my renters, I described their reactions to Bob's chest—a mocking story, one that showed how I saw through them, these people who claimed to be sexual deviants but who really just enjoyed light spankings.

I told only Johanna how awful it was being in the house with them and how lonely I felt listening to their grunts and screams. And I didn't tell even her how Don had taken to leaving the rent on my pillow, despite my closed door, or how if I came home in the middle of a session, they got louder, much louder, once they heard me.

Though they were careful to pay in cash and not to use last names, details emerged. Don mentioned that he practiced aviation accident litigation, which seemed like a particularly odd niche of ambulance chasing. Ten minutes of Googling, and his face was smiling up at me from his practice website, along with his bio, which emphasized Don's belief in the importance of marriage, family, and church.

One day, Melinda revealed that the woman Don had brought to the house—she was still angry about them starting without her, though Don had asked what else was he supposed to do, sit around and make small talk?—was a prostitute.

Can you be bought?

Melinda saw the look on my face and begged me not to tell Don she'd said anything. It was a college student call girl, she said, not some hooker he picked up on the side of the road. For the next few weeks, I debated kicking them out, picturing a prostitute in my house. Then I pictured my mortgage bill. I needed the money. Could I be bought? It seemed that I could.

———•—•———

It wasn't until I fell in love that things unraveled. The night I met Jim, a PhD student in poetry, I told him about Bob, who'd since moved on, and the renters, who'd been with me for close to eight months by then. In a sort of flirtatious sexual one-upmanship, he described his ex-girlfriend, a grad student who sold her dirty underwear on the

Internet under the name Molly Masters. He was seven years my junior, and I assumed that ours would be a short fling. I worried at first that all we had in common was sex and writing, but to my surprise, things got serious.

Don and Melinda had always emailed to tell me if they planned to come over at an unusual time of day. I did the same, letting them know if I was going out of town in case they wanted to spend the night. Once I began spending more time with Jim, the courtesy emails abruptly stopped. Don and Melinda seemed to make a point of coming over when I said I would be home, and they wouldn't share Melinda's new work schedule, no matter how often I asked. I stressed that I wasn't trying to keep tabs on them; I wanted to give them more space by staying at Jim's during their rendezvous. I eventually realized they didn't want space; they wanted someone to hear them scream.

Of course, there was more to it than Don's power games with the schedule. Perhaps unsurprisingly, my stance on monogamy had changed. I'd also learned that my friend Johanna's breast cancer had spread. Although all she would say was that there was "involvement" in her liver, it became apparent that her case was terminal and had been for a long time. Suddenly I had even less patience for Don's juvenile jokes. In my grief, I began fantasizing about calling his wife, or his pastor, or the police.

Instead, I set to work icing Don and Melinda out. I'm not proud of this. I behaved the way I might have in high school: I hid in my room. I avoided eye contact as they came and went. I didn't smile at Don's innuendos. I'd call Jim and say, loudly, "Forget about coming over. *They're* here. . . . No, I didn't expect them, either. They were here yesterday and the day before that."

Finally, Jim, my levelheaded boyfriend, the man I eventually married, stepped in. "Is this any way to live, dreading pulling into your own driveway?"

He had a point. Wasn't that why I'd gotten divorced in the first place?

He suggested I send a coolly worded email. No pleading. No explaining why: *If our arrangement is to continue, I need to know when you will be using the house.*

Within an hour, I had a response. Don and Melinda would be moving out at the end of the month.

———•••———

After the movers were gone, I stood inside the empty guest room. Large metal brackets remained in the wall where the mirror had hung, and there were holes where the paddles had been. I took a deep breath. For the first time in seventeen months, the house felt like mine. I had no idea how I was going to make up the four hundred dollars a month, but I didn't care.

I opened the door to my bedroom and left it open. Nestled in my pillow—exactly where I expected them—were Don and Melinda's keys.

Circles of Light

Sheila Raeschild

Out beyond ideas of wrongdoing and rightdoing,
there is a field. I'll meet you there.
—Rumi

Once, in my late twenties, I went to visit my folks in their retirement condo in Miami Beach. The hot, humid day of my arrival, I hurried down to the ocean. My parents were having a leisurely breakfast and would join me later.

The water sparkled and shimmered, and I jumped up and down in the breakers before retreating to my beach towel.

A beautiful young stranger dropped to his knees on the edge of the towel and said, "You looked like Venus rising from the sea! Come away with me," he begged, "right now."

I laughed, feeling wonderfully sunlit.

Out of the corner of my eye, though, I spotted my mother and father trudging toward me across the sand, lugging striped plastic folding chairs, a yellow beach umbrella, and an old, beat-up picnic hamper.

"I can't," I whispered, already breathless. The thrill of his asking had turned my voice into a wisp of smoke that rose from a pile of twigs about to burst into flame. "My parents . . ."

"Tonight, then. Here. At sundown. Say yes. Please say yes." His rush of words fell into the rhythm of my heartbeat.

He leaned toward me, touching my bare knee with his index finger, like God stretching out his hand to bring Adam to life.

Someone else might have said, "Who the hell are you?"

But not me. If I heard a line from The Script, I had to respond appropriately.

"Yes," I said.

He rose and turned in a single graceful movement. I watched him walk across the sand as my parents arrived. I saw my mother look after him, too.

"Who was that?" she asked.

"I don't know," I answered, and that was the truth. "Just some guy." But I knew he was more than that.

What is sin? Is it the snake tempting Eve with the apple? Is it Eve offering the apple to Adam? Is it God asking, "Who told you that you were naked?" and Adam blaming Eve and Eve blaming the snake? Or is it an unforgiving God saying, "Get out of here, both of you"?

My Jewish mother's definition of sin was generic and all-encompassing. It ranged from the crimes reported in the newspaper to someone being rude to her on the street.

"*Treyf*!" my mother would say when anyone or anything disgusted her, or when behavior struck her as wrong. *Treyf*, the Yiddish word for everything that was unclean, garbage, trash. She would turn her head and pretend to spit. "Poo-poo," she would say. Her eyes would burn holes through my chest as she judged me. "*Schande*," she would say. "Shame."

But my definition of sin was far more focused and closer to God's. To me, sin meant erotica and sex, a delicious blend of excitement and desire. It was a tasty mélange of wanting and being wanted. Even as a curly-haired moppet I had drawn men's attention. They wanted to hold me, hug me, have me sit on their laps. By high school I was giving it away to anyone who begged for it. In those moments, I knew I was special, unique; I knew I was not like others. Filled with erotic momentum, I was living a life that was not like the life of an ordinary person, a boring person. I had always been the black sheep; every kid in my family had a label, and that was mine. Black sheep. I always managed to live up to it.

Occasionally there would be a flare of shame, like the electric shock I used to get from my daddy's home-built crystal radio kits. But that evaporated into my feeling that I was Aphrodite, goddess of love.

———•·•———

The sun was setting as I told my parents that the day had exhausted me. I was going to turn in early. I kissed them goodnight like a dutiful daughter; then I retreated to my bedroom and changed into a cleavage-revealing yellow shirt and a short gold skirt. Silent as a cat, I snuck out the back door to meet my unknown lover.

He was already there, wearing a gleaming white wifebeater under an unbuttoned flower-print shirt. His dark trousers completed the *Miami Vice* look. He lay sprawled across a blanket on the sand. The slight chill in the evening air was not even partially responsible for the goose bumps that rose on my arms. As though he sensed my presence, he stood up, came toward me, and took me in his arms. We kissed passionately, pressing our bodies together. Kissed without ever speaking a word and without even knowing each other's names. We kissed as though we were lifelong lovers, reunited after years apart.

He drew me toward the blanket, and we sank down on it. I slid my hand down his beautiful chest, down below his waist. I lowered the waistband of his trousers, and then I lowered my head toward his exquisite penis. Opening my mouth, I took it in with the sense of homecoming a bird must feel when settling into her nest.

Later, he'd say, "When you took me in your mouth without my having to ask, I knew you were the woman I'd been searching for. The woman of my dreams. A woman I would want to make happy."

That was later, though. At that moment, I only knew that I was already happy, and I wanted to make *him* happy, too.

He cupped my head with his hands and groaned in pleasure. Then, after a too-short time, he pulled me up so we were face-to-face and rolled on top of me. His trousers were down even farther; my skirt was pulled up and my skimpy Victoria's Secret panties pulled down, and he was in me in a single, swift thrust. Oh, God, what bliss.

"My name is Tom," he whispered, licking my ear.

"I'm Sheila," I said, wrapping my legs around his smooth back, "and I'm yours."

"*Treyf*," my mother would have said, but I would say, "union with the beloved."

He moved in me, thrusting rhythmically so that my back pressed into the sand with each movement. Then the night became as bright as midday. *This is it*, I thought. *This must be the illumination of perfect ecstasy.*

But I was wrong. The night really had become as bright as midday!

"Get up," a gruff voice commanded—a male voice.

My eyes sprang open. There was a ring of light surrounding us. No mystical ring, but one created by the flashlights of half a dozen policemen.

"Put your clothes on and get up," the cop said.

That's when one of those rare lightning bolts of shame shot through me.

But then Tom said, with a calmness that belied our half-dressed, brightly lit bodies, "Get your lights off her."

They were his first words spoken out loud that evening. They were noble words, the words of my man defending me. I felt amazed by him, and as scared and embarrassed as I was, I had to smile. Even as I was grappling with my panties, pulling them back up over my hips, I smiled.

And his words worked. The lights slid off us and over to the bare sand. When we stood up, the cops divided like the Red Sea for Moses. One wave of blue-clad men swept my hero, my stranger, to a Miami Beach Police Department patrol car parked at the edge of the sand; the other blue wave swept me away to another.

I don't know what they said to him.

To me, they said, "What's a nice girl like you doing in a place like this?"

It was a phrase I'd heard over and over throughout my life. Whenever I was caught, whenever I was in an odd or questionable setting, whenever anyone looked at me and saw the girl next door doing things the girl next door wasn't even supposed to know about.

"We know him, and he's bad news," one of them added, leaning so close that his breath blew one of the tendrils of my hair out of my eyes.

I suspected this was another one of those standard lines—sort of parallel to the "nice girl like you" line. I suspected they didn't know him any better than they knew me. I suspected they didn't know him any better than I knew him—which is to say, not at all.

Finally they drove off, leaving us there like two seashells washed up on the beach, alone and apart. But not for long.

"I can't believe it," Tom crowed, his laugh telling me how to interpret the entire event. "During that whole time, I never lost my hard-on!"

I laughed in relief. It wasn't a tragedy. It wasn't the kind of scene where the community circles around the girl and cries out "Shame!" Where people throw stones.

It was a comedy.

He rushed to me and once more wrapped his arms around me, and we shared the long wet kiss that ends the traditional romance novel. And that wasn't all we shared.

In *The Teaching of Buddha*, under "Defilements," it is written that "human desires are endless. It is like the thirst of a man who drinks salt water: he gets no satisfaction and his thirst is only increased." I don't know about the lack of satisfaction part, but our desires that night were endless; and like two people dying of thirst, we did drink.

By mutual and unspoken consent, we left the beach. I had walked from my folks' condo, but Tom had a car. So we drove. We drove straight into the heart of Miami Beach. He pulled up at one of the ritziest hotels on the strip, letting a valet in a silly red vest park the car for us. With his arm around my waist, we sauntered into the dimly lit lobby like a couple of swells. We could have been a normal couple except for the heat that emanated from us and the aura I felt must certainly be surrounding us. Then, the pressure of his hand against my waist told me we weren't checking in.

No, instead of aiming for the registration desk, he steered us toward a plush sofa set in front of the mock fireplace. And we weren't about to seat ourselves demurely, either. As soon as we sat down, Tom pressed himself onto me and slid me down onto the soft velour surface. In plain view of the guests and passersby, he lifted my short skirt, fingered my panties to the side, and pushed himself into me. It was shocking. I was shocked. Shocked and thrilled—so thrilled I almost came the minute I felt him in me.

Over and over he thrust himself into me, and in the background I heard gasps that weren't mine.

"My God," a woman exclaimed. "Do you see what they're doing?"

"Pay no attention," said a man, no doubt her husband, rushing her past the scene.

I laughed out loud. It was so outrageous and unbelievable and insane and wonderful. Here I was, fucking a divine stranger in the lobby of Miami Beach's best hotel. I knew that the man hurrying his proper wife past the scene would later be jerking off under the covers as he replayed the scene in his imagination. In his mind's eye he would be the man on top, pumping away at the promiscuous woman under him. Me.

Tom laughed, too. Laughed and shuddered to a stop.

"Time to go," he whispered.

He pulled me up, and we headed for the door. A raging passion for the madness of the night with this lunatic set me alight like a fir tree in a forest fire.

Soon we were in the car again, heading away from the crowded downtown scene.

"What next?" I asked, and repeated the question to myself, within myself: What next?

"You're as gorgeous as a thousand stars," Tom said, gazing at me. "Graceful and daring. A perfect woman."

His murmured words soothed me, lulled me. Yet at the same time I felt more awake than I had ever been. I felt as though I had been asleep all my life and was just waking up. This was it! I was Sleeping Beauty and he was the prince, the perfect lover. I felt as though my life were truly beginning, my insane new life with this stranger, about whom the police had said, "Watch out; he's trouble."

The Teaching of Buddha also says this: "The world is like a lotus pond filled with many varieties of the plant; there are blossoms of many different tints. Some are white, some pink . . . some spread their leaves on the water, and some raise their leaves above the water. Mankind has many more differences."

Well, that about sums it up.

I spent the next three days and nights with Tom, and we made love over and over, in every position either of us knew or could invent, creating in our bodies blossoms of many different tints. We made love in every place I had ever imagined, and in some places I hadn't.

I called my parents to say I was alive and well—more alive and well than I could possibly explain—and hung up before my mother could demand an explanation. I returned to their condo only long enough to pack in order to make my plane home.

"*Treyf!*" my mother hurled after me as I spun my way out the door to Tom, waiting in his car to drive me to the airport. I knew we would find time and space for a few more grapplings before my plane took off. After all, the bland, sterile environment of an airport would surely be a perfect place to experience delight while we shocked everyone else.

"Let's go," I said, throwing my bag into the back seat.

As he pulled away from the curb, I lowered my head into his lap, unzipping his pants. When we got to the airport, we kissed and hugged and fucked on benches and against the wall and waiting in line on the way to the gate where we would be separated.

How could I ever bear to leave him?

But I had a life back in Atlanta. Of course. And he had a life here in Miami. Or at least I assumed he did. We still knew nothing about each other except our bodies.

All we'd had, and all we would ever have, were those three days in the Garden of Eden—sans snake, sans apple, sans God.

Love in the Worst Way

Aaron Gwyn

She was five eight in stockings, five nine in heels—brunette and shapely and extraordinarily fit. She had the high cheekbones of a model and she moved with a model's poise, though I don't know if she ever modeled for anyone but me. She had tattoos on both shoulders, tattoos encircling her waist, an elaborate dragon inked on her lower back, and paw prints walking up the inside of her right thigh. Two weeks before I met her, she'd turned forty, but she looked my age, which, at the time, was thirty-one. I was six years into my first marriage, and within twenty minutes of meeting Kyra, I was having sex with her on my apartment floor.

We were introduced at a pool party thrown by one of our mutual students. She was a philosophy professor at the university where I was just finishing my first year as an assistant professor in English. My wife had flown back to Oklahoma to visit relatives when the semester ended, and this student who'd been in my spring workshop invited me to his party. I remember discussing it with Rebecca. I didn't really want to go, but we'd been in Charlotte for less than a year, and she wanted to meet some more couples our age. We'd run into my student, Shawn, and his wife at a local bar, and Rebecca had liked them and thought the four of us might become friends. On the phone that evening, I told Rebecca I'd drive over, make an appearance, and then come back home.

My second book was under contract, and my agent was breathing down my neck. I'd been staying up at night writing and then sleeping from about four to ten, though I didn't really feel the need. I'd been on an antidepressant for five months, and a manic electricity ran through my nerves like a current. I can remember lying on the futon late at night, with my wife asleep in the next room and the television muted and flickering, feeling as though I was falling through the sky. I'd started boxing again, going to jujitsu, and I felt better—stronger, stranger—than I could remember feeling.

I'd never experienced mania. I didn't know it was an actual thing that happened to people—like ingrown toenails, or bone spurs, or gout. I didn't know there were symptoms. I didn't know it was a potential side effect of the medication I was taking. I didn't know it could kill you as dead as the depression I'd gone to the doctor for in the first place.

Shawn and his wife, Sarah, owned an impressive house: large and expensively decorated, with an enormous backyard. A hot tub. A pool. Anyone with both would normally have set off my radar right away, but my radar was on the fritz, had been for several months. I went up the sidewalk and knocked on the door.

Sarah answered in her bikini. She had a red plastic cup in one hand and she was smiling drunkenly.

I walked inside. I didn't know a single person other than Shawn and Sarah, and I was escorted through a living room full of people and then through the kitchen to the backyard. There were people in the hot tub, people in the pool. People sitting around on lawn chairs drinking and smoking pot. A very beautiful woman sat in a lawn chair next to a table talking to an African-American man with dreadlocks. She wore a brown two-piece, and her hair was the color of syrup. Sarah walked me over to her and said, "I'd like you to meet Kyra."

Kyra looked up at me and smiled. She took my hand. I didn't remember offering it.

"I've heard about you," she said.

Sarah stepped between us and offered me a drink, but I told her I was allergic.

"You have an alcohol allergy?"

"Yeah," I said. "Makes me break out in handcuffs."

Then we were in the hot tub: an exchange student from Germany, a guy who taught high school, Sarah beside me. She sloshed her way closer and began whispering. Her breath smelled like whiskey. Her lips brushed my ear.

"Shawn's afraid you're going to be offended," she said.

I looked around. At a table on the patio, three girls were snorting cocaine off a paper plate.

"Offended by what?" I asked.

"What's about to happen," said Sarah.

"What's about to happen?"

"Drugs," she told me. "Sex."

I waved her off. I lied and told her I was impossible to offend.

She raked the nails of one hand down my shoulder and then across my biceps and forearm. She reached back, undid her top, took it off, and sat up on the edge of the hot tub. Her breasts were fake. She stuck them out.

The pool was separated from us by a low concrete wall, and she executed what was supposed to be a seductive back roll and slunk into the pool. She backstroked away, staring at me, her nipples protruding from the water like turtles' heads.

I was trying to figure out how to make an exit when I heard a voice beside me.

"Hey," it said.

I turned to look. It was Kyra. She knelt down on the lip of the hot tub.

"I think we shouldn't be here," I said.

"Because we're professors?"

"Yeah."

She glanced over at Sarah. She told me I was probably right.

Then she said, "You teach fiction?"

"Yeah."

"And you have a book out?"

"Yeah."

"I saw it at Barnes & Noble. I was going to buy it."

"It's a story collection. No one buys it."

"*I'll* buy it."

"That makes one of you," I said.

She smiled. She said we should get a drink sometime.

I told her I didn't drink.

"Do you drink coffee?"

"Sometimes," I said.

"Would you like some coffee now?"

I climbed out of the hot tub and stood there dripping.

"I don't have any clothes," I said, pointing at my swimming trunks.

"Did you bring a shirt?"

"I brought a shirt. I forgot my towel."

She stared at me a few seconds, the corner of her bottom lip in her teeth. Then she placed a hand on my chest, the other between my shoulder blades and, brushing down with her palms, squeegeed off the water.

"Now you don't need a towel," she said.

Then we were inside the house, in Shawn's office, kissing. I'd never cheated on my wife. Now I was.

We stopped for a second. I was sitting in an office chair at a desk and she was sitting on my lap.

I said, "Would you like to go back to my apartment and fuck?"

She squinted at me. I didn't know if I was about to get lectured or slapped.

"Yeah," she told me. "I kind of would."

"I know you would," I said.

We stood and I took her hand and led her down a hallway toward the front door. Shawn caught us in the living room.

"Whoa, whoa, whoa," he said. "Where are you two sneaking off to?"

"Back to his apartment," said Kyra. "To fuck."

Shawn studied the two of us.

"Oh," he finally said.

We went outside into the humid spring air, walked across the front lawn, and made it to my car. I unlocked the doors and we climbed inside.

I said, "Let's talk STDs."

"I've never had an STD."

"I haven't either."

I started the car, turned on the lights, pulled away from the curb.

"I think we just talked STDs," Kyra said.

We were driving through an old neighborhood, trees on both sides of the road. It was just dusk and the windows were down. North Carolina this time of year smelled rich and humid. Mist rose from the blacktop.

"Why are you *married?*" she asked.

I told her I loved my wife. Which was both ridiculous and true.

When we walked into my apartment, the air conditioning prickled the skin along my arms.

We stood at the kitchen counter, kissing.

"Where's your bathroom?" she asked.

I motioned toward the next room and she kissed me again and said she'd be right back.

I remember walking into the living room. All the lights were on and I thought about turning a few of them off, but I turned on the television instead. I flipped around, selected the music channel that plays songs from the '90s. Then I just stood. I was about to betray my marriage vows, and those were vows I'd always taken seriously. I asked myself if I knew what I was doing, but before I could answer, Kyra came into the room and we started kissing again.

I turned her around and began kissing the back of her neck. When I pulled off her shirt I saw she had Hebrew characters tattooed on her left shoulder blade.

"What's that?" I asked.

"What's what?"

"*That,*" I told her, putting my index finger on top of it.

"It's Hebrew," she said. "It's *kavod.*"

"What's *kavod?*"

"It means *respect,*" she said.

I started laughing. It was too much even for me.

She turned around to face me and snaked a hand inside my waist-band. "Why don't you sit down on the couch and let me suck your cock?" she said.

We walked around to the other side of the futon, and she knelt on the carpet and pulled my swimming trunks around my ankles. I don't remember it feeling good when she took me inside her mouth. I remember thinking, *this is what adultery's like.*

"It's good to respect yourself," I said.

She didn't answer. Her head was going up and down.

"I think, if you're going to blow a married guy, self-respect is pretty key."

She slid one hand along my stomach and pushed against my chest.

"I'm sort of a fellatio-heckler," I admitted.

She took my penis out of her mouth and started laughing. When she was finished laughing, she put my penis back.

After several minutes, she stood, pulled off her shorts, pulled off her bikini bottoms, and started to mount me.

"Wait a second," I said.

I walked back into the bedroom, went into the closet, and dug down in my underwear drawer. I had all these different-colored condoms I'd gotten at the University of Denver when I was finishing my doctorate, but I never used them because my wife and I didn't use condoms. We only had sex about every six months anyway, so we'd have died before we'd have gotten through them all. I selected a green one, put it on, and walked back into the living room.

"You have a green condom on your dick," Kyra said.

I told her that her PhD from Syracuse was really paying off. She took me in one hand, and, squatting, tried to put me inside her. She was still wearing sandals, though, and my first thought was I didn't want to get my futon dirty. I didn't want my wife to see sandal prints on the fabric. I grabbed her and put her on the floor. As soon as I touched the head of my penis to her vagina, she came.

I knelt there, watching. Her entire body convulsed and she screamed very loud and then she lay there shivering. It frightened me in a way I didn't understand.

"Did you just have an orgasm?"

"Yeah," she said.

"Jesus," I told her.

"I'm a push-button girl," she said.

I didn't know what that meant.

I never asked.

———•——•———

After we put our clothes back on and were headed for the front door, she said, "So, I should maybe get your number," and I scribbled it on a Post-It. I remember thinking she wouldn't call. I remember *hoping* she wouldn't.

When she rang me up at nine the next night, we talked for three and a half hours. After about fifteen minutes, I was glad I'd given her my number, and after another thirty I'd made plans to see her Monday evening. We ended up at North Carolina's largest tourist attraction: a 1.4-million-square-foot indoor shopping mall called Concord Mills. It's a living monument to Capitalism and Teenagers and Fried Food. There's a miniature train with real tires and a fake chimney that ferries children around, a bell ringing when it comes up behind you.

We had dinner at a really bad restaurant with an indoor bowling alley and we tried on clothes we had no intention of buying, made out in the dressing room of Victoria's Secret, went to a Vin Diesel movie, had sex in the back row, and left. At one point, we stopped in at the bookstore and checked to see how many copies of my book they had in stock (eleven). It would have been ridiculous behavior for an unmarried man in his early twenties, and it's likely the best time I've ever had.

Our third night together she leaned across the table in this restaurant where we were having dinner and said, "I'd like to see you fuck a girl right in front of me."

I sat staring a few moments, trying to determine if it was a trap.

Then I told her I'd like to see that too.

My wife was due back from Oklahoma in three weeks and in those twenty-one days Kyra and I acted out scenes from an entire manic marriage. We stayed up all night watching porn; we picked up girls at restaurants, strip clubs, tattoo parlors, and once at a bagel shop just down the road—that one looked so young Kyra made her show us her driver's license.

At the end of the second week, we got tattooed. I'd grown up doing martial arts—tae kwon do, jujitsu, the traditional Japanese sword-art, *Iai*—and there was a kanji from Miyamoto Musashi's 17th-century treatise on swordsmanship, *The Book of Five Rings*, that I'd always loved. The character looks like this:

I showed Kyra and tried my best to explain—not like she didn't have the intellectual horsepower to understand. She'd been trained in the Western philosophic tradition. She'd had numerous courses in Eastern philosophy, and when she was recruited by the university, she'd been teaching English in Japan. I'd never had a philosophy class of any kind, had never been to the Orient, and whatever I'd been trained in was hardly cohesive enough to be called a *tradition*. The character I'd chosen can be translated as *emptiness* or *no-mind*. I prefer the more ambiguous *nothing*, and this is the translation that most appealed to Kyra.

Up to this point, all her tattoos had been done by a man she'd dated, Vic, who had started a prominent parlor in Charlotte, then sold the business and moved to Wilmington. Since Vic was no longer in town, we went to a parlor just down the street, a place called University Tattoo, where a morbidly obese man inked Musashi's symbol first on the inside of my right forearm, then on Kyra's left hip.

Back in the car, giddy from the endorphins, I held my forearm against her waist and kissed her. I studied the tattoos. Identical, but with my arm angled down, inverted, reversed.

"Nothing," I told her.

"Nothing," she said.

———•·•———

She was twice married and twice divorced. She told me she didn't know how many sexual partners she'd had. She said she was open to all comers. The course she taught at the university—the course she'd been recruited to teach—was titled "Philosophy of Sex." It was the most popular course on campus and the most controversial. Her area of research was trauma and sexuality. She authored papers on bioethics. She served on the board of Carolinas Medical Center as a liaison: I was never sure for exactly what. Her father was Jewish, her mother was Catholic, but she told me both were irrelevant, because she didn't believe in God.

She said that at the age of nine, she'd been raped by two men in her front yard in Estes Park, Colorado, but that she didn't tell anyone until she was an adult. She said the night before this happened an angel had appeared to her, the Russian angel Tatyana. I didn't want to hear this, but she told me anyway. She had a tattoo of this angel on her right deltoid, a mermaid-looking figure with the Cyrillic letters ТДТГ. After she explained the tattoo, it scared me so much I tried not to look.

She said her father had molested her. She said her grandfather had too. She'd been institutionalized three times, and she took an antipsychotic every morning. They came in capsules and were small and green.

When I asked her what happened if she didn't take them, she told me she'd go insane.

———•·•———

When I pulled into her drive the afternoon after we got the tattoos, she was pacing around the yard, weeping. I got out of the car and walked over and tried to hold her, but she twisted loose and started toward the woods in back of her house. I followed her up a trail, through a grove of post oak and pine, and she stopped in front of a patch of poison ivy, dropped to a squat, and held her face in her hands.

I knelt beside her. I kept asking what was wrong. The streaks of mascara down her cheeks made her look like a figure from Kabuki.

I can't recall the conversation well enough to quote, but here's the gist:

She'd spoken to Vic that morning, her former boyfriend and tattoo artist. Kyra had told him she'd fallen in love with me and that, the day before, we'd gone to get tattooed. He hadn't minded the fact she'd fallen in love. He didn't even care she'd let someone else tattoo her. But when he learned who'd done the work, he was furious. He told her the artist was an HIV-positive heroin addict who'd already had two of his parlors shut down.

I managed to listen for about a minute. Then I couldn't anymore. The questions started tumbling out:

Could you pass HIV through tattooing?

And if so, how did she know this?

And why was she talking to Vic?

"I thought you said the relationship was over?"

"It *is* over," she said. "But we still talk. We're friends."

It clearly wasn't over, but some things definitely were. The laughs were over. My witty repartee had deserted me completely. I turned, leaned to one side, and threw up. I felt like I was falling, and I put my hand in the grass to keep from pitching over.

When I came to myself, her hand was on my shoulder. She was saying it was going to be all right.

It wasn't going to be all right, but I didn't know what was worse: the fact that we'd been tattooed by someone who got HIV sharing needles, or the fact that I'd fallen in love.

I looked at Kyra. I asked what we were going to do.

The question could have referred to so many things that she just shook her head.

That was on a Tuesday. Rebecca's plane was scheduled to land on Thursday evening. I took Kyra with me to pick her up. I know how that sounds—or now I know—but this was our thinking at the time:

I'd come clean to Rebecca. I'd tell her I loved her and that nothing between us had changed. I'd tell her that now I loved Kyra too. I'd tell her Kyra was a part of us. Kyra kept saying she loved me like she'd never loved anyone, and that if I loved Rebecca, she would learn to love her too.

We'd be a family, she said.

We discussed this over and over. You'd think two adults with PhDs would be able to see the madness of this. You'd be very mistaken.

I remember that drive to the airport, Kyra gripping my hand when I took it off the gearshift, her knuckles white. We were excited and eager and almost high from the fear. We kept saying how much we loved each other. We kept saying everything would be fine.

We parked on the bottom deck, went inside and up the escalator toward the security checkpoint. When we passed the screen showing arrivals, I saw my wife's flight had been canceled. We walked over to the US Airways counter and asked them what had happened, and a man in a blue uniform told us the flight had been diverted to Atlanta because of the weather. Kyra and I looked at each other. We'd not gotten back to the parking deck before my cell phone started ringing.

"It's me," said my wife. "I'm fine."

I asked her if she was in Atlanta.

"Atlanta," she said. "Getting a room at the airport. They got me on a flight that leaves at six tomorrow morning. I don't want to wake you. I'll just get a cab."

Kyra and I drove back to the apartment like inmates granted a stay of execution. The giddiness was gone. There was a calm in its place. We had sex on the floor beside the living room window, and when she came she began to cry. We lay there and I held her. Outside, it started to rain. The storm that had rerouted my wife's flight had finally reached us. Kyra looked at me. I always smoothed back the strands of hair that covered the wrinkles on her forehead and she always raked them back into place.

She said, "I feel like God gave us one more night. I feel like tonight is a gift."

"Thought you didn't believe in God."

"You brought me back to Him," she said.

I didn't know what to say to this, and I don't know now. She reached out and brushed her hand across my face. I believe, because of what she'd been through, that I'd thought of her as being damaged. The look in her eyes said she thought the same of me.

———————

I remember waking up alone the next morning on the futon, turning when I heard Rebecca's key in the lock, watching as she came through the door.

"Hey," she said. She put down her bags and came over to give me a hug. Her hair smelled like espresso. I realized I'd forgotten that.

There were a number of things I'd forgotten, but they came rushing immediately back. And there were some new things rushing along with them.

I knew the affair was over. I knew my marriage was over. I knew the tattoo was the least of my worries. I knew this was how it felt to lose your mind.

I couldn't know that two weeks later I would put a knife to my wrist and watch as my wife ran screaming from the apartment. I couldn't know that Kyra would be fired that coming semester for sleeping with one of her students, that she'd leave Charlotte in December, that afterward, I'd never see her again. I'd rightly guessed Rebecca and I would get divorced, but I didn't know how much it would hurt, how much I'd relied on her, how much of my bullshit machismo came from her support of me.

I still don't understand my frame of mind that summer, but I can tell you at the end of a manic episode, your muscles ache worse than they would from any beating. That *despair* is no longer just a word in the dictionary. That when the dopamine and serotonin plummet, you need love like you can't imagine. You need it in the worst way.

Fat

Sarah Einstein

Neil and I rented a side bedroom from his brother's girl-friend for fifty dollars a month. We called it our afternoon home—it was where we lived between the end of my school day and my ten o'clock curfew. I was a junior in high school (he a college sophomore) both of us lived with our parents. We bought a hot plate, a stockpot, and a tea kettle. I stole things from my mother's house: a white hobnail bedspread; mismatched flatware; chipped mugs; and an elaborate, gold-encrusted finger bowl I used as an ashtray. He repaired broken radios and clocks on a card table near the door; I made boxed macaroni and cheese for our dinner. Playing house. That old game.

Mostly, though, we made love on the old pull-out sofa under the big picture window, afternoon light streaming in through the batiked cloth that we had rescued from a nearby dumpster and hung as a curtain. We lived naked on the lumpy mattress, swathed in the hobnail bedspread. We ate, read, fucked, talked, smoked cigarettes, and learned to drink coffee without our feet ever touching the ground, like children playing at alligators-in-the-carpet. We were a tangle of arms, legs, mouths, hands, and skin and could not say where sex began and ended.

We did not always remember to stop and find a condom. This was before AIDS taught us all that lesson the hard way.

I was queasy from the moment I got pregnant. It had only been three weeks since my last period—too soon for symptoms, according to the handouts from health class—when the smell of gas from the Warm Morning heater in the bedroom's old fireplace knocked me to my knees. Neil scrambled to find a pail while my stomach roiled, and when at last there was nothing left for me to sick up, he put my head in his lap, tucked a damp tendril of hair behind my ear, and whispered, "Oh, fuck, baby, what are we going to do?"

We gave up the extravagance of the room in his brother's girlfriend's apartment. I carefully snuck the bedspread, flatware, mugs, and finger bowl back into my mother's house. Neil called the assistant principal's office and pretended to be my father so that we could drive to the state capital and see a doctor at the state's only abortion clinic. Neil said that the assistant principal, who knew my father and couldn't have been fooled, said, "Of course, John, I'll go get her from class now. Just call whenever you need to take Sarah out of school for a doctor's appointment." He then said, in a less collegial tone, "We've noticed she hasn't been feeling well these last weeks. We hope you're going to see someone about *that*," and slammed down the phone.

The doctor at the women's clinic said, yes, I was pregnant, and probably had been for five weeks or so. She never asked what I planned to do; no one showed up at that particular clinic for neonatal vitamins or obstetric advice. She handed me an appointment card for a Saturday four weeks later, patted my shoulder, and said, "See you then, kiddo."

For a month, Neil and I scrounged for change in between our parents' couch cushions, begged from friends, and did odd jobs in a panic to raise two hundred fifty dollars. I took money for a prom dress from my mother, but never bought the dress. Neil stopped eating. His father didn't keep food in the house and even the subsidized lunches at the student union cafeteria would have taken too big a chunk out of the tips he earned delivering pizza for Domino's for him to save anything. In the afternoons, when he picked me up from high school, we sat on the floor of his bedroom, rolling pennies and listening to David Bowie.

I fed him the bag lunches my mother packed—bologna sandwiches, bags of Fritos, Little Debbie oatmeal cakes—which I was too queasy to eat. He brought me tall glasses of club soda and sleeves of saltines.

"It's all going to be okay," he said, every time I let the coins dribble though my fingers and dissolved into tears. "It really will be okay."

I don't remember if he promised me we'd have children someday, when we were ready. It seems he must have; we were always talking about the future, imagining for ourselves the kind of life that only seems possible if you are young and privileged. A house with turrets, dormer windows, crystal chandeliers, and, oddly, composting toilets. I would be a writer, Neil a brilliant engineer. And so, with that impossible life shining brightly on the horizon, we never considered allowing the pregnancy to go to term.

Neil drove me back to Charleston, the two hundred fifty dollars in his wallet, on the Saturday I was ten weeks pregnant. A woman in scrubs gave me two Valium and took me back to a small room with an examination table, a metal stool on casters, and a steel rack full of paper robes. I undressed, slipped into a robe and onto the table to wait for the doctor. In the next room, I could hear the quiet hum of the vacuum aspiration machine, one woman crying, and another mumbling encouragement. I wanted to run to the nurse's station and insist that they allow Neil to stay with me, but the Valium weighed me down. I could not move. I waited, though I can't say if it was for a long or a short time.

I curled up in the back seat of Neil's Honda Civic on the way home, staring through the window, still lost in the sedative. I must have slept. I remember nothing about the trip home. I awoke swaddled in a nest of blankets on his father's couch. I do not know how Neil managed to get me from the car to the house—he was tiny then, and I never was. Noises from the kitchen must have been what finally roused me. Neil was making me lunch.

He came into the living room after what seemed like a long time, carrying plates heaped with brown rice, shrimp, and broccoli in a rich brown sauce.

"Here," he said. "I know you haven't been able to eat much lately, and I thought now maybe . . ." He trailed off, looking at me hopefully.

The food smelled like brine and garlic; it made my head swim. But he was so sincere, so wanted to comfort me, that I ate it. The taste lingered in my mouth for days.

We stayed together for another few months. Because we had given up the room to pay for the abortion, we met in coffee shops. Years later, he was my husband for a few months. He made the shrimp and broccoli dish only once while we were married. When he asked why it made me cry, I didn't have the heart to tell him. Taste, like smell, carries memory in a way I cannot guard against. After that dinner, we never made love again.

———•—•———

Putt and I drove from Huntsville, Alabama, to Atlanta for the First National Lesbian Conference without a single argument, which for us counted as an accomplishment. We were always fighting, mostly about the gap between my vaguely defined bisexuality and her lesbian orthodoxy. We had been trying, off and on, to be lovers for five years, and couldn't seem to find a way to live comfortably with our differences.

The idea of attending a gay rights conference made up entirely of women—though, back then, we undoubtedly spelled it womyn or wimmin—thrilled us both, and that the conference was in the Deep South seemed particularly transgressive. The Radisson Hotel in which the conference was held was a very modern, very urban sort of place; neither of us had ever stayed in such an aggressively corporate environment. We were in our early twenties, not yet old enough to have those sorts of jobs. My luggage was a ripped army knapsack; she wore frayed jeans and a T-shirt from a women's music festival she'd gone to the summer before. We were insurgents, smiling aggressively at the middle-aged businessmen in the elevator and roping our arms around one another in triumph. I was at my best as a faux lesbian when it was a political act, though I wouldn't have admitted it then.

The conference itself was a little tedious. We went to different sessions; I to ones with enough theoretical content that I could later write about them for my Women's Studies courses, and she to ones with names like "Goddess Spirituality" and "Sacred Drumming." There were women at the conference whose official job was to "watch the vibe," to be certain that the almighty process moved forward. More often than not, this meant silencing any voice that sounded even a little like mine; one of these *vibe-watchers* escorted a young, crew-cutted woman out of a session when she insisted that maybe there was something positive in the butch-femme traditions of 1950s lesbian culture. I heard another tell a woman who identified as "not yet sure of her sexuality" that this was lesbian space, and although she was welcome to stay, she should sit quietly and "let the process continue."

It was 1991, and we tossed around words like *phallocentric* and *gynocide* with revolutionary abandon. Radical lesbian separatism still seemed a viable option, and we quoted Andrea Dworkin with grave seriousness. ("Only when manhood is dead—and it will perish when ravaged femininity no longer sustains it—only then will we know what it is to be free.") I was, I knew, a snake in the grass. I brought the *male gaze* into the room; I enslaved my would-be sisters with my disloyal lusts; I gave succor to the enemy. At the end of every session, I slunk into one of the bathrooms (there were no "men's rooms" in the conference area—we had liberated them) to whisper at the beige walls all the snarky comments I had swallowed.

We would meet up again in the afternoon for the plenary sessions; Putt, high on sisterhood, me furiously scribbling notes in the back pages of my dog-eared copy of *Gyn/Ecology*, feeling like a sex offender. It was there that the real skirmishes broke out. A group of women claiming to speak on behalf of all the Black Lesbians in attendance took the stage before one afternoon session and demanded that all the Jewish Lesbians leave, because they could not have "lesbian safe space" when surrounded by those who were oppressing their Palestinian sisters. There was an ongoing debate about whether or not the bisexual women in attendance should have to self-identify—perhaps, it was suggested, by wearing a ribbon or button of a specific color—and abstain from voting on any of the conference's referendums. The gap between who I was and who the lesbian community would accept as a member of the tribe widened into a chasm.

The vendors' room offered the only respite from the unrelenting seriousness of the conference. There, and only there, did sexuality rise up above the din of politics and make itself heard.

Putt and I leafed hungrily through back issues of *On Our Backs*. Maybe somewhere in those tastefully shot, mostly black-and-white photographs of real women loving real women, we would find a rubric that would let us be lovers. Oh, we'd each had stormy, tempestuous love affairs with *other* women, but somehow the alchemy of sex never worked between us; we never stopped being a clumsy tangle struggling toward intimacy; we never dissolved into a single, fluid being. At best, we soldiered on until the effort left us exhausted enough to fall asleep as comrades-in-arms. More often, attempts at sex simply reaffirmed our belief that things could never work out between us, because I had loved a man or two and could not say I never would again.

We purchased buttons with slogans like "Sisterhood Is Powerful," and "Grrrl Power." We did not buy the ones that said, "Jodi Foster Made Me Do It" or "Vagiterian." We were not that bold, nor that crude. I bought rainbow bracelets, a totebag silk-screened with a photograph of the Venus of Willendorf, pink-triangle earrings, and twice as many books as I could afford. I hoped to educate and accessorize myself into what Putt needed me to be. I loved her; it was painful to be told that I was her oppressor.

For the first two days, we walked by the Good Vibrations table without stopping. One of our earliest arguments had been over my suggestion that we just cut through all the trouble we were having and take my vibrator to bed with us. Putt was horrified. She was not, she made it clear, going to let something that could best be described as a *contraption* anywhere near her sacred yoni, and could not believe that I would even suggest it. We had still been teenagers then, and she was the *real* lesbian, so I apologized and never brought the subject up again. But there we were, five years later, still confused and frustrated. Finally, on the next to last day, I grabbed her hand and pulled her over to the table.

"Look," I said, gesturing to the table full of dolphin-shaped dildos and Wahl coil vibrators. "If this stuff was anti-lesbian, the conference organizers would never have let them set up here. I mean, they've banned perfume, alcohol, and men. It's not like they're shy about excluding."

"I don't care what they think." She gave me a long, cold look. "I told you how I feel. Why are you pressuring me?"

I picked up a silicon statue of the Virgin Mary, showing it to Putt. Maybe I even shook it at her, though I like to think I didn't. "How is this phallocentric? I don't understand." The woman sitting at the table, who I now think might very well have been the queen of lesbian sex herself, Susie Bright, laughed at us and shook her head.

"Of course you don't understand," Putt said. "You have sex with men. You WANT us to have a penis in bed with us." She turned away, and I followed, reminding myself that I had no right to be angry, that I was—as I'd so often been reminded since we arrived—in danger of defiling her with my own impure desire.

That night, we went to a little Ethiopian restaurant that everyone at the conference had been raving about. We were shy going in; it was comfortable in the hotel, but we had lived with the harsh stares of the Deep South for long enough to be cautious. But inside, women huddled around the small, low tables in multiples of two. It seemed everyone at the conference was here with a partner.

The owner, a short middle-aged man in a starched white shirt and dark polyester slacks, smiled and led us to an empty table in the back corner of the restaurant.

"Have you eaten Ethiopian food before?" he asked. We had not and agreed to let him pick out the dishes for our dinner. "You will like this very much," he assured us, and then, after asking if we ate meat, and whether or not we liked our food spicy, he walked off to greet the next table of conferees.

Putt and I looked around, amazed to see so many women openly holding hands, even kissing, in a restaurant smack in the middle of Atlanta. We were tired, less certain of ourselves, not as brave. The uncomfortable afternoon weighed heavily on us, and we had little to say to one another. Finally, the owner came back carrying a huge *mesob* covered in thick lentil and spinach porridges, chunks of meat and fish, and a large oval of *injera*.

"Watch how they do it," he said, pointing to a family sitting at the next table; a family who, amazingly, seemed completely at ease in the company of fifty affectionate lesbians. As we watched, they used small pieces of the *injera* to scoop up the porridges and stews on the outer edges of the *mesob*. "You do it like that, no knives or forks." He shook his head and laughed. "But, really, you should feed each other. It's called *gursha*. In Ethiopia, if you love someone, you feed them." He smiled at us—a kindly smile, not a leer—and went off to wait on another table.

We sat for a moment, staring at the bread and the thick porridges, considering. Did we love each other? Before the conference, we would have each said yes, and now neither of us was certain. But, finally, we could not resist the charm of the custom or the heavy scent of spices that hung over the table. We fed one another small mouthfuls of lentils, lamb, fish, and vegetables. After a few warming bites, we grew playful. Putt was immoderate in the size of her *gursha* and fed me more than I could chew; I became clumsy and spilled *azifa* down her chin, into her lap. We laughed. We laughed some more, and then we ate and kissed and talked and forgot to worry about whether or not I was oppressing her. We left the restaurant holding hands.

But we went to sleep that night in separate beds, and never made love again, though we are still friends. Every Christmas she sends me her famous Cayenne Cashew Brittle, and I send her jars of grape and cherry jam made during the summer. If I am in the South, we meet up and take one another to restaurants famous for their barbecue, or grits, or pastries. We swap recipes, and the only contraption we fight over now is her KitchenAid mixer, which I insist she should leave to me in her will. She says she hasn't, but I don't believe her.

On our first date, we ended up at Nobu even though we had no reservations and the restaurant was always fully booked weeks in advance. I do not know how he got us through the door, but James seemed to know every maître d' in Manhattan. He fed me bigeye tuna and fresh fluke with dried miso while we sipped at lychee martinis and I tried to look sophisticated. Afterward, we had Champagne at the Top of the Tower in the Beekman Hotel, across from my apartment. I had left the lights on, and we could see from our table that I was not a good housekeeper. He laughed about that, saying it didn't matter. He had a cleaning woman. Later, at my door, he gave me a halting, chaste kiss before scurrying off. I thought I would never hear from him again.

I was wrong. We began a love affair that was more passionate in the city's best restaurants than in our bedrooms. James introduced me to the voluptuary pleasures of Manhattan's finest dining. He fed me an amuse-bouche of asparagus soup with frog leg at Les Celebrites, warm octopus salad at Le Bernardin, and pan-seared fois gras with concord grapes at Jean-Georges. I learned to identify tastes in wine like *tar*, *leather*, and *smoke*. We met for lunch on Saturdays at Caviarteria—a silly place that became emblematic of the excesses of dot-com-era New York. They served Osetra with crème fraîche on toast points and a glass of Champagne as a lunch special. By the time we finally tumbled into bed, I had gained ten pounds.

When James stopped kissing me and calmly opened a night-table drawer and pulled out a syringe, I was mildly thrilled at the idea that I'd ended up in bed with a junkie—so New York, and I was trying very hard to be a New Yorker. But it wasn't heroin; it was something called *Caverject*; a pre-Viagra answer to erectile dysfunction, which was, frankly, a lot less romantic. It smacked of infirmity rather than dangerous hedonism, and the idea of his actually sticking a needle *into* his penis made me queasy. But I went gamely on, pretending not to notice, afraid to embarrass him. And he went gamely on, afraid to admit he didn't think it worth all the hassle either, and would rather just go out for a drink or dessert. And so, for several months, we had wonderful meals and terrible sex.

I grew fat. When food is sex, and you're in love, it's impossible to eat moderately. Our weekends were protracted gastronomic orgies; we often had lunch and dinner at five-star restaurants on both Friday *and* Saturday, each a many-coursed affair. We wandered into Chinatown on Sunday mornings, paper in tow, and settled in at a table at our favorite dim sum restaurant—its name long lost to memory, because everyone knew it by its address: 60 Mott Street—and meandered through the small dishes from morning till afternoon. The more I loved James, the more I ate, until the night when we had to cancel dinner with the Michaelsons at Le Cirque because I was too fat to fit into a single one of my cocktail dresses, and jeans simply would not do.

James, who I think loved me too, took me to a shop for big women the next day, bought me three flowing silk dresses that I would fit into no matter how large I got. They were tents in muted shades of gray and black with elastic waistbands and voluminous sleeves. I wept while I tried them on, and because he did not want me to cry, James made a phone call. That night, instead of food, we made love through a gram of coke. It was hotter, more intimate, and more invigorating than any sex I had ever had. I remember thinking: *ur* sex.

Three months later, the cocktail dresses that had been too tight weren't even snug, and I had left James for a man with better drug connections who did not love me and so did not care that I was rushing into disaster. I think we had sex all of the time, but I'm not sure. The days from that year are a blur, the memories bruised, and I never call this man by his name. If I talk of him at all, I call him "my coke dealer." And when I think of him, I also think of James, who was kind and sweet and should have just let me grow fat.

Tonight, I'm making rigatoni with seafood cooked in a pink vodka sauce. Last night, it was linguine with sundried tomatoes, sausages, capers, and broccoli rabe. The night before, simple spaghetti with a meat sauce. I spend twenty dollars a week on Parmesan alone.

I fill one of the huge Fiesta Ware bowls from the cupboard with the layers of pasta, sauce, and cheese, then carry it out to my husband, Scotti. He is lying on the couch, watching the same episode of *The Daily Show* he has watched every afternoon this week. He will eat two bowls this size in the next fifteen minutes, and then fall hard asleep. He won't remember having watched any part of the show, and tomorrow we will watch it again, our routine as set as the show's script. Only the pasta will be different; farfalle with eggplant, buckwheat, and truffle oil; fusilli with a wild-mushroom ragout; spaghetti Fra Diavolo.

Scotti is unhappy. Not with me; the mess his unhappiness makes of my life is collateral damage. But he is unhappy enough that all the anti-depressants in the pharmacopoeia only make a dent, and our family doctor has urged me to convince him to try electroconvulsive therapy. Shock treatment. The idea of it frightens me, and although I've mentioned it, it would be a lie to say I've tried to talk him into it. In truth, his depression is so dark and all-encompassing that I don't try to talk him into much of anything these days. Instead, I work to be the buffer between what he needs and the sharp truth of things. Food is my little white lie; it is the "everything is going to be all right" that I cannot bring myself to say.

I am five foot seven, and I weigh 208 pounds. When I married Scotti, I was five foot eight and weighed 157 pounds. Gravity is pulling hard on me.

Scotti weighs almost 350 pounds, more than even his square, six-foot-six skeleton can comfortably carry around. He's a striking man—when we are out, children confuse him for Hagrid from *Harry Potter*, and old hippies holler, "Look, it's Jerry Garcia." But his knees hurt all the time and his feet look frostbitten. He cannot feel them. Diabetic neuropathy, near as the doctor can figure, although he isn't diabetic. It's just one of many puzzles. His hands are nearly as numb; half the time when he reaches out for me affectionately, he hurts me, unable to feel that he is touching me unless his caress has the force of a slap. When I cry out, he looks bewildered and does not reach out again for days. This is just one of the many ways I fail him.

The bowl of pasta piled high with grated cheese is another of those ways. We would feel better if we were not so heavy, but it would be a long time coming, and I can't wait that long to comfort him or myself.

Even our dogs are fat; we love them, too, and each has grown old and crippled in a way we cannot do anything about, so we toss them chunks of the sausage or pieces of pasta while we eat.

We have forgotten the ways of showing affection.

In the summer, when the vegetables are fresh, I will put us on a diet . . . again. We will eat salads piled high with tomatoes from the garden and onions from the farmer's market. Scotti will lose thirty pounds; I will lose fifteen. But it won't last. Soon enough, it will be fall again, the melancholy season, and we'll put the pounds back on. I will gain twenty; Scotti will gain forty-five. This is how we lose the battle.

In truth, I like him fat, though not myself. I like that even when he is too sad to put his arms around me, I can curl around his back and the sheer bulk of him creates an illusion of safety. And there is so much we need to feel safe from, these days. I like to watch him eat; to see the veil of depression lift for those few minutes; see him go at his dinner with a single-minded passion that I imagine, in his younger years, would have been the hallmark of his lovemaking. I can't give up this shadow of sex, a remnant of passion, and doom us to becoming distant bodies in the same house.

He jokes that I am killing him with kindness; I say, "No, oh-my-love, I am just killing you." I am afraid it may be true, but I am more afraid to let the pot grow cold, to let the bowl stand empty, for very long. My resolve is nothing compared to the way his sadness weighs us down. It does not matter that I know what I am doing to the both of us; I am not brave enough to stop. I am afraid that both hungry *and* sad, we would turn mean, or cold, and drift away. And fat is not as bad as that. Fat is soft and comfortable; fat stands between us and everything that is not us. Fat softens the blows. Fat, at least, feels safe.

Mad Love:
The Ballad of Fred & Allie

Sonja Livingston

The sin was not so much the taking of the throat as the wanting of it in the first place. And what a fine throat it was, the way it captured those who saw it: men loitering at the Customs House; boys down by the river, who stretched their own necks to catch a glimpse of its fine whiteness; eventually the entire nation. But Alice Mitchell was the first to be lassoed by Frederica Ward's charms, becoming hooked while they were still schoolgirls.

It must have been the way Frederica walked into the music room at the Higbee School for Young Ladies. The Higbee School took only the best girls, from the best families in Memphis—not always the first families, those with places at the Cotton Exchange on Front Street, mind, but always the most respectable families, which is how Frederica's people were set, a touch heavier on the respectability than the money. But my God, how that girl could twirl her hips like the women selling their wares down on Pontotoc Avenue, laughing like a child before breaking into song. And the voice! Frederica could catch a river full of fish with her singing, hooking a finger in her lips between songs, walking haughty and making fun when the mistress wasn't looking. Known to her friends as Freda or Freddie, but mostly just Fred, she had brown eyes and a body like a new branch in spring, thin but coming together with new growth. Like the petals of a magnolia, Fred's body was all silk white and cupping.

The brick building on the corner of Beale and Jessamine was shaded from the afternoon sun by a stand of slender elms. All seventeen of its classrooms provided wide, cool spaces for lessons in art, literature, Latin, and Greek. There were French lessons, a music room, even a governess named Miss Aurelia Lane: how could the girls not emerge from the Higbee School more charming than when they'd entered? All that poetry and music in their heads, roses climbing outside their windows. Three hundred of the best girls in Memphis attended the school in 1890, among them Alice Mitchell and Fred Ward.

All they did at first was look. Just look. Something moved in Alice while following the hair gathered at Fred's neck, the turns of it, the lone dark curl tucked behind the ear, and yes, the throat, as if made of marble. Memphis had not ever seen a finer child, and she knew it, Fred did, piling that hair and running a finger along her mouth as she swallowed, smiling all the while, smiling at her dearest friends, including Alice, who replied in kind. Until it was only Alice, the girls talking in a code they'd devised, a universe unto themselves, appearing to speak no words, but saying everything with the work of their mouths.

How I love thee; none can know.
—*Letter from Alice Mitchell to Fred Ward, 1891*

———•◦•———

The girls could not have been more different. Fred embraced music and drama and flitted from room to room while Alice's passions seemed limited to baseball and horses. Despite their differences, the girls became fast friends, and in at least one way were a perfect match: Alice adored Fred, who, in turn, demonstrated great skill at being adored. They had pet names, Fred calling Alice "Sweetheart" and Alice calling Fred "Petty Sing."

The girls twined round each other in the hammock for hours, held hands, and spent so much time in each other's clutches that, at times, friends called them disgusting. But these complaints were launched lightly; such relationships were not only accepted at the Higbee School, but were also encouraged by society as they kept girls from good families from ruining themselves with men before marriage. Neither Allie nor Fred would likely have been allowed to interact with boys or the world outside of home and school without strict supervision. But with each other, they would have enjoyed nearly limitless freedom.

———•◦•———

> Sing, I have a rose for you; if it is not withered
> by the next time I see you, I will give it to you.
> I have been trying to get one for a long time. It
> beats all other roses.
>
> —*Letter from Alice Mitchell to Fred Ward, 1891*

———•◦•———

But good God in heaven, what but what was up in Golddust, Tennessee?

Nothing but mud fields and shacks set onto stilts and row after row of cotton. Fred's father had changed his business to planting and moved them all upriver, Fred and her sisters. Golddust was a romantic enough name, and Fred might have tried to make it sound pretty in her letters to Alice, writing of horned larks or the stand of pecan trees just outside her window. But Alice's daddy must have been up that way and would have told Alice there was nothing about Golddust but mud. Mud and cotton. But if he tried to console his daughter with such images, Alice did not oblige. The girl wouldn't touch a thing on her plate—no matter how her mama and Lucy, their cook, begged, the reality of Golddust itself had become a cake of dirt on her tongue.

Golddust was all Alice could think of, the place that held what she most wanted to hold. It killed her to think of Fred with her pretty dresses and feathered caps, sitting in a stilted shack sixty miles upriver. Fred could still come to visit Memphis, of course, but there would be no more regular dances at the social club, no more nights together at Miss Higbee's school. Alice must have tortured herself with memories of nights they'd sneaked away to stare up at the stars, the moonlight guiding them. And surely there were other memories, secrets held tight between the girls. Either way, there was nothing to do but stand at the levee and look across the river to Arkansas, waiting for steamers to carry letters to and from Golddust.

Fred was miserable, too, without Allie, or she at least claimed to be. Her letters from Golddust confessed flirtations with young men, coupled with promises of fidelity to Alice, whose anxieties multiplied with each new letter:

> Fred, do you love me one-half as much as you did the first winter? I believe you loved me truer than you ever did. You didn't fall in love with every boy that talked sweet to you then. Sweet one, you have done me mean, but I love you still with all your faults.

Yes, Fred replied, she did love Alice still:

> Sweet love, you know that I love you better than anyone in the wide world. I want to be with you all the time, for I more than love you. Good-bye until tomorrow.
>
> —*Sing*

There were visits, weeks when Alice went on the steamship to Gold-dust, times when Fred stayed at the Mitchell home in Memphis. Satisfying exchanges, evidently—so satisfying that by late July 1891, the newly seventeen-year-old Fred began to wear a piece of jewelry, a gift sent up from Memphis by her eighteen-year-old beloved.

———•◦•———

> I received the ring all OK. I know you are true
> to me Love and I more than idolize you. I will
> be so happy when we are married.
>
> —Letter from Fred Ward to Alice Mitchell, 1891

———•◦•———

Something must have threatened to spill from Alice—what joy she must have felt, to have secured such a promise from her love. At heart, they might have known how hopeless their engagement was, and perhaps it was this that led them to act too quickly—though there was no particular schedule that would have improved the chances for two women eloping in 1891. Such a marriage was impossible, but what is impossibility in the face of love?

They hatched a plan: Fred would take the steamship *Rosa Lee* from Golddust to Memphis, where Alice would be waiting. Fred might not recognize Alice straightaway, for she might be already dressed as a man, wearing trousers and a Norfolk jacket, hair set under a bowler hat, and answering only to the name of Mr. Alvin J. Ward. The girls knew enough to know that one of them would have to pass for a man if they were to marry, and Alice was the natural choice.

They might have heard of women posing as men at Miss Higbee's school, whispering in the dormitory, giggling in the corner of the drawing studio. Their parents had lived through the Civil War, and the girls might have heard stories of women who dressed as men to fight, women such as Mollie Bean and Cathay Williams. Fred, who delighted in the theater, would have known of Viola posing as Cesario in Shakespeare's *Twelfth Night* and Portia as Balthazar in *The Merchant of Venice*. With no boys to fill the roles, the girls might have even played male parts during productions at the Higbee School.

However the idea arrived, it came to them strong and sure, so that the girls had no trouble imagining Alice in trousers and short hair. It became the ticket to freedom for them both, Alice's manning up, the one thing to allow them to say good-bye to Memphis and board the steamer, holding hands and heading north this time, to St. Louis, where they'd disembark and say, "I do." A date was set for late July, and what thoughts the girls must have had as the hour approached.

The heat hangs heavy along the lower Mississippi River in summer. Both girls must have wiped their brows as they packed their cases, Allie in Memphis and Fred up in Golddust, each girl preparing for a new life to the backbeat of crickets, the whir of cicadas. How short every breath, how humid the air. The scent of jasmine wafting from verandas, the air thickening as evening arrived, expectant as a descending storm.

This was the moment, the point at which they were still girls, half drunk on possibility, all jittery and looking forward, hearts flung foolish and wide.

Miss Allie Mitchell:

Ere now you must fully realize that your supposed well laid plans to take Fred away have all
gone awry. You should have taken into consideration that Fred had a sister watching over her
who had good eyes and plenty of common sense. .
. . I return your 'engagement ring' as you called it,
and all else that I know of your having [sent] Fred.

—*Letter from Mrs. W. H. Volkmar, 1 August 1891*

They were caught. Of course, they were caught.

If their friendship seemed more affectionate than usual, it was tolerated. Even when the girls were separated, no one thought of them as anything but the usual chums until the night they packed their bags and tried to insert themselves into the wide, moving world without the permission of fathers, brothers, or husbands.

Who knows what girls dreamt of in 1891? Perhaps the very idea of dreaming anything other than roles as wives and mothers was a radical act. In this way, Fred and Alice were absolute renegades.

It's said that Fred dreamt of the stage, an impossibility for a girl of her social class, whose wedding day with its garland of orange blossoms and stacked cake would be the most drama she could expect. But she dreamt of it anyway, the sway of glittered hemlines, the never-ending change of costumes, the beauty of art in motion, a northern city, far from the sand and muck of Golddust, far from the snarls of men baling cotton, far from lines of women grown tired with waiting.

As for her dreams, Allie seems to have wanted most of all the sight of Fred in a bridal dress, a tree to climb perhaps, a shared bed, night after night, the sound of horses galloping in a nearby field, the freedom of running, the freedom of trousers.

But it was not to be. Fred's brother-in-law saw a light on in her room late at night, found her packed and waiting, and stopped her from leaving Golddust, a Winchester in his hand. Did she protest? The sight of all those fields cracked dry in the summer, the cotton starting to open, miles of white dabs clinging to the plant in all directions but the river. And what of Alice waiting downriver? Where did she fix her eyes? How many stars in the sky that night? How many times must Alice have retraced the contours of the past, remembering them together under the cloak of night sky as she waited for the sight of Freddie—oh would she, oh would she, oh would her one true Sing come?

Sing, I don't do a thing but have the blues all the time.

—*Letter from Alice Mitchell to Fred Ward, 1891*

The blues were nothing new to Memphis. W. C. Handy hadn't yet written "The Memphis Blues," but by the 1890s, there was already plenty of soulful singing on Beale Street. Freed people had come from all parts of the Deep South to the shops and storefronts along Union and Beale. And to the fields. It was the Delta, after all. Cotton was still king, baled and stacked by the river, as it had always been, graded and sold in the same places where, a few decades prior, human cargo was unloaded. Buggies and mules shuddered beside the levee while men made deals along the riverfront and streetcars screeched through packed streets, competing with the sounds of the new railroad bridge going up over the Mississippi.

No, Handy hadn't written his famous song yet, but Memphis had already endured its share of the blues. The city had been broken by yellow fever epidemics, the last of which hit in 1878 and claimed so many lives that Memphis collapsed under the weight of its losses.

By 1890, the city was booming again, but even as the girls sat studying Latin at Miss Higbee's school, it was not uncommon for violence to erupt in the streets surrounding them. Alice and Fred would have grown up with stories of the saffron-colored skins of relatives lost to the Fever. They would have heard talk of black men hanging from trees, would have absorbed the sounds of the lonesome singing on Beale, the strumming of strings. Yes, even those girls at Miss Higbee's school, wrapped in their ruffles and lace collars, would have understood what it meant to have the blues.

When Alice was cut off from Fred and the engagement ring returned, she threatened to kill herself with laudanum. She cried to her mama and told her troubles to the cook in the kitchen, must have struggled to make sense of the way her heart was caving in on itself. But no one seemed to understand, especially not the cook, who only replied that at "least you have plenty of money."

No one could raise Alice from her bed. She continued writing to Fred, but received no response. No matter how those around her tried, Alice refused to budge from her grief, becoming so thin that her dresses began to float about her as summer moved into fall. The crepe myrtles lost their flowers, the water oaks dropped their acorns, and even the holiday season, with its firecrackers and gunshots, did nothing to rouse her. Alice could not bring herself to care about a thing. Until Fred came to town.

A freeze settled on Memphis that winter, a rarity in the part of the state that leans upon the Mississippi Delta with both its knees. There had been snow and ice for weeks, and when, finally, the weather relented enough to allow travel, Alice took a buggy out. She asked her friend Lillie to join her, and together they clopped up and down the streets near their homes, including Madison, where they passed the Widow Kimbrough's house, and imagine Alice's surprise when there at the window sat Fred!

After the shock of it, after keeping herself from clawing through the window, Alice must have pulled back and taken stock. She would have smarted at seeing Fred come to town without so much as a word. As if Alice no longer mattered. As if Alice would not find out. As if Miss Frederica Ward could puff her sweetness over Memphis and think Alice would not know. The world must have felt as if it were in ruins, Fred so close by and never once come to call. It would have hit her then, all of it. When she returned home to her small box of special things, the box she liked so much to mull over, she would have found the ring Fred had worn when she promised to be true. How Alice must have stared at that small band, setting it into her own hand, pushing her finger over its cold surface, going round and round, thinking of what to do.

In January 1892, snow fell white as cotton as three girls walked past the Custom House toward the steamship docked at the landing. Fred, her sister, and a friend were headed back to Golddust; the girls must have shivered as they huddled together and crossed toward the levee, none of them noticing the buggy trailing them.

Alice, with her friend Lillie once again beside her, followed the trio toward Front Street, the buggy moving in their shadow, Alice saying to Lillie as she jumped, "Oh, Lil, Fred winked at me . . . I'm going to take one more look and say good-bye!"

Had she winked? Was Fred playing a game with Alice, teasing the girl who was loyal as a dog in her affections? Or was the wink a lie, something Alice only hoped to see? Something she wanted so badly, she actually did see? Either way, no one in Fred's party paid much mind, none of them seeming to notice the fair-haired girl as she jumped from the carriage and ran up the stone path, none of them noticing the wild look in Alice's eyes until it was too late, none of them recognizing just how serious she was until the razor was unfolded and in her hand.

A Most Shocking Crime.
A Memphis Society Girl Cuts a Former
Friend's Throat.

The New York Times, 26 January 1892

A Tragedy Equal to the Most Morbid Imaginings
of Modern French Fiction

Memphis Public Ledger, 26 January 1892

That Alice killed the one she loved best was never disputed. Lillie described Alice's return to the buggy, the way she refused to wipe away the blood on her face because it had belonged to Fred, and how she asked only about the quickest way to kill herself. Alice herself admitted to the killing, saying she'd planned to cut her own throat as well, but had been thrown off course when Fred's companions interfered.

In fact, the trial, which captivated the nation, was not for murder, but for lunacy. Alice admitted her love for Fred in open court, speaking of their plans to marry, her own idea to dress as a man and take a job to support them. She spoke of these things openly. In 1892 Memphis. Without a speck of shame.

The press descended on Memphis. Public interest in the "Memphis Girl Murder" was so great that the judge had his courtroom enlarged with a special stand for the press. The room was said to be the largest in Memphis, outside of the local theaters—an apt comparison, since the room was jammed each day with men and women, black and white, craning their necks as the prosecution attempted to paint Alice as a cold-blooded killer. And given the way she'd cut a throat in broad daylight, with witnesses, and her own confession, it seemed a fair enough portrayal.

But the defense's claim that Alice Mitchell was insane was supported by witnesses who spoke of her preference for sports, her skill at baseball. They testified about a sack of marbles found in her room, the lack of dolls. One young man testified that Alice had refused to dance with him at a picnic. Another claimed that when he called her a tomboy, Alice had not seemed to mind. Out and out insanity.

———•—•———

A girl that thinks to assume the mask of a man, can shuffle off the baptismal name given her and take the name of Alvin J. Ward, take the place of a man and marry a woman—Your Honor knows there was madness at the bottom of that.

—*Colonel Gantt, testifying for the defense*

"*The Pity of It*," Memphis Appeal-Avalanche, *26 February 1892*

———•—•———

THE APPEAL-AVALANCHE

WILL CONTAIN

FROM

DAY

TO

DAY

A

COMPLETE REPORT

OF THE PROGRESS

OF THE UNPARALLELED

MITCHELL-WARD-JOHNSON
GIRL MURDER TRIAL

IN ALL

ITS DETAILS,

FULLY ILLUSTRATED.

MEMPHIS APPEAL-AVALANCHE, 24 FEBRUARY 1892

In the end, there were no surprises. Alice's love for Fred was considered more outrageous than the act of murder, and she was found to be legally insane and was committed to the Tennessee State Insane Asylum in Bolivar on 1 August 1892—a year from the day she'd stood waiting for Fred to step from the *Rosa Lee*, a year from the day on which her prospects for a wider world were shown to be as small as the mud-flat town where Fred sat crying sixty miles upriver.

Perhaps Alice was truly a lunatic and would have killed Fred anyway. Maybe something was loose in her head, so that even if they had made it to St. Louis and she could coax a mustache from her face, an episode of violence might have occurred. But who would have ever remembered it then, a man killing his wife? No, it is only the fact of their shared girlhood that shocked the world. Nice girls from good families, so that people were left to wonder over those nights at Miss Higbee's school, the neck and the blade, the claims of love. What could they do with such a girl but send her to the madhouse, Alice perhaps stealing one last look at the wide bend of the Mississippi before turning in her seat and leaning into her mama as the carriage headed east, away from the singers along Beale and the river Alice would never see again.

There goes that Alice Mitchell,
With arms tightly bound down,
For the crime she did in Memphis,
She's bound for Bolivar now.

—from "Alice Mitchell & Freddy Ward"
Sounds of the Ozark Folk, vol. II. *Collected
by John Quincy Wolf, Jr.*

The ride east seems to have been gentle, given the circumstances, and those in the carriage complied when Alice asked to stop to say good-bye to Fred. They pulled up at Elmwood Cemetery on the way out of town, likely stopping for a moment near the gate, taking whatever shade they could get under oaks that had been standing there longer than the cemetery itself. When they could go no longer by carriage, they would have passed bald cypresses on foot, treading through limestone angels and stone anchors, the air filled with the sound of whistling as trains pulled coal from one side of the country to the other, Alice leading the way until, finally, she stood over the square of turned earth that had not yet settled back into the space over Frederica Ward's body.

Did she hear her voice then? As she stood beside the grave, did the sound of low and hard whistling give way to Fred's voice? That sound must have been to Alice what the singing of birds is to the sky. If she closed her eyes right then, was she back on Jessamine and Beale, where nothing was so true as the light coming through the windows of Miss Higbee's school, the sound of hooves on the stones beneath the music room? Could she feel the heat of the other girls, their laughter and delight, as Fred practiced her flirty walk? It might have seemed, for a moment, as if Fred had never left. And if she closed her eyes just right, Allie might have even allowed herself to imagine that they'd boarded that boat to St. Louis after all, that she stood not before a new grave, but at the very edge of the river, aboard a steamship, holding her love's hand, watching the levee disappear as they headed north, the world opening before them.

No Other Gods

Sarah Gilbert

Y ou are 19 and you are beautiful.

You are 19 and you do not believe you are beautiful. Or if you do, it is beautiful . . . but. But: you are not really sure; you are pimply and freckled, and your clothes are not quite right. But: your shoes betray your status, poor kid in a school of Richie Riches. You sit between two oil heirs in your British Lit survey class. Oliver North's kids and Dan Quayle's kids went here, too.

You walk into fraternities and your face turns hot with *I don't fit in.* You do not drink beer because you believe drinking is a sin, and this does not help you fit in. You go home to your apartment and you kneel by your bed and you pray you will be forgiven for your sins and you will be loved; you pray you will fall in love and be forgiven for your sins.

Still, you dance. Surely this, among your sins, is forgivable.

They watch you dance, the fraternity brothers and the law students and the Keydets who come to party at Phi Psi, because the brothers there are cool, and the house is the closest to VMI. You dance to "Rump Shaker," and they watch you—maybe because you are making a fool out of yourself, or maybe because you have a great ass (you've heard this said before), or maybe because you can dance. You decide to believe it is the dancing.

You go home with too many of them this year in your search for love, and your need for forgiveness multiplies. Later—much later— you will find them on Facebook, and you will still feel wrong for your promiscuity. William. Ben. Michael. Joseph. You knew them, instead, by their last names because that is how your boyfriend—later, when you began your confessing—would refer to them.

Maybe you should not go home with them, but they are beautiful or powerful or funny, and they seek you out and one of them (at least) gives you a venereal disease and it is easily enough healed though the sin is everlasting.

This is 1993, and you are 19 and you do not yet see past 21. You believe you will be married by 27, but you do not yet believe you are worth the love. You do not believe you are marriage material.

Your classmate Gamble is marriage material. Lenora Gamble Timberlake Parks, she of the stacked deck of family names and the prep school and the considerable wardrobe probably purchased at full price at Dillard's in Dallas. She has an easy, confident way with boys. You think she is marriage material because she believes she is, and let the one who is without insecurity cast the first stone. You watch her walk around parties and you see her sitting in the Commons when you are setting up for a barbecue or an alumni function and you watch her shaking her hair and tipping her head back and laughing and, without quite realizing it, you shake your hair and tip back your head.

Later, right before graduation, you will see her on the arm of a townie, with her glorious helmet of walnut hair bleached bright blonde, and you will be shaken and humbled by her downfall but it will be too late.

You will have fallen, too. You are 19, and you are headed for a fall.

You are 19 and you are working for the school's catering department because it is better money than any of the other work-study options, and way more hours. You work intimate dinners for visiting speakers, and whole-school barbecues on the lawn behind the chapel, and parties for trustees at deans' houses, and weddings.

You work the law school formal, the Barrister's Ball.

You remember the oddest details about that night. Carrying trays of food to and from the buffet table. The dining hall, with its tables swept to the side, its black-and-white checkerboard tile floor thieving the romance that might have been. (After all, power is romance and law school stinks with the presumption of power to come. It is sandalwood and gardenia—heavy, righteous, unstoppable.) Your shirt smells like too many washes and splashed cooking oil and stale coffee. Of the black skirts at your disposal, that night you wear the pleated one, flouncy and coming right above your knee, bought at the J. Crew catalog outlet around the corner from your apartment and stained by candle wax and Virginia wine, subtly enough so that you can still get away with wearing it.

How you skim the crowd at these functions, looking for boys' eyes to catch and older men to impress. (This fills something open and yawling in you. You will continue to desire the admiration of much-older men for many, many years. You will continue to hope their attention is about your smarts and charm but you will eventually believe it is not only because of your youth, your smile, your legs.) You find several likely candidates, including William and Ben.

And then you find another. He looks back at you. Appraisingly at first, then hungrily. And finally possessively. He reaches into you with his arms and his lips and his power.

You fall. There is an arm around your waist and you let yourself fall into it, you part your lips in the way of the Good Kisser, with a little tongue, and you taste chicken strips and honey mustard. This is another thing you remember: chicken strips and honey mustard. When you think of it even now, 19 years later, you can taste it: his tongue, the chicken, the sauce sold in gallon containers with handles. You are hot, half with sex and half with shame, and you wonder when the shame will overtake the sex or if it will always be this. Sex/shame, honey mustard, want, and rage.

Wait for the rage. It is not in the story yet.

You want to break now. You take a break for moralizing, for de-moralizing, for the unleashing of those old morals. Look at your watch, take five. Take all the time you want. You swallow hard and get more wine (Spanish, *rioja*, which—did you know?—can be white in Spain, even though "rioja" sounds like it should be "rojo," red. You bought your first bottle of Marques de Caceres rioja at Harris Teeter in Charlotte to share with Mr. Honey Mustard, that first summer you cohabited, and the grocery store sommelier taught you both about the white rioja, and later, on your honeymoon in Spain, you would tell your husband, leaving out the bit about how you learned it. An omission is a lie. Toss it. The lie; the guilt. That's part of the break. Go on, end the parenthetical).

Sin. It's not what you used to think, sin, somehow. After decades of this pounding—you even started out drinking down the grape juice of your Original Sin far away from the South, in Portland, Oregon, where you now drink Marques de Caceres white rioja in a bed with your oldest son sleeping next to you—you began with this Christianity here, seek and you shall find, ask and it shall be answered to you. Judgment Day. You will be judged for your works but not given salvation for your works, reckoning, every word and thought and Yes This Sex You Had with Mr. Honey Mustard a reckoning—after decades of this, you have stopped believing. Don't stop believing? No. The feeling you were holding onto was bad, shame, regret, unstoppable unwanting of yourself. How could there be a god who could at once be the guiding light behind "turn the other cheek" and at the same time have ordered the raping of women and slaughtering of children whose husbands and fathers just tripped into the path of the Israelites? How could he let Mr. Honey Mustard put your head under water in the tub in Charlotte because you were "bad"? You weren't bad.

You kiss Mr. Honey Mustard and taste the food you served into rectangular metal catering trays with sharp lips that sometimes cut into your skin underneath your catering shirt as you carry them to the table. That kiss is what begins the sin.

He tells you it is OK, his date is ugly and a lesbian. At 38, you think back and wonder whether she really was a lesbian. Indeed, it wouldn't have been altogether unlikely; in the South at that time and probably even at this time it was/is hard to be a lesbian at a law school at a conservative university under whose freshman dorm Robert E. Lee's horse was once buried.

The kiss turns into a late-night visit to the apartment you share with a senior who is dating a libertarian who (you discovered later) is good friends and politically aligned with Mr. Honey Mustard.

Oh, let's just say it. His name is Jeffrey. Naming names is a sin for which you have come to forgive yourself.

You are Sarah and he is Jeffrey and you have sex and you have more sex and it is several months before you give up on Ben (he is so beautiful but he does not love you) and you discard William (he has funny-shaped lips and is not as smart as Jeffrey) and you finally send off the other one, who is on the law school council, the day before his graduation. He is too formal. He is too tall. You do not quite have sex with him in an apartment whose furniture has already been sold to undergraduates. You do not quite have sex with him on blankets on the floor, looking at a line of law books also on the floor.

Jeffrey it is. You are in love with him.

You have sinned too much. You have failed too badly. You have fallen too hard.

You are a bad girl.

He says this, over and over, for years. For eight years. He says that you are a bad girl, and he uses this as a reason to send you home and a reason not to invite you to parties and a reason that he sleeps with other women and hits you sometimes and shoves a gun into your mouth. Because he invites you to other parties and loves you with fierce animal possession and kisses you, over and over, with his mouth tasting like whole wheat toast or bourbon or shrimp etouffee that you have made for him, you either believe him or let him or decide that this is the wages of your sin.

His penis in your mouth is your penance.

You want to marry him. You want to be his; you imagine a ring that is the size of . . . what? A chunk of coal. A pencil eraser. A communion wafer. The size of your self-confidence now. You dream of this and nothing else for years.

That is not entirely true. You also dream of fast running, and beautiful wool suits that show off your legs, and a perfect bottle of wine, and admission into the top business school, and the plate of brownies or fry-up of crab cakes that will open his eyes to your perfect marriage-ability. There is no one more perfect for him than you. You get into a business school that is ranked one. In the world. You order many tran-scendent bottles of wine. You buy beautiful Italian wool suits with your Wall Street signing bonus. They call you a "superstar" and you make him crab cakes and you bake him brownies and you run in Central Park on the Fourth of July in 102-degree heat. That is the only day you have off.

You help him to buy condos, first in Manhattan and then in the fastest-growing county in Northern Virginia. You fly from Dulles to La Guardia every other weekend, and in Virginia you install a parquet floor all on your own. The floor is beautiful. You walk in your stacked heels on it, and the neighbors downstairs complain. You toss your hair and you throw your head back.

Finally, he hits you and makes you have sex on the beautiful par-quet floor of the condo in Northern Virginia, where he has ordered you to live because if not he will leave you . . . and you leave him.

He says he will buy the ring.

He tells you about the children you will have, he gives them names, he giggles in the way they might giggle and scampers across the room in the way he imagines they might scamper. You can hear those future giggles but know, although you try to laugh too, that they will hide the cowering, under the covers, as he rages at you. You know that playful run contains the day you will fill a suitcase, listening to his threats of custody battles and arrests, as you drag your two girls out, arm slung around their waists, your face white with terror. No.

You have learned to say "no." You have learned that your sin was your own thing, a self-inflicted judgment. Your day of reckoning has come and gone, and your judge, prosecution, and defense were all in your imagination. You were being good and believing yourself to be bad. You reckoned wrong.

The sin is yours and yours alone. It stops with you.

You have been punished already, the sackcloth and the stoning and the tearing of hair. That's done, that's accounted for, that's added up. You have been measured, *mene mene*, you were not found wanting by anyone but you.

Take the crowns, take the treasures, take the kingdom of heaven. It is all yours. Take it now and whatever you do, submit it not to anyone.

If you prostrate, sinner, prostrate before an idol in your own image; if you lust, lust after your own joy. If you submit, submit to your son, who also has suffered enough the sins of his father and his father's father and his father's father's father before him.

Make unto yourself a new temple and give unto yourself a new sacrifice. Take, drink of this wine that is nothing but wine. Take, eat of the chocolate of the new covenant. Covenant to yourself: thou shall not bow down to any image but that of unconditional love.

Do not cast out sin or sinner. Forgive yourself for your transgressions, and forgive those who transgress against you. Forgive Jeffrey.

You are 38 and you are beautiful. You will have no other gods before you.

In-Training

Ellen Hagan

The year is 1994. The place is Bardstown, Kentucky—which would be voted "Most Beautiful Small Town in America" by *USA Today* in 2012. Had you told me that in July of 1994, when I was 15 and so reckless you'd have been afraid to drive or hang anywhere with me, then I'da told you *Bardstown can suck it.* For good measure, I'd have blown smoke from a Marlboro Red that I wasn't really inhaling, just holding the sticky smoke between my burning cheeks, then letting it float slow from my cherry-lip-glossed mouth.

Bardstown is small-town Kentucky, "the bourbon capital of the world" if you want to be specific. If you've never been to Bardstown, then you probably don't know that the distilleries look like lonely, whitewashed, shot-out hotels with dark windows, and that they line the roads from the suburbs out to the hills. You wouldn't know that the whole town smells like sour mash in the late afternoon and that when the Bardstown High School marching band practices you can hear the trumpets and trombones in your backyard. You wouldn't know that Big Al's will sell you a case of beer even if you're wearing your cheer-leading uniform, and maybe because of it. You wouldn't know what it's like to spend your mornings swimming butterfly in the public pool—letting both your arms jut wild from their sockets while you wait to be told you are certified to save someone from drowning—when really it's you who needs saving.

———•·•———

Every morning my mom drives me the five miles from our house to the Bardstown City Pool, which smells always like too much chlorine and vomit—not strong vomit, but vomit just the same, though it might be the nacho cheese. I'm on the swim team. We wear bright red Speedo bathing suits, and I have mastered the backstroke and butterfly. I am fast but sloppy, an assessment you could apply to almost every area of my life. It's the summer after my freshman year; I'm too young to get a job, too old to do nothing, so along with joining the swim team, I'm in lifeguard training. Two weeks ago I nailed the physical test—rescued a brick in seconds from the deep end of the diving pool, swam the length and width of the pool with ease—but I failed the written test. I couldn't remember which arm to use with the buoy, or the commands to call out and in which order. What I knew was that if someone was flailing or calling my name, I would save them. Easy. But to my mom I wasn't taking it seriously, so I was grounded with the Lifeguard Training Manual and forced to read the chapters I'd intentionally skipped. When I took the test again a few days later, the swim coach let me use my notes. He knew I'd never let anyone drown, so he let me cheat on the final and here I am: a lifeguard in training—certified.

It's already past the middle of July, and all, all I want to do is put my tongue in some hot boy's mouth—taste his menthol cigarette or beer or spearmint gum, rub my tongue along the fine ridge of his teeth, and feel the weight of his breath in mine. I want to spend an afternoon just kissing. And I am in love with everyone—pretty much. But mostly I am in love with Ryan Lynch. He's from out of town—Ohio, Indiana, I don't think anyone knows the real story. He's been staying with Dr. Bradford and his family. He's either a distant relative or a friend of the family, but the point is he's fucking hot and there's a rumor he used to be a model. It's true that no one has seen any of his modeling portfolio, but no one really cares. Also, he's 18, and there's another rumor that he's saving his virginity until marriage. *What?* Every girl in town is obsessed with him, and, somehow, he likes me. Sure, I know it might be short lived, and I know he's definitely hooking up with every other girl in town. But what matters is that he likes me, and he's a fully certified lifeguard and it's true what I said before: I need saving.

"So, y'all wanna meet up tonight?" he asks, walking up to my best friend, Nina, and me on the sidelines of the swimming pool. I am stretching, my legs stretched spread eagle. Mike Manning is with him and I know Mike is in love with Nina, who has a pixie haircut and perfect breasts. I know she doesn't want anything to do with Mike, but I have a suspicious feeling that if she doesn't go, neither one of us will go.

"Yes," I say immediately. "Where?" I ask, perfecting my lean, smiling as wide as possible. The whole town is spread out behind us—the rusted picnic tables next to the concession stand and the sloping hill behind the urine-filled baby pool, and behind that, downtown with its Hurst Drugstore and soda counter and its Courthouse Square and the Old Talbott Tavern where drunken ghosts supposedly haunt the guests, and further still is the yawning sprawl of the suburbs with their two-car garages and their second refrigerators full of Bud Light. *Yes*, is what I say. What I don't say is: *I would meet you anywhere. For real. Any. Where.*

We agree to meet at nine at the Subway in town. In the meantime, I have plans. Our friend Leah, who moved to Tennessee last year, is flying in for the week, so Nina and I ride with my older brother's best friend, Eric (who's our best friend, too), out to the Louisville Airport. The windows are always down in Eric's car, and it always smells like weed. As soon as Leah gets in we take the long way back, through country roads to High Top where they'll sell beer to anyone. We pull up to the drive-through window and order a case of Natural Light. It's four in the afternoon outside of New Haven, Kentucky. Leah, Nina, and I are 15. Eric is 17. And we have just ordered a case of Natural Light from the High Top Bar, where last Halloween the two guys at the window were dressed in Beavis and Butthead masks. This is my life. We take the scenic route home and stop in a field of tall corn to smoke some of Eric's stash. Already I am aware that this will be a summer unlike any as I inhale, hold my face to the sky, and exhale.

After the drive, Leah and Nina come over and we get ready in my bedroom. We get a bottle of Smirnoff vodka and use my mom and dad's shot glass to take shots chased with grapefruit juice. The taste is bitter and sour at the same time, and the more I drink, the braver I feel. I know it's a cliché, but I don't care. I take another shot, and spill some vodka on the carpet and use the L'Air du Temps as a carpet cleaner, which makes my bedroom smell like rubbing alcohol and my grandma. It's possible I don't care about anything, which makes me lie to my mother about our plans and where we'll be for the night. I do tell her Eric is giving us a ride to the county fair (which is true), but I don't mention the Subway rendezvous. Besides, it's fair to say that after we meet up, I have no idea where we'll go.

The Nelson County Fair is alive and wild. (If you've never been to Bardstown in the dead of summer, then you wouldn't understand the sweaty filth of the county fair.) We go for the something to do of it. We go so we can drink beer from Styrofoam cups and cruise the circus-like atmosphere. The fair is full of rednecks from the county and rides like Scrambler, Zipper, and the always-there Dragon, all run by out-of-town freaks—we fit right in. I am most likely wearing my cut-off jean shorts, which I have worn for approximately 32 of the 48 days of summer so far, and probably some tight black shirt. I have no breasts, really, but that doesn't mean I don't like things tight.

It's around 10:00 P.M. when we finally meet up at the Subway. Mike drives a van that, in another scenario, could be transporting massive quantities of methamphetamines or could be the home of sex traffickers. (If Nina and Leah hadn't been with me, I would never have gotten into that van.) We pile in. It's me, hot-ass Ryan Lynch (who, remember, was/is a model in some Midwestern state), Nina and Mike Manning (who is a total dick), and Leah and Eric (who's totally a nerd, but totally awesome). Almost immediately there are beers in all of our drink holders and we're driving out to the Farm, which is basically a cul-de-sac near a mossy pond at the end of a subdivision out near I-64 on the way to Louisville. We talk about nothing in particular, and somehow there is always a beer in my hand. I'm not sure who has the idea first, but finally we decide we're bored with the Farm and our lukewarm beer, and decide it's time for a dip.

It's nearing 2 A.M. when we pull up to the pool. Mike and Ryan are both lifeguards, but neither has a key to the front door. They go back and forth about our best entrance option and settle on the wire fence near the diving pool—there are three boards, two of medium height and one that stretches into the sky. It's my favorite one to plummet from, my body sky, too, in that moment before I hit water. So we climb the fence. I'm probably faster than anyone since I've spent the past few weeks amping up on my certification. Once over we all just stand, watch the water ripple over the buoys, and laugh. Ryan realizes he's cut his hand. He remembers there's a first-aid kit in the office and tells me to join him.

It's in the pool manager's office that we start to kiss. Among the life preservers and concession-stand receipts and boxes of Band-Aids and Neosporin, Ryan starts to kiss me and kiss me. We move to the boys' locker room. I have no idea where everyone else is. For all I know they could be in desperate need of my lifeguard assistance—I don't care. In the locker room you can smell sweat and mildew. We keep kissing. We take all our clothes off, but keep our underwear on. I'm wearing a bra that doubles as a swimsuit. Ryan turns the shower on and I can taste the spearmint menthol I've been waiting for, and I can touch his shoulders and his waist, and he has his palms on my stomach. I am dying, it's possible I am dying because I am 15 and drunk and taking a shower in the boys' locker room of the public pool with an 18-year-old model/virgin who has his tongue so deep in my mouth that I am pretty sure that at least one of the rumors is false. I hope. And then we move to the shallow end of the Olympic-sized pool. I can vaguely see the others, but my focus is on Ryan and the heat of his breath on me. He puts his fingers inside me and holds my small breasts in his hands and kisses the sweaty salt from my neck and tells me he wants me. I lose track of all the other girls and their necks and breasts that he's put his mouth on, and how I could ever top this night and this summer right here, in this chlorine haze. I don't think about fall or algebra or the 10th grade, because I have his hair in my fingers and my legs wrapped around his waist and we are buoyant, floating in this middle-of-July morning.

We don't have sex. We don't get caught. Finally, someone mentions it's time to go, and we manage to find our clothes on the benches and climb back over the wire fence. On our way to the van I study the pool and its concrete decks, imagine its stench and glory, its chlorine and bleach, its slushy grape Icees and Blow Pops, its lines of county kids waiting with towels slung around skinny necks and bare feet and goggles on tops of heads with their dollar bills and their endless holding of breath as they seep into the water and become weightless, silent. It doesn't matter that Ryan Lynch will become a total asshole in about 17 days, and will leave town—still a model (maybe), possibly still a virgin—and that I will go back to being single. It doesn't matter that the whole summer I'll wonder how it's possible to both love and hate where you come from. What matters is that in the morning I will go back to swim-team practice and freestyle back and forth for hours and that I'll win blue ribbons for the pull of my back muscles during the breaststroke. What matters is that I have all the rest of July and August to drink beer from plastic cups and to ride in cars with the windows down and to smell sour mash in the afternoon. What matters is that I passed my lifeguard tests, all of them, and next year, I won't be in training anymore.

The On-Ramp

Amy Thigpen

She is honeysuckle dripping with milky juice. She is magnolia-sweet air and hot crawfish boiled in backyards in 100 percent humidity. She seeps into my skin, my hair, my molecules, until I am hot and wet with sweat that doesn't ever evaporate, and I don't mind because this is the most alive I've felt since the last time I was here.

She doesn't have to be the place you were born to seduce you this way. She can be the place where you feel at home even if you're a Yankee. You're going to succumb in the end, and she knows it with the certainty of a voodoo queen. It may be the food, or the music, or the fog settling in on the French Quarter as if the Mississippi River has finally come to claim her gas lamps and wrought iron and all those French doors shuttered to the night. New Orleans is many things, but if all of those things were simmered down to an essence, clarified like butter, what remained would be pure aphrodisiac.

The exact origin of the seduction has always been a mystery. She works on me slowly, from my first steps out of the airport gate, every time. In the spring of 2005, as I deplaned in New Orleans and slowed my feet to a stroll, I looked to my left and noticed a tall, good-looking man in his late twenties, with long red hair and a lanky gait. He started chatting me up on the way to baggage claim. We were both home for the New Orleans Jazz & Heritage Festival, and the flirtation went down easy, like the cold, wet bodies of oysters sliding down my throat. The redhead introduced himself—"I'm Andrew, Andrew Babylon"— and reached his large, freckled hand toward me. I laughed as I took his hand. I'd just set foot in this town, and already it had begun. Is it that I look better here? Do I sway my hips further from this side to that side? Am I just sexier in this city of sin, this city that care forgot, the Big Easy? Yes, yes, and yes. It's not just me; everyone is sexier in New Orleans.

In the Bay Area, where I live, my dates are few and usually disappoint by dessert. Strangers won't speak to me even when I smile and say, "Good morning." It took three years and an earthquake before my neighbor would return my smile. I blame the cold of the Pacific, the bundling up against the damp, turning us inward. In New Orleans, we are all soft-shells. We are moist and open; maybe it's the heat. By the time I reached Babylon, it had been five months since my last visit home, and I was starving for someone to let me know I was still a woman and had some powers left, and that being single and fairly young and alive was a good, good thing. Oh, yes, New Orleans began to feed me five minutes after I landed at the airport. It was like this each time. If there were no red-haired Babylon, it'd be a middle-aged airport porter with a paunch, asking, "Honey, you need a cab?" or the clerk at the rental car place, drawling, "Awright now, baby, you want INshuurance with your car?" As I smiled at Babylon, I found I was sliding down the inevitable slope. There was no use fighting it.

I arrived at Mid-City Lanes Rock 'n' Bowl on my first night in town, having chosen it from a city full of bars with smokin' hot music playing all night long. I parked at the far edge of the parking lot, right up against the bus stop. The place was littered with crawfish heads and tails, as if someone had just had a crawfish boil right there, next to the on-ramp of the I-10. I turned to see a seafood restaurant behind me and smiled, imagining people eating crawfish and drinking beer while waiting for the bus.

Feeling like I didn't belong, I climbed the long staircase to the dance hall, which is also a bowling alley. I'd had this feeling too often in hip San Francisco bars. I was still moving too fast and worrying too much, swimming against the current of the town. Even for me, it's not easy to let the South seep in all at once. It's an adjustment, slowing to Southern time, which drifts and stretches out like the Mississippi River delta. I wasn't used to going out alone, but I told myself I was never really alone in New Orleans. I always ran into a cousin, or a sister's ex-boyfriend, or I made new friends real easy.

At the top of the stairs, I breathed in and smiled, surveying the twelve lanes running the length of the room and a small dance floor with a stage on the right. The bowlers spun to the zydeco music the DJ played. It was a raucous room, with bowling balls banging and rolling, and folks talking and dancing and carrying on. Tab Benoit was only one of four acts scheduled upstairs that evening, and four more would play downstairs. Really, there should be a law against so much hot music in one place. But there aren't any laws that interfere with having a good time in New Orleans. There are drive-through daiquiri shops all over town, making literal the meaning of the phrase *Laissez les bon temps rouler*, which is more mandate than mantra in the city. Let the good times roll.

At the bar, I wrapped my hands around my first Abita Amber, found an *Offbeat Magazine* with the subtitle "Jazz Fest Bible," and snuggled into the crowd waiting for Tab Benoit to resume. After a while, a blond man about my age, in a baseball cap and alligator shirt, returned from the bar and handed me a cold one and smiled, and I smiled back. He took my empty bottle, and I thanked him with the sweet recollection that as a woman in the South, I did not have to buy my own drink. It's one of those tacit Southern rules, like putting *Miss* or *Mr.* in front of a person's first name as a sign of respect.

I eased onto a long bench and heard, "May I sit next to you?" I looked up to see a handsome blue-eyed brunet gesturing toward the spot next to me. He started up a conversation with, "This is just what the doctor ordered," pointing toward his feet in their Converse low-tops, saying they were sore from the festival that day. I had to agree about the whole thing being just right: the bar, the beer, the sweet anticipation of bayou blues, and the fact that this was the third attractive man starting something up within a few hours, ummmm hummm.

His name was Will, and he was from Houston but lived in the West. His accent was gravy-smooth and peppered with *darlin's*. Sure enough, the conversation was easy. I told him about my job as a hospital social worker. He was a graduate student struggling toward a PhD. We found, somewhere in these tellings, a mutual story of the bliss of finding this city as she was and finding in her just what we both needed, a respite from the world of death and deadlines.

By the time Tab Benoit came to the stage, I assumed the night would only improve. I went directly to the dance floor while Will went to the bar to buy me another Abita, and with the first strains of the slide guitar, I felt an early symptom of succumbing: my lips curling up into a smile that stayed put.

Tab Benoit had thick curly locks that would amount to whole handfuls of hair if grabbed. He wore a pink cotton shirt. I loved that such a masculine man wore pink, as if to say, "I got everything y'all need right here, *and* a soft side." He stroked the strings and howled the blues with a Cajun lilt, all muscle and rhythm. His jeans were tight, and his big belt buckle signaled the size of what lay below.

My feet, which just a few hours before had been rushing down the jetway at the airport, shifted easily to the barroom shuffle, the brass-band bounce, the swamp-boogie saunter. I learned my first dance steps on the French Quarter streets when I was in grade school. My father, a jitterbug man, taught me. I picked up my brass-band stomp in high school, from the marching bands at Mardi Gras. Later, in the clubs on the edge of Rampart Street, my jazz musician friends showed me how to second-line. For a white woman, I move all right. At the Rock 'n' Bowl, I brought my feet down to meet the hardwood. My hips followed their lead, and I let the town take me.

A few sets later, Will and I were hula-hooping along with the twenty-one-year-old barmaids to the twang of John Mooney's relentless blues guitar. Many sets later, they finally stopped playing music but hadn't closed the bar, though it was four in the morning. Will and

I made out under the full moon, on the hood of my rented sedan, by some crawfish heads, overlooking the on-ramp to the I-10 going west toward Baton Rouge.

After that, I expected the seduction to gain velocity and accepted the fact that there really wouldn't be any getting off the freeway of the city until I "fell out," as they say. I didn't care because I was too busy smiling that nonstop smile and letting it all happen.

The next morning, the hangover set in. My ears rang, and my feet ached from dancing. I perked up when I remembered I was having breakfast at the Jazz Fest with Will. I eased through the festival gates with all the other music lovers in sundresses and shorts. I strolled toward the food stands and began to salivate. Crawfish quesadillas. Spinach oyster salad boudin balls. I asked the lady at the first meat pie stand for directions to the Natchitoches meat pie stand and told her, "I'm meeting someone there." Twelve hours in the city had loosened my tongue. I'd begun to talk to strangers about all my business.

The lady laughed and said, "Oh, it's not just a tasty treat; it's a destination."

"It's a date," I added. I was late, because time already seemed superfluous. After I had strolled up and down the food stands awhile, reading the signs and trying to decide what to eat first—Crawfish Monica? Oysters en brochette?—Will appeared in a blue oxford shirt. He was energetic, having already eaten a meat pie. He had also had a Bloody Mary, with beef bouillon, for breakfast, and he held that this was *the* hangover cure. We moved on to the soft-shell crab po' boy stand. He pumped layers of mayonnaise like a meringue onto the French loaf and doused the crab with hot sauce and lemon, and we sat down in the grass, facing each other cross-legged. He told me the story of his dissertation, and I ate the po' boy, hearing only his Texas accent mingled with the flaky crabmeat. Will's eyes got bluer, and his story of erosion and tectonic plates became increasingly compelling, as the sweetness of the meat and the tangy hot sauce tingled on my lips.

Somewhere between the Gospel Tent and the Jazz and Heritage Stage, Will and I moved into that neutral ground where the strains of electric blues guitar and the jazz trumpet's ecstatic blast blended on the breeze with the climactic chorus of the Zion Harmonizers' "Meet Me on the Church-House Steps," and I felt it. Held in the space between the stages, the musical mix that could have been cacophony became a kind of heaven. The divergent rhythms melded into a gorgeous, disorganized whole, like the city herself. After eighteen hours, something in my step, something in my nonstop smile, in the lingering aftertaste of the crabmeat, and in the promise of the warm hand in mine, settled it. I had truly arrived. In that moment, I sounded like myself again; my Southern accent slid on, and my step was a saunter. I was home.

Will had to leave for the West the next day. I did lament his absence for a good few hours that morning after I put him in a cab. Then I realized that, after all, I was a woman, and fairly young and alive, and I was in New Orleans. So I put a honeysuckle sprig in my hair and a slinky sundress on the rest, and I headed back to the Jazz Fest with my sister, Juju, who had just arrived from Portland.

That evening, as the sun set on the fairgrounds, we ran into our old friend LeClaire, who told us where to go next. At the corner of Esplanade and Moss, a Shell gas station hosts the annual after-party. "Shell Fest," LeClaire said, "is for the drunks that don't want to go home." I conveniently fit in to both categories. He went on, "The beauty of it is that people are doing so many illegal things all at once."

Now, it's common for New Orleanians to find excess and a disregard for the law attractive. It's also common for them to hold in high regard activities that are just plain stupid and dangerous, if not technically illegal—like smoking by the gas pump or doing the limbo in an impossibly short skirt. According to LeClaire, these were some hallmarks of the Shell Fest.

We strolled toward the Bayou, not fully believing a party at a gas station could be a good time. As we arrived, some SUVs were leaving what had been a parking lot, revealing a cement dance floor. The "Shell girls," good-looking blondes in their fifties, danced to disco music and called me "baby" as I bought my Bud Light, which I wouldn't ever drink in California, but here at the gas station, cold beer was good beer.

My sister and I joined the others on the cement dance floor, grooving to Sister Sledge's "We Are Family," and I noticed a white man in his mid-twenties, dancing like a black man born right there. He was shorter than me by a good three inches and younger by about ten years. He had blond hair and wire-rim glasses, looking real intellectual on top, but, below, all muscle, not too stocky and not too lean. He was just right.

I smiled and looked away, having remembered how to flirt. Soon, I got too hot. With all that sunshine and sticky air, I was layered with sunscreen, Jazz Fest dirt, and sweat. When the DJ announced, "Have a COOOOOLD shower at the Shell Fest," I danced over toward the barbecue grills, to where an upturned water hose pumped a powerful spray of water into the air. It came down cold and clear, and I plunged straight into its thundering circumference, in my cotton sundress, squealing, raising my face to its goodness, eye makeup be damned. Then, the man with so much soul appeared outside the shower and held out his hand toward me. *Yes* was all I could say. It was all I had been saying for two days. I grabbed his hand, and he spun me in and out of the spray. The man turned out to be a salsa-dancing fool on top of all his funk prowess and general good rhythm. He spun me to bliss and back. Our hips and arms intertwined and pressed for a moment right up almost into each other, and then with a snap of his wrist, he spun me out and back under the shower. In the spinning, wet blur, I saw that the crowd on the dance floor had turned our way and bright flashes of light came from the cameras of people in lawn chairs perched on the flatbeds of their trucks, parked on the perimeter.

Breathless at the end of the song, we joined Juju and LeClaire and his friends, and I twisted the ends of my dress to wring out the water. Everyone laughed, and LeClaire said, "You *are* the Shell girl." Somehow, this was a high compliment. The man introduced himself as Dave from Brooklyn, and he couldn't explain how he got so much soul. He said good-bye and left with his friends. The rest of us stayed and danced until the crowd thinned. At the grills, they were selling "Shell Burgers." The DJ said that all the proceeds from the burgers were going to "the poor orphans at Shell Beach," because political correctness just never caught on in the South. The price went down to a dollar, and I bought two. The smarmy, unshaven men flipping burgers looked at me knowingly through half-closed eyes and said, real slowly,

"We loved watching you dance, baby. You want cheese on that? Yeah, we really loved watching you dance."

They said it like they'd seen me make love. I wondered if I should be ashamed, but I laughed as I put onions on the bun, thinking I hadn't done anything I wouldn't do on the salsa dance floor in Berkeley. It was the shower that made people gather and take photos. Showers are usually something you take for a small naked moment in your house, but sensuality isn't reserved for private spaces here. It's out on the street; it's the thrill of honeysuckle scent, the burst of a mango freeze on your tongue; it's everyday life with all of its fragrance and flavor. So I didn't mind that these men had watched me succumb to the pleasures of the Shell shower any more than if they had watched me do something as natural as exhaling.

On the final night of the Jazz Fest, my head was full of music from the entire week, from jazz to blues to zydeco and funk and a little African and folk and bluegrass. I thought I couldn't take in another note, thought I might boil over or burn up. In between howling, ripping slide-guitar riffs, from the stage at Mid-City Lanes Rock 'n' Bowl, John Mooney said, "We were arguing before the show 'bout who was gonna fall out first, the crowd or the band."

Nobody fell out because the music propelled us up, though it was three in the morning. My feet couldn't stop moving because John Mooney's guitar beat set a foundation for Theresa Andersson's soaring, wild fiddle melody, which electrified the air. Her voice asserted itself above it all, singing, "I take what I want, and I want you." As if on cue, Dave from the Shell Fest shower appeared on the periphery of the crowd. The city, despite her slow pace, is always on time. Her timing is borne not of minutes or hours, but of notes and phrases, of chords and refrains, climaxes and resolutions.

Dave took my hand and pulled me close, I mean real close, and I didn't push him to an acceptable distance like I would on the salsa dance floor in San Francisco, no. I'd been home about ten days, and all resistance was gone, or almost all. I mean, we didn't do it right there on the dance floor, but we may as well have. He added a little swing to his salsa, and blues to his funk, and ummm ummmm ummmmm.

I put my drink down for this, and he alternately spun me dizzy and pulled me so close I was almost behind him. I could feel everything, and everything was satisfactory and in just the right place, and then he kissed me. The kiss was half sugar and half muscle, like a cocktail, the very one he put to my lips during a brief interval between the songs, so brief we barely had time to clap. John Mooney couldn't stop. He pressed on. Atomic, that's how the kiss was, and my pent-up, thirsty self was sucking on him like he was honeysuckle and I was a bee.

"Yeah, you right!" screamed John Mooney when he finally gave in and played the last note, holding on to it while we clapped. "Yeah, you right," I screamed back, meaning not only "Yes!" but also "Hell, yeah," and "Amen," and "Hallelujah, I'm home."

I couldn't cling to the final note or the festival or the city forever. I had to leave the next day. I couldn't live in New Orleans year round. I wouldn't survive. I'd die of a heart attack from the mayonnaise and fried food, or of cirrhosis or something.

Back at my favorite café, a week after my return to the West Coast, I noticed something. It seemed I still smelled of honeysuckle, still had a soft shell. I kept smiling and talking to strangers, as if a friendly conversation wasn't a commitment, as if it didn't mean marriage or anything more than we're both alive and isn't that a good, good thing? Sure enough, I met more men in the two weeks after my trip to New Orleans than I had in the entire six months before.

Too quickly, my scent faded, my pace sped, and I closed up like night jasmine at dawn. As much as I tried to cling to myself, the saucy openness evaporated into the summer fog. I made up my mind to go home every three months for an adjustment, to let New Orleans slow my step and soften my shell, and not only to be seduced but to become the seduction myself, if not by way of the on-ramp or the Shell shower, then some other part of the city just as unlikely and just as fine.

Out of the Woods
Gail Griffin

Forty years later I can't think of the place without smelling boxwood, the urinous stink of boxwood in the heat. It was all over the campus, all over the town, and when I got a whiff it felt disturbing, like something lurking.

In the steaming late August of 1972, I moved into a small apartment complex two blocks from The University, as everyone called it, so that you heard the upper-case T, as if it were the sole post-secondary institution in the known world. The complex consisted of two buildings, each with six units. One of its attractions was that it was framed in green: on the north and west, lines of trees blocked the streets. On the south, a well-worn path through a brief woods took you quickly to The Corner, the area of busy shops adjacent to The University. On the east side, the rear of the building abutted a thickly wooded hill.

The apartment itself was contemporary and generic, but affordable and furnished and air-conditioned. A door opened from an open-air landing into a living room carpeted in avocado green, featuring a brown vinyl sofa and a brown vinyl chair, lamps, and wood veneer tables. Sliding doors opened to a small balcony overlooking the parking lot and woods.

There was a windowless galley kitchen with avocado-green appliances, a dining area, a windowless bathroom, and a bedroom with a double bed, a bedside cabinet and bureau, a lamp, and one small window.

Searching for a place to live, I'd had in mind something like Mary Richards's Minneapolis apartment, in the turret of a rambling Queen Anne, but two sweaty days of visiting apartments earlier in the summer had yielded plenty of nightmares and only this one clean, well-lighted, and utterly anonymous space.

As I signed the lease and opened a bank account and arranged for utilities, I emphasized that I was a *graduate* student to distinguish myself from the uncouth hordes called, I'd already learned, Wahoos. I would be spending my nights in the library, thank you very much. I had serious studies to pursue. I was beginning a life here.

I had come to Charlottesville to study nineteenth-century English literature, and this was the first problem. I'd landed in an Americanist's paradise, and I fell deeply in love with its presiding ghost, William Faulkner. He had taught at The University shortly before he died, when he was well pickled and well past the novels that shimmered with his peculiar genius. People remembered him. He was a presence, something like Mr. Jefferson himself (who was always called "Mr.," as if he might walk around the corner any minute, a cultural quirk that struck me first as endearing but quickly grew tiresome). I plunged into Faulkner's world—the heat, the obsession, the secrecy, the family madness, the twisted sexuality, the grotesque humor, and, above all, the guilt, the seething racial anxiety. The more he tries to talk through it, kneading it with words, the bigger it gets. It's the tar baby, viscous and implacable. It seemed to me that all the other manias in Yoknapatawpha County— from incest to castration to barn-burning—boiled down to the spectral essence of white anxiety. It was like a deep, pervasive scent.

And for me, the arriviste, the scent was distinct. It smelled like secrecy, like something unspoken. In my mind it belonged to the South the way I had learned that racism belonged to the South. Growing up in the suburbs of Detroit, watching television, I had seen the fire hoses driving people into buildings, the police dogs lunging. I was thirteen when the four girls died in the church basement in

Bombingham. Clearly, we all agreed up North, this segment of the country was demented. Racism was a distinctively Southern growth, like the kudzu that swallowed entire trees. And here I was, landed among the Compsons and Snopeses.

Well, not really. As any Virginian would tell you, there is no Yoknapatawpha there. Virginia is the north of the South, and the east of the South. Faulkner may have taught there and left The University his manuscripts, but the "Deep South" is elsewhere. The local accent is soft, clipped, famous for turning *house* and *about* into *hoose* and *aboot*, Canadian-style. It doesn't wallow or drawl. And traditionally, The University was where Southern boys of Good Family were sent when they failed to get into Princeton or Harvard.

Why was I there? I know, I said that: to study nineteenth-century British literature. But I could have done that anywhere, or at least somewhere more suited to that branch of literary study. Truth be told, I was there because of the dark-haired, mustached, corduroyed young man who taught my senior honors seminar in British Romanticism, and whose doctorate had come from The University. He was the latest in a long line of men—real and fictional, all unavailable—into whom I had plunged my whole sense of self. Falling madly and obsessively for charismatic male icons—rock stars, actors, writers—was, for me, something like reading huge, engrossing Victorian novels; my entire imagination was subsumed, absorbed. When I was accepted by his alma mater, I spoke to Mr. Ineffable, who said I'd love it there.

I was also there because it was time, I had decided, to kiss the Midwest good-bye. Time for life to get interesting. Time for new horizons, with mountains—albeit very soft, low mountains.

And I was there because at the time, The University scrabbled for the top spot among graduate English Departments. Pickings were slim for PhDs in English; degree prestige would count. I was flattered, thrilled to be accepted, though the offer came with no money. I didn't care; they wanted me.

One graduate English Department of the Ivy variety had turned me down with a letter that explained their gender quotas, right up front. There was a women's movement, as I remember, though it was born in ridicule, christened "women's lib" before it could even speak for itself, and I wanted no part of it. I would have marched for the vote, but beyond that, I didn't get the point. I thought I was a child of the times—the miraculous sixties, that is—and in many ways I was. The only thing I loved as much as English literature was rock music. I was pretty sure the pigs should be offed, the US should get out of Southeast Asia, Bobby Seale and everybody else should be freed, pot should be legal, and Power should go to the People. But in all these ways, I was following the lead of the witty, kind, poetic men who had brought me to the pinnacle where The University would want me. In shying sharply away from the movement that was my birthright, I was only following orders. There were women in the professorial ranks, all of them young, occluded, marginal, deeply uncharismatic. I never took a class from any of them. Not a one. I knew where my allegiances lay. What I wanted was to be among the Brethren.

I began to acclimate. I learned to say "JPA" for Jefferson Park Avenue, and "Grounds" and "Lawn" for "campus" and "quad." I subscribed to the *Daily Progress*, or, as we snottily called it, the *Daily Regress*, accent on the first syllable. One of its ongoing stories that fall covered serial rapes in the neighborhood to the north—my side—of the campus. The story barely grazed my awareness; rapes were, I'd learned in college, part of the landscape of what we liked to call a "student ghetto," as if we were all deeply oppressed.

As the fall progressed, the Blue Ridge turned rusty, sure enough, but the heat only barely abated. The cicadas' drone seemed to voice the thick air—the sound of madness, I thought. I yearned for the sharp clarity of a Michigan fall. I was embedded in classes, trying to convince myself I knew what I was doing. Sometimes the little seminars fell into the sparkling exchanges I remembered from undergraduate literature courses, but mostly I seemed always to be missing some nuance, some shade of meaning, as if I were proficient in the language but not fluent. I was furiously striving to assimilate—learning the faculty names and reputations, the in-jokes, the allusions. I was titillated by the talk of which woman student was sleeping with which professor. A gay man had a "coming out party," which seemed deliciously hip. I had something like friends; I was invited to the bars and the parties. But mostly I felt as if I were looking in through a window, just shy of visible, even to myself. For the first time in my life, I felt acutely Midwestern.

It never occurred to me to link my alienation to the demographics: In a department of sixty-something faculty, there were several women, but none over forty. None ever tenured, as I would discover. Only one faculty face was not white, that of a young African-American fiction writer who looked generally grim and quickly went somewhere else.

I'd come expecting the whiteness of The University, of course. I had grown up with the battle for the integration of higher education in the US. In fact, the first African-American student had entered The University's Law School in 1950, aided by the formidable efforts of Thurgood Marshall himself. After a year of hostility and exclusion, he departed. In subsequent years, African-American students matriculated in—though did not always graduate from—other graduate programs, and it wasn't until 1955 that the undergraduate program was integrated. A student named Robert Bland stuck it out to become the first African-American to take an undergraduate degree, the sole black graduate in the class of 1959.

But beyond these circumscribed corners of the institution, The University Board of Visitors fought like the gray-coated Cavaliers for whom their sports teams were named. Throughout the early sixties, they were dragged toward the inevitable, heels dug into the ruddy earth and *Dixie* playing at every football game. When Martin Luther King spoke in Cabell Hall in 1963, only one university official attended, and the event was sponsored by the Virginia Council on Human Relations rather than any campus organization. But The University was integrated.

Or was it? At some point during my first fall there, somebody finally told me that the first women had been admitted as undergraduates just two years earlier, in 1970, and then only under threat of a class-action suit. Ah. That explained the restroom doors with "Wo" added to "Men" in Magic Marker. In fact, it explained a lot. Black men came first—and probably because their arrival spelled the end of the world to the Wahoos, the advent of women was only another phase in the general Götterdämmerung. But it occurred to me to wonder: given the resistance to black men among the Wahoo brethren, what did it mean that it took even longer to admit women? The "separation" of the races (meaning the subordination of one to another) had been justified by appeals to Southern Ideals and Jeffersonian Values. But much older laws dictated the "separation" of the sexes (meaning the same). In a stalwart and unambiguous statement of refusal to accept reality, the fraternities still honored the old custom known as "Rollin' Down the Road": pilgrimages to Mary Baldwin or Sweet Briar in search of women. Women living on campus and going to class alongside you—that spoiled the fun. You can't hunt domestic animals.

Sometime that fall I'd first driven the winding road up to Monticello, from which Mr. Jefferson had surveyed, through his telescope, the construction of his Academical Village for Gentlemen. The small, friendly scale of the house surprised me. It vibrates with quirky ingeniousness, sharp intelligence, tokens of enormous industry. In all the tours I took of the place—and by the time I left the state I could have given one myself—I never heard anything about slaves. Two years after I arrived, Fawn Brodie's biography, asserting Jefferson's long-term liaison with Sally Hemings, burst on the Grounds like some kind of leftover Yankee shell. Dumas Malone, Jefferson Foundation Professor of History at The University, on the edge of a Pultizer Prize for his six-volume biography-in-progress, led the sputtering chorus of eminent Jeffersonians adamantly maintaining the impossibility of such a lapse on the part of the Author of American Freedom, and assailing the impudence of Brodie in suggesting otherwise. The Hemings story raised the old taboo in these parts—white, black, sex. Even when the unholy trinity didn't involve a Founding Father, it was like an explosive chemical compound, potentially lethal. And Brodie, like Hemings, was a most unwelcome intruder into the Jefferson saga. Who was she who broke the code, this upstart (aged 59), this female Pretender named, for god's sake, Fawn? Who was she to creep up to Monticello and proclaim that the Emperor frequently had no clothes?

By November I had come to know at least one of my neighbors, a woman across the landing. One Saturday I was in the middle of a recipe and realized that I lacked an ingredient, so I headed to her door. It was a windy afternoon, gusts whirling up the open stairwell. Too hurried to bother finding my keys, I pushed the button on the lock to keep the door from locking when it blew shut behind me. I got whatever it was I needed and headed back to my kitchen. The heavy door swung shut with a *thunk*.

I was deeply asleep that night when I wakened, sharply and fully, to the sound of my front door opening.

Immediately I remembered the lock, and then, even as my stomach lurched and my heart rate surged, I knew what I must do: on the chance that he would seize my stereo or my purse and leave, I must be perfectly still. And on the chance that he had a gun. Listening to his footfalls around the living room, I thought of my mother, hearing that I was dead. This chapter, this odd, uncomfortable new chapter of my life, would end here. My time in this surreal place would end surreally.

Time bent and stretched. Half an hour, five minutes, thirty seconds, and now he was in my bedroom doorway, a shadow against the dark.

My mind worked sharply: now, what I must do was feign sleep. He might yet leave without hurting me. I watched him through nearly closed eyes. He was down on the floor beside my bed, near my feet. I didn't know what he was doing; later it would occur to me that he was probably masturbating. When finally he touched my leg with his right hand, I exploded like a roman candle. I had always wondered, oddly, whether I had a scream in me. Now I shot up in bed and I shrieked. He stood, grabbed my arms. I flailed and screamed and struggled and then he was running and I was out of bed running after him screaming *Get out Get out Get out*. I was Fight and Flight united, pure adrenaline, terrified and probably terrifying.

The police came, two white guys, not well coordinated and not particularly interested, so I had to repeat my story more than once, obligingly implicating my own stupidity. *Young black man. Maybe five nine. Yes, young black man. Under six feet, yes, definitely. I saw only the back of his head as he ran. Young black man. Door unlocked. Yes. I think. No, I only saw the back of his head. I know. I know I left the door unlocked. Yes, young black man.*

They dusted for prints. They used their walkie-talkies. And before they finally left, one of them suggested, with barely disguised exasperation: "Listen, if he comes back, try and get a better description, OK?"

As if I had failed.

If he comes back?

------·•·------

Nothing happened to me. He touched my leg, grabbed my arms, that's it. But there ensued six interminable weeks of insomnia, the first and last time in my life I would be unable to sleep. Darkness and the end of my evening's schoolwork ushered in a dismal ritual of window-checking, door-checking, closet-checking, drapery-checking, ultimately giving way to the running of an empty dishwasher, sometimes more than once, to replace the random, slight night sounds with the white noise of churning water. Sometimes I dropped into exhausted, tense slumber around 3:00 A.M. The skin around my eyes became weirdly inflamed, and every ointment I tried made it worse, so I wore sunglasses everywhere, even to class. Finally I staggered into the student health center and was referred to a counselor, an aged pale-gray man who told me I was not afraid of being raped; I was afraid of being alone.

But nothing had happened.

The first fellow grad student I told was a third-year eighteenth-century scholar with Coke-bottle glasses and acne who had been kind to me. He said, "Listen, don't tell anyone about this. You don't want to get a reputation for being unbalanced." When I told others, mostly to break the soundproof bubble of isolation, I narrated the story as a kind of adventure, an odd nocturnal comedy-drama in which nobody was hurt, really.

And really, nothing had happened.

I stopped walking to and from campus, because it would involve crossing through the shallow woods. They had been part of the apartment's appeal, curtaining it protectively from traffic and noise. Now they had become The Woods of lore and legend, dangerous and obscure.

And I had become a person living in fear, as if fear were an ambient element. As if I had crossed into some new level of reality, I began to see and hear stories of sexual assault everywhere. They rose from memory, from news media, from gossip and hearsay, to meet me. It was as if some membrane had been torn away to reveal, everywhere, women in fear. It was intolerable. It was inescapable. I didn't know how to live there.

Especially since, as I kept reminding myself, nothing had happened.

And then, perhaps three weeks later, something happened. I came home after dark and was walking from my car to the building. I stopped briefly to talk to a neighbor. Suddenly the woods rustled and cracked, and a girl spilled out onto the concrete walkway, entering our light. A young African-American woman, tall and bony. Her short hair and sleeveless white blouse were disheveled. Was her face bruised, or did I paint the bruise in later? Was she holding her head?

"Can I use a phone?" she asked, quietly.

It was as if my throat constricted. But it was my heart constricting, and my mind. How many seconds passed before I shook my head? "I'm sorry, I can't, I—"

My neighbor said something. "I'm just in some trouble," the girl responded. "I just need a phone." She started to turn away.

And I suddenly woke up. "Wait. Wait, I'm sorry. Sure, you can use my phone. I live right up here."

She followed me silently. As I turned the key, I said, "I'm sorry, it's just that we've had . . . I had a . . . somebody broke in a couple weeks ago." This made no sense, I realized. She nodded, moved to the phone, made a brief, quiet call, hung up, and thanked me, turning to go.

"Listen," I said, "are you OK?"

"Yeah," she said flatly. "Thanks."

And then she was gone.

———•———

Over the ensuing months and years, I began to believe that something had indeed happened to me that fall. At some point along the road I wandered into a sexual assault prevention group and started folding and distributing flyers—the first time in my life I had aligned myself as a woman with other women. I began to notice that the English Department functioned very effectively as a grist mill for brilliant young women who were hired, ground up, and expelled. I began to think a lot of old jokes and stories weren't terribly funny—for instance, the one about the legendary department Eminence who emerged from an oral exam to share a three-word assessment of the candidate: "Cupcake's got brains." I started to have some questions concerning which authors were thought "serious" or "important" and which were not. In fact, questions sprang up like spring mushrooms. As answers began to solidify, so did I. I began to occupy my life, and to construct the story of what had happened to me.

But here's the thing: all coherent narratives depend on selection, and thus on exclusion. Whether it's the saga of the Sage or the story of the grad student, some things and some people have to get axed for meaning to emerge. And if we're not careful, we do murder in the name of meaning.

For years I wrote and rewrote, told and retold this story as the story of my own coming to identify as a woman with other women in order to save my own life. Which is true. The problem is that it's a lie.

The story I have told and written is the story of a man who came out of the woods. This story factors out the second stranger who emerged from the woods to crash into my life. Excising her was easy, especially because the memory bore a sour whiff of shame. When I told her, "I can't," I spoke the truth: I was unable—to allow her into my apartment, my life, my understanding. She was a young woman in obvious trouble, frightened, breathless, probably hurt, very possibly in grave danger, running through the woods. The odds are overwhelming that she was running from a man—an abusive father? Boyfriend? Pimp? Police? Perhaps the same man who came through my front door. But when she confronted me with her need, I failed to see another woman. I told her, by way of excuse, that there had been an intruder. What was I saying, except that I saw her as an intruder as well? That I saw her as another version of him? That her race trumped everything else about her? What was I seeing except a black stranger, stumbling out of those woods that surrounded and smothered my imagination?

In my mind she stands there in her trouble, her terror, in the yellow circle cast by memory's light. She was about my age. So was he, the other stranger, so far as I could tell. Forty years later, I move toward the end of a life whose losses and suffering have always been cushioned by what, in the context of general human experience, can only be called enormous privilege. And where are the two of them? Not nearly as likely to be alive, or healthy, as I. The odds are very good that he, in particular, is either incarcerated or dead. Both of them crossed the woods from black Charlottesville into the world of Mr. Jefferson's University and its disciples, its corner bars and antique shops and music stores. They crossed into the story of my life, where we all flailed around, unable to recognize each other. The chemistry of disaster: Black, white, sex. Male, female, violence. Black, white, female. Male, sex, violence. One accidentally open door that could never again be closed.

After five years, I would drive up and over the Blue Ridge in a tightly packed Toyota, leaving the South behind. Within a few hours I would be in Ohio—the Midwest, terra cognita. The South would become for me what it became in the white American consciousness: Attic for our dangerous memories, repository for our fear and shame; the Woods of our collective fairy tale, from which no one emerges unscathed, unchanged. And it would always smell like boxwood.

Rum-Running Queen

Louella Bryant

A while ago I was a guest at a garden party in Kentucky. A meadow rolled down from a stone patio to the Ohio River, where a hundred fifty years ago steamboats would have lazed along, smoke drifting from their tall stacks. From a covered porch, a fiddler and a guitarist played some sprightly tunes. When they took a break, I noticed the guitarist picked up a mason jar at her feet and took a sip.

Moonshine, probably. Everyone has a bit hidden in a kitchen cabinet, and entertainers are usually offered a few shots—always from a jar—to help them find their groove. That afternoon I preferred to visit the bartender, who was pouring expensive whiskey from bottles on which the host had paid the appropriate federal tax.

Not that I have anything against moonshine. In fact, for generations my family tended a still in Virginia's Shenandoah Valley. My mother told me the story of her Uncle Shorty, my grandfather's brother, who burst into the house one night panting, "Archie, they're after me." My grandfather was an honest man who worked as a foreman for the local paper mill. Having always suspected his younger brother would get into trouble one day, however, he was ready. The back seat of his Model A Ford lifted up on hinges. He emptied out the tire iron and fishing tackle, stuffed his brother into the compartment—no easy task because Uncle Shorty was as round as he was tall—and settled his two children, my mother and her brother, on the seat cushion as decoys. Then he took off, careening around mountain switchbacks through the towns of Healing Springs, Hot Springs, and Warm Springs, into West Virginia and up through Maryland, not stopping until he arrived the next morning in Harrisburg, Pennsylvania. There he pried Shorty out of his cramped compartment, dusted him off, and put him on a train to Kentucky.

When men drank, they perched on a sawhorse or on overturned buckets out behind the barn. Women, on the other hand, drank around an activity like a game of gin rummy. At the garden party, a guest told me of attending a quilting bee with five other women. Previously, they had stitched the blocks of fabric together, fitted the batting, and attached the backing. Now the quilt was on its frame, and the women gathered to sew the scrolling design that holds the quilt together.

They'd just begun when the host's husband, a deputy sheriff for the county, returned home from busting up a moonshiner's still. The offender had been sent off to jail, and the sheriff had confiscated a gallon jug of moonshine as a souvenir. He presented the jug to his wife, who poured each of her friends a tumbler. The women sipped while they sewed, getting happier with each stitch. The more they drank, the lovelier their designs, vines curling and whirling gracefully over the fabric. As it grew late, the women agreed to meet the following week to finish the quilt, and gave each other cheery hugs before leaving.

When they reconvened the next week, they found the quilting frame empty. The unfinished quilt had vanished. The women scoured the house, but found no quilt. Finally someone spotted a bundle tucked up into the kitchen rafters. When they had retrieved the package and unwrapped the bundle, they found not the beautiful quilt they had labored over earlier, but a wretched mess with uneven stitches meandering in haphazard directions. No one remembered hiding the quilt, but patiently (and soberly) they pulled out the misbehaving threads and started again.

Kentucky was once part of Virginia, where I was raised, and the two states share a common heritage that includes a partiality to moonshine liquor. In the 1960s, my family purchased a vacation cabin in Virginia's Jefferson National Forest, not far from the Kentucky border. To get there, we had to ford a few streams where bridges had not yet been built. Those crossings, when water sprayed up around the car windows, were my favorite part of the trip.

When we opened the cabin for the first time, we had to fight our way through cobwebs hanging from the ceiling. Mice scurried through the kitchen. Antiques and dust-covered junk were piled everywhere. The stone fireplace was unusable because squirrels' nests clogged the chimney. Moths had eaten holes in the carpet, under which the linoleum peeled and cracked. Spiders had to be swept from the casings to pry open the windows and let in the mountain breezes that chased away the must and mildew. Honeysuckle, pawpaw, fermentation, and loam scented the air wafting from the surrounding Blue Ridge Mountains.

The cabin, built in 1925, during Prohibition, held evidence of some good parties—pictures of movie stars taped to the walls, a stack of 78 rpm records next to a wind-up Victrola, and dozens of empty whiskey bottles on the kitchen shelves. My parents called the place Pine Cliff because it perches on a cliff surrounded by evergreens. Below the cliff, Jennings Creek cascades over a drop-off into a deep swimming hole. This is moonshine territory, for sure—a location that would have been hard for federal agents to penetrate unless they were willing to deal with rattlesnakes, copperheads, and thickets wiggling with ticks. My brother takes his buddies there for hunting and trout fishing. Don doesn't drink much, but he does support the local economy. The last time I visited him, he opened the door of the old oak icebox he'd taken from the cabin porch and restored. From the lower compartment, he pulled out several gallon-size mason jars. Preserved peach halves settled on the bottom of one jar of pinkish fluid. The others held liquid colored with damson plums, blueberries, and elderberries.

"What is this stuff?" I asked.

He grinned. "It's moonshine whiskey."

"Where'd you get it?"

He didn't want to reveal his source, but I waggled it out of him. His daughter was a student at Ferrum College in Virginia's Franklin County, which has been called "the moonshine capital of the world," and a friend of hers was paying his tuition by selling the stuff. Don had donated twenty dollars to the boy's scholarship fund in exchange for the white lightning.

He unscrewed the lid of the peach jar and poured some liquor into a shot glass.

"Have a taste," he said.

Moonshine is usually very potent, as high as 180 proof, or 90% alcohol. A proof of 180 is strong enough to double as an effective cleaning agent, and I've heard that moonshine can be contaminated with toxins, but I trusted my brother not to poison me. The first swallow was like liquid fire. My throat blazed. My eyes watered. I coughed. After a few more sips of the firewater, I excused myself and went to bed. Moonshine may be an acquired taste, but I don't think I'll ever get used to it.

The writer Sherwood Anderson moved to the mountains of Virginia in the 1920s. He described people like my Blue Ridge relatives who stuck "tight to their barren hills like fleas on a dog. Little houses tucked away on some side road . . . a cow and a barn right close up against the road. Every man with a bottle of moon whisky in his hip pocket . . . " Moonshine was the main cash crop for many Appalachia dwellers, and women not only tolerated the work at the stills but were involved in it. When it comes to their liquor, Appalachians feel entitled to drink what they produce from the corn and rye they've grown in their own fields in stills they've forged with their own hands. For many of them, putting a tax on corn liquor is like taxing the corn itself, and they won't stand for it, even if it means serving a jail sentence. If the women spied alcohol and tobacco tax agents, they "called the cows" by yelling out, "Come, Boss." "Coooommmme BAAAAASSS!" A "whoop" or a honking horn carries across a field, and a revenuer might have thought a woman was rounding up the herd for feeding rather than alerting her menfolk about an intruder.

Selling moonshine makes good economic sense. A superior tasting whiskey is aged for at least two years in barrels, which take up space and have to be rotated in a warehouse to compensate for fluctuations in temperature. And not only is the whiskey not bringing in money during that time, but the alcohol is seeping into the wood and evaporating. When a bottle of the finest finally does go to market, the price for a bottle of legal liquor can be staggering—and half of the money goes to the federal government in taxes. Many moonshiners have considered applying for the license to sell their goods legally, but the regulations and the costs of licensing have sent them back to the deep woods.

Anderson wrote in a 1934 issue of *Liberty Magazine* that Franklin County "fairly dripped illicit liquor." For decades, thousands of jars of the precious liquid were transported to buyers in northern cities. The contraband was bottled in gallon jars painted white, as if it were milk. Savvy moonshiners recruited women to run the shipments. They told revenuers who stopped them that they were delivering milk from the family farm.

One woman in particular was notorious for hoodwinking the police; her name was Willie Carter Sharpe, and her daredevil tactics earned her the title "Queen of the Roanoke Rum-Runners."

In her twenties Willie was good-looking, if not beautiful—the type of woman men admired rather than desired. She was solidly built, five feet five and weighing 157 pounds. Some called her "mannish" because she liked a smoke and a drink after work with her boots up on the table. She was anything but dainty and feminine, and she'd spit in your eye if you called her a lady.

One afternoon in 1920, Floyd Carter, the son of bootleg baron John Carter, walked into the dime store where Willie was working. Most people avoided the Carters, who had amassed a fortune in the liquor business and were known to be dangerous if you crossed them. But Willie was not cowed. She looked Floyd straight in the eye the way she would any other customer. Floyd liked her spunk and asked her out. After a brief courtship, he was smitten. When he popped the question, Willie considered her options. She had grown up barefoot on her family's farm and had done the work of a man until she was sixteen. Floyd could give her things she'd only dreamed of. She would not be deprived again.

She took immediately to the bootleg business and talked her father-in-law into letting her drive for him. Willie had learned the nuances of farm machinery, and to say that she could handle a car was an understatement. She would get up a head of steam and then slam into second gear, jerking the steering wheel to the left to spin the car a hundred eighty degrees and pass the pursuers in the opposite direction. Soon, she was making runs every night. She drove for the sheer thrill of it.

It never felt to her like breaking the law—she hadn't made the hooch, after all, and she wasn't selling it. Sure, she was speeding, but she'd have to get caught to get arrested. And catching Willie Carter was no easy task. Willie reputedly ran more than 220,000 gallons of illicit whiskey from Franklin County as far north as New York.

When John Carter saw how cleverly she could work a vehicle, he assigned Willie the job of pilot—the driver of a decoy car that lured police cruisers into a high-speed chase, leaving the roads empty for convoys of illegal liquor to be delivered across the county line. Willie was the middleman—middle woman—having a good time behind the wheel of a quick machine. It was a rule to have a faster car than the law, and so moonshine runners spent hours on their autos, muscling up an engine by adding three two-barrel carburetors to a Cadillac motor installed in a Ford body. Carburetors had to be shortened in order to close the hood of the car. A supercharger rammed additional air into the cylinders, and some vehicles had as many as fifteen forward gears. Mechanics installed a sixteen-gallon fuel tank and extra suspension springs to hold the vehicle level even when carrying a full load of whiskey. It was not unusual to see an unloaded auto with its hind end kissing the sky. With a trunk stacked full, including a hidden compartment under the trunk bed, a load of liquor could weigh over a thousand pounds. If you heard the sound of a big engine, you made sure to get out of the road quick.

Some runners used delivery vans or pickups with a tarp over the hooch and a load of mulch or topsoil piled on the tarp to look like a routine farm delivery. Cars could be fitted with bright rear-facing lights to blind pursuing revenuers, and it was common to switch license plates to confuse the Feds.

Willie preferred a car. With the flick of a special switch, she could turn off her taillights, which made her harder to spot from behind. When revenuers shot at her tires, she took to country roads and lost them on deadly curves and steep ascents. She came alive when she drove, adrenaline rushing through her veins, every nerve alert.

Willie could make fifty dollars a night driving through town streets at speeds of seventy-five miles per hour. She enjoyed the money and bought silk suits and shoes of Italian leather. It was said that she had diamonds set in her teeth. She once had nothing, but now nothing was too good for her.

And then, one night in 1931 as Willie was driving pilot, something went wrong with the brakes on her car. Federal agents were tailing her, and she careened down a side street to lose them. Doubling back, she whirled into an intersection and, unable to stop, rammed the side of the agents' car. She crawled from the wreck, her arms sliced and bleeding. The men were cut up pretty badly, too. Any runner worth his salt would have taken to the woods, but Willie had a soft spot. She stayed and helped the agents out of their banged-up vehicle. There was no liquor in her car, but the agents put her under arrest for reckless driving, and a judge sent her to federal prison for three years.

While she was behind bars, Willie had visitors, many of them women—some blue-blood Virginians dolled up in expensive dresses. She had become a sort of romantic muse, the kind of wild spirit other women dreamed of being but didn't have the gumption for. One woman asked if she could ride with Willie when she got out of jail. The young woman wanted the thrill of a high-speed chase, making tricky maneuvers, getting away with lawlessness. Outrunning cops had become the new extreme sport. Willie told the woman she was finished with driving—but within a week of her release, she was behind the wheel and running moonshine again.

Between 1930 and 1935, moonshiners in Franklin County were the recipients of thirty-seven tons of yeast, seventeen thousand tons of sugar, and thousands of tons of malt, meal, and other materials used in making whiskey, along with a million five-gallon cans made specifically for liquor. As the illegal distilling business picked up, so did federal investigations. In 1935 a federal grand jury indicted thirty-four people for conspiracy to defraud the government. Those indicted included a Franklin County sheriff and several of his deputies, a state prohibition officer, a House of Delegates member, the Franklin County Commonwealth's Attorney, and Willie Carter Sharpe. (By then she had divorced Floyd Carter and moved in with a bootlegger named Charlie Sharpe. Although they never married, she added his name to hers.) The trial lasted forty-nine days, and one hundred seventy-six witnesses were called to the stand.

Some of the witnesses admitted to moving more than a million gallons of whiskey, and it was estimated that one hundred million gallons of moonshine were transported out of the county each year. The prosecution estimated that the conspirators had defrauded the federal government of five and a half million dollars in whiskey excise taxes, and argued that a conspiracy to avoid taxes was akin to robbing the government treasury, thereby robbing people served by that government. But one witness countered, "Anyone would tell you you cannot legislate morality, and you certainly can't stop people from drinking."

Willie wore a white tailored dress with brown ruffled sleeves, with a white hat and shoes to match, and had pinned the front of her collar with a cameo brooch. Her fellow bootleggers defended her. One testified: "The illegal liquor trade is worth tens of billions . . . and it's not Willie Carter Sharpe who's in charge. It's gangsters. Organized crime has a stranglehold stretching across the country." He listed half a dozen mobsters in major cities, including Chicago's Al Capone, whom he called "the most notorious gangster of all." Capone, he said, earned over a hundred dollars a minute from illegal alcohol.

The testimony was convincing. Obviously there were larger fish to fry, and Willie was free to take to the road again.

Eventually, Willie gave up running moonshine. She had paid her dues with jail time and court testimony, and left Franklin County to live out her life in anonymity. But in the mountains of Virginia, Willie Carter Sharpe and her lawless driving are legend.

Sherwood Anderson called southwest Virginia "a gracious country," and it is. My Uncle Shorty and many other residents of the Shenandoah Valley made good money from their stills and always offered their guests a sampling. Even today, if you visit any of my relatives, they'll insist you stay for a meal. And if you're lucky, they'll unearth a mason jar from the root cellar and pour you a drink. Just don't ask where they got the whiskey. Down that way, traditions die hard.

Sportfucking in the South

Suzanne Roberts

I came home with a bladder infection.

I told my husband that I had eaten too many carbohydrates—doughnuts, bagels, croissants, dinner rolls. You know how those writing conferences are: starchy foods for breakfast, lunch, and dinner. And the weather—humidity is bad for female parts! I know I am not fooling you, and I only fooled him because there are times when the truth, though obvious as a raindrop, is too hard to accept, even if it has landed on your nose.

You and I both know that bladder infections are usually the result of too much sex. Now, I am not usually the sort of person who tends to modify the word "sex" with the words "too much." My sister tells me in that sense, I'm just like a guy, though I know plenty of women who like sex. Plenty who like sex more than men do. Is that a big secret? I sometimes think so. Because when I had the chance to have too much sex all weekend, I bought myself a plane ticket and headed south. Yes, I have read *He's Just Not that Into You*, and yes, buying my own ticket is also against *The Rules* (I have read that, too), but I didn't want the guy to marry me. I just wanted to fuck. I justified it by telling myself I was on the way out with my husband.

I should stop lying. He wasn't my husband but my live-in ex-husband, which makes some of this seem better; some of it, worse. Anyway, this live-in ex-husband of mine and I were not exactly having a fairy-tale romance, so when this poet I knew said, "Come see me," I didn't wait around for him to ask twice. The plan to sportfuck all weekend wasn't explicitly stated, but in our emails, he had made his vasectomy known, and I had made clear that my crotch was a no-fly zone unless he submitted to a battery of STD testing beforehand. He complied, and we set a date.

This poet wasn't exactly a hunka burning love. He was (and I assume still is) a wisp of a man, older than me by at least 10 years and what you might call very delicate. He has girlish wrists, and the bones of his spine line his back like pebbles. He is famous enough that I won't use his real name. I will call him Werther, not because of any suicidal tendencies, but because I wanted to think of him as a Romantic, even though I knew that wasn't anywhere close to the truth. Months earlier, Werther had come to my hometown to give a poetry reading, mostly because we had engaged in some email flirtation, and it seemed exciting—a little thrill to break up the monotony of grading papers, committee meetings, and a live-in ex-husband. So, he had come, along with another poet, whom I had no interest in fucking. They both read, and afterward, I offered to show them some good old-fashioned hospitality by taking them across the state line into Nevada to the casino dance club, where at midnight all the bikini-clad cage dancers do away with their tops.

My live-in ex-husband wasn't about to let me go off to the dance club alone with two poets and my recently divorced friend, Kitty, so he came along as well. Kitty was, at that time, engaged in what she called "serial dating." Middle-aged, but hardly frumpy, she caught the eye of all the 50-year olds on Match.com who were tired of looking at women in mom jeans. So Kitty was getting plenty of action, but action begets action, and she, too, was impressed by Werther and his verse. To be fair to old Werther, he's good-looking in a scholarly kind of way, and smart and fake humble, which tends to go a long way with women.

Anyway, Kitty and Werther were grinding up a storm among the twenty-somethings on the dance floor, and I was glad for the moment because I thought this somehow proved to my live-in ex-husband that I, myself, was not at all attracted to the poet. True, we were already divorced, but we had moved back in together, had agreed to try to make it work. Divorce or no divorce, this was betrayal. But I sat smugly drinking something sweet and strong. Soon enough, my live-in ex-husband was satisfied that I wasn't interested in Werther, and so he left. By this time, Kitty and Werther had made out on the dance floor (and, I later learned, in the parking lot, too), and he had begged her to drive them both to his hotel. Kitty was drunk, but not drunk enough, so she declined. At that point, I am ashamed to say, I did what any mean girl would do: I swooped in on Werther. After that, I have to admit things are a margarita blur. I knew that if I didn't come home, I would be in big trouble with my live-in ex-husband and even bigger trouble with Kitty, who had jumped in a taxi home once she saw me flirting with Werther. I know Werther begged me to come to his hotel, and I said no, though I promised to visit him to finish it off.

The next day, everything seemed to settle back into place. My live-in ex-husband didn't say a word, Kitty was more mad at Werther than at me (and probably herself, though in that little triangle, I don't think any of us was without guilt), and my hangover was finished by evening. However, I didn't feel mad at Werther. He was an opportunist. I was not available, as he had planned, so he went for someone who was.

A few months later, when Werther picked me up at the airport, he was wearing his usual poet black. He held wilting red roses and a little box of chocolates, which were already melting in the heat, and I ended up giving the sad chocolates to my students to make up for missing a day of class to go to a "writing conference." In my mind, the writing conference excuse wasn't an entire lie: I went to spend time with an established poet. Werther carried around his notebook all weekend, at least the few times we left his bed. God only knows what he was writing. Yet, being with him made me feel like less of a poet, not more of one. At one point, he told me he thought that the poet bares the world, and I still don't know if he meant bares or bears. I was too embarrassed to ask. Maybe he was baring the world while I was bearing it? I didn't write a word that weekend. Later, I wrote humiliating, self-indulgent poems.

I thought the wilting roses terribly romantic, which made me a little nervous. When I am nervous, I talk. A lot. I talked the entire trip from the airport, telling Werther one embarrassing thing after the next about myself, until the moment we were almost killed. We were on a two-lane highway, behind a giant truck. In the opposing lane was another giant truck. I suppose the pickup that tried to pass the giant truck in the other lane didn't see us behind the giant truck in our lane. Or didn't care. We couldn't go into the other lane because of giant truck number one, and just then, we were traveling across a bridge, so there were no shoulders on either side. With the pickup coming straight for us and nowhere to go, Werther and I both did the most logical thing: we shut our eyes and screamed. We should have hit the pickup head on. We should have faced a shattering of glass, our organs bungled by steel. We should have been in a terrible accident. But when we opened our eyes, we were past the bridge on the opposite shoulder. Don't ask me how that happened. There are very few incidents in my life for which I don't have rational explanations, and this is one of them.

We sat on the side of the dark road and shook with disbelief, fear, relief, and adrenaline. A blizzard in my veins, an icicle for a spine, despite the heat. I am sure we must have said something to one another, something like "Wow" or "Holy shit," but I remember only the shivering, and then the driving in silence.

We arrived at Werther's rancher, crossed the lawn, went inside, took off our clothes, and went to bed for two days. This is an exaggeration, of course, but just barely. I remember eating pancakes while Werther read me a horrifying David Foster Wallace story about a child's genitals being badly burned. And a steamy afternoon walk under flowering dogwoods, where I nervously talked and talked, telling Werther that I had been to a psychic who told me that someone on the other side of the country was thinking about me, and didn't he think it must have been him? And a trip to the university, where Werther had to pick something up from his office. There, he introduced me to a woman, and at first glance, I knew he was fucking her, too.

Other than these small errands, we spent the time in bed. Not until that weekend and never after it has fucking felt so much like sport. Werther must have been in his late 40s at the time, and I can't imagine he pulled off this feat without some pharmaceutical help, but he denied it. At first, I thought this frenzy of fucking was due to the accident. The fact that really, we ought to have been dead.

I figured all we wanted to do was to prove that our bodies were still alive, that our hearts were beating, and other things, too. That on a hot Southern night, we had cheated death. Maybe even witnessed a miracle. A God that neither of us would claim had saved us. There's the unspeakable—pushing back the presence of God with the pleasures of the body. Or maybe it's the search for God in the moment of sweaty, bodily ecstasy. The ancient religious poems are full of erotic imagery; the ecstatic can only be reached through God or through fucking. Were we in touch with something more spiritual, or was it really just sportfucking? I can turn anything into anything else if I think about it long enough.

But I want to tell the truth.

On the way back to the airport, I tried not to chatter on and on, which wasn't that hard because I was tired. Werther didn't ask to see me again, and I didn't mention it. Good-bye was just that. I never saw him again, at least not like that. Life is full of all sorts of surprises, though, and a few years later, we ended up in the same plane and then the same taxi on the way to a real writing conference. *Why don't we all share a cab?* someone suggested. Squeezed in next to him in the backseat of the taxi, the only word that came to mind was *impossible*.

After Werther dropped me off at the airport, I sat on my carry-on at the gate. I called Kitty, who tried to make me feel better. I think she may have asked why I went, what I was looking for. I felt like a balloon that had sailed across the room, spurting air. Once loud and ridiculous, now finally still. Empty and crumpled. The airport is an appropriate place for loneliness. No one makes the pretense of staying. Everyone is going somewhere and usually with great haste.

I suppose I went to see Werther because I wanted to have a life that was exciting and free, though as I write this I see how contradictory it all is. I wanted to be more than myself. When I came back from my trip, my sister said, "It's as if you are in a car, and you have pulled your hands off the wheel, ready to crash." Everything at that time in my life was like that. Going to visit Werther was like pressing on the accelerator. Waiting to crash. Almost crashing, as usual. Close your eyes and wait. Somehow, I had managed a series of near misses. How do we escape what we deserve?

I didn't—and still don't—care that I was one of many of Werther's women. He wasn't my only affair, either. What I wanted was to be someone who could take charge of her life, though really, I was doing just the opposite. I wanted to believe I would look in the mirror and think, *Why, who is that woman who can jet off to the South for a clandestine affair in a 1970s rancher with a man who weighs less than she does?* That's what I ended up doing, but I suppose what I really wanted was to believe that I wasn't the sort of woman who talks too much about crazy things when she is nervous. I wanted to be the woman who could go off and fuck someone who cared nothing about her and feel just fine. The truth is, there is no woman like that, and if there were, I am not sure I would admire her. I am not trying to be moralistic here. I am not saying sex without love is an awful thing, because I don't believe that either. I don't regret my sportfucking weekend. Antibiotics took care of the infection, and my live-in ex-husband and I were on our way out anyway.

Here I am at the end of this, and there is no universal theme, no surprise. I have crossed years to get here, and still, I am not sure why I did the things I did.

One more try: a friend of mine said that if it isn't true, it's just noise. Here is the truth: I wanted Werther to like me. I didn't want to have a relationship and get married. In fact, I wanted to be free to do whatever I wanted. But still, I wanted him to like me. He didn't. He didn't like me or Kitty or his colleague at the university. What I can see now, after all these years, is that I didn't like him, either. I used him, too. I needed an escape from my humiliating living situation. I used him, and that doesn't make me like myself very much, either.

I have a friend who hasn't had sex in years. He is ambiguous about his sexuality, and so he has been walking the fence for a very long time, which has given him the chance to take a look at sex from quite a distance. He says you can't just give yourself to someone you don't love. I don't think that is exactly right. I think you can. Anyway, people do, and I don't think there is any useful separation here, except maybe in culture's eyes, between genders. I think you can have sex with someone you don't love, but I am not sure it's such a good idea to have sex with someone you don't like, and that's what Werther and I did for an entire weekend. To be nice, he would say he liked me, but it isn't true. And I didn't like him, which feels worse to admit because it means I should have just let Kitty have him in the first place, though in truth, she didn't like him much either.

"You're a crazy girl," my sister finally said. Maybe that's what I was looking for: crazy. To be crazy means you get to erase so many other things. To be crazy means that the other stuff is there, but no one gets to see it. It means people will like your stories, but the problem is that when we don't get past crazy, there is no point to the story. Crazy is an easy, dishonest way out.

I was jogging this morning in Florida, and if you have ever been to Florida in July, you know the prickly stars of a wet heat on your cheeks, the stinging fire in your lungs. The body's machine working against the heat. The body remembers things based on feel, based on the temperature of a landscape: I ran and I remembered that walk through a late afternoon glare, how I talked about "my psychic," how I must have sounded like a crazy person. How I let my sweaty hand dangle next to his, hoping. It all comes back, whether I like it or not: the near-accident on the highway, the football announcer's tinny voice coming from the cracking loudspeakers at the nearby stadium, the dogwoods, the afternoon heat seeping through the blinds, the weight of my suitcase.

A Lesson in Merging

Rachael Peckham

All along route 52 the train chases evening into haze
of field smoke. And it is steel and iron and bitter. I want
you. I want you. I want to breathe you in and sweat you
out like fever . . .

—Joel Peckham, "You Tell Me All My Love
Poems Are About Myself"

*T*he semester before my mentor, Susan, and her husband, Joel, were in a fatal car accident that would kill her and their oldest child, Joel taught me how to merge onto US-441—nicknamed *Suicide Stretch*—on the outskirts of Milledgeville, Georgia.

At twenty-two years old, I had followed Susan and Joel by moving from a small private college in Michigan to a graduate writing program in Georgia, trading "the country's breadbasket" for the Bible Belt; the Great Lakes for cotton country and hilltops edged in longleaf pine. And perilous two-lane highways. US-441, flanked by roadside stands selling two-dollar pints of boiled peanuts (*bald peanuts* on one sign), careens around Georgia's swamps and forests like it's trying to buck you off its back. A driver learns to anticipate its throws—a blind entrance around the bend, a logging truck barreling by or, worse, edging out in front.

"You can't be passive on this road," Joel once coached from the passenger's seat. We were stopped at the mouth of Coral Road, one of the many tributaries flowing into 441, on our way to his faculty picnic. Joel had called me, desperate for a ride after his family's Ford Escort station wagon—*a very sexy car*, he often joked—had broken down again. I was happy to help out, even as I silently cursed the left turn I would have to make onto 441, where the road shakes loose from the forest's grip and the lanes multiply and the speed limit feels 20 mph too fast. Where a string of drivers, relieved at the opportunity to finally pass a sputtering pickup or tractor-trailer, make a break for the open lane in both directions.

After I had spent several minutes inching out, retreating back, inching out again, Joel threw up his hands. "You have to make up your mind, Rach."

———•—•———

My decision to move to the South had unfolded over poetry and peanut butter sandwiches with Susan two years prior in Michigan. Her office was a magnet for those of us in search of some quiet counsel, feedback on a poem, or simply lunch in her company. It felt good, sitting in the soft light of her office, which she filled with personal treasures: her books, of course; two Tiffany lamps; a collection of small rocks her boys had collected and painted, one of which now sits on my own desk at home. Even her perfume still lingers in a book I borrowed, as traceable as any signature.

I had enrolled in Susan's workshop during my sophomore year of college. And like everyone Susan met, I was immediately struck by her beauty, her grace—by the way she twisted her black waist-length hair into a knot at the nape of her neck and then untwisted it, repeatedly, in a mindless dance of the hands; by the velvet red hair tie she stored on her wrist for such habits; by the chime of her laugh when she excused herself for the third time to use the bathroom; by the cotton tunic hugging her pregnant form.

Two months later, Susan gave birth to their second child, Darius, named after the Persian emperor in honor of Susan's Iranian heritage. If I wasn't already completely mesmerized by her at this point, I most certainly was when she returned to school hugging a bundle of baby with a crop of black hair as thick and lustrous as her own. I took every class Susan taught, and lit up when she asked me one day if I'd watch the boys during her department meeting. I still have pictures of that fall day, when I pushed their stroller across campus to the public library, with Darius asleep in the back and three-year-old Cyrus in front, dangling one hand over the edge to brush a sidewalk blanketed with leaves.

Eventually, I would graduate from college and accept Susie's invitation (I took to using her nickname, a gesture both intimate and possessive) to join her at a small MFA program in Milledgeville, Georgia, where she had taken a position teaching graduate-level workshops. Joel had accepted a position at the nearby military college. Soon we were packing our respective U-Haul trailers, bound for the South and its legacy of great writers.

From the start, the move took on a mythopoeic tone. I had placed Susie atop a pedestal, ascribing to her all the values and virtues of the ideal academic life. She was a poet, an abstract expressionist painter, and a classically trained pianist—a living model of the Liberal Arts, in my mind. In Georgia, I lingered even longer in her office, sitting across from her in the blue armchair that now stands like a monument to her memory in the program's department. I can picture her elbows resting on her knees, which peeked out from beneath the hemline of a cotton summer dress. We'd be talking about something poignant in a book we'd read, maybe a film one of us had seen that weekend, and she'd pause to ask me, "Have I ever told you about Cyrus's birth?"

The gravity of this memory—the memory of her first child's birth—made Susan's eyes fill and widen, her voice quiver like a violin string, both delicate and layered. I knew the story well, at this point, but was still mystified by it. Or maybe it was the way she told it, with a fragility that she entrusted to the listener. As though its ending could shift and shatter in the space between us. Her voice always caught at the part when Cyrus was pulled from her, *not breathing, the words trailing off, I thought he was . . .*

I would wonder, much later, if she foresaw the ending, not to this story but to another one hovering in the distance. But in this moment, this memory, there was only Susan—her black hair, her round dark eyes, and the smell of her perfume so lush and full that even as you exhaled, you felt the urge to breathe in again and hold her there.

———

I liked the way Joel rubbed Susie's feet while they watched television, kicking back after a day of teaching and attending university events and parties that required me to babysit frequently for Cyrus and Darius. And when Joel and Susie returned home, I was always asked to *stick around a while*, to *hang out*, even stay the night on a few occasions when it was quite late and dangerous to be on the road and I felt too tired to argue with them.

On nights like those, we'd sit in the living room around the TV, chatting about the graduate program. Joel always held a beer in one hand and Susie's foot in the other. It's tricky, he'd say, to grip and rub a foot with one hand, but he had played offensive center in college. "See?" he'd hold up a hand. "Small but strong." And within minutes Susan's eyes would close. "Isn't she beautiful?" he'd whisper.

She was. And *they* were, this little family who had adopted me, far away from my own. The first day of my graduate student orientation, everyone took turns, both students and faculty, introducing themselves and the story of their arrival at this MFA program. Susan explained that she came from a small college on Lake Michigan—"along with Rach, my star student."

I shook my head modestly, but it felt good being her star, when really it was *she* we freely orbited around. When it was Joel's turn to introduce himself, he said without hesitation, as though the sentence had been formed a long time ago, "I'm the one who's married to the most beautiful, talented, most wonderful woman in the world."

For a second there was silence, followed by a few sighs and nods. But I bristled. *Come on.* For some reason, the display felt disingenuous every time, even though I delighted in the little moments of affection I was privy to when he rubbed her feet on the couch. But this grand gesture—which offered no introduction at all to who *he* was—read to me like a subtle trick at self-effacement, and it irritated me.

What did I expect, though? He was always deflecting the attention, turning his focus back on her, even as she slept ("Isn't she beautiful?"). And isn't this what I loved about him—no, about *them?*

————

The turn signal tapped steadily. "Just use the turning lane," Joel repeated a little more sharply. But I couldn't see a break, in either direction. Just weeks before, I had driven this road on my way back from Atlanta with a friend, and we'd come upon a long line of stopped traffic dissected by a pendant of flashing lights. Before we'd even reached the scene of the accident, my friend—who reads Tarot cards and sees auras—instructed me not to look to the right because *somebody's dead up there.*

I whipped the steering wheel a half-circle and gunned it, throwing Joel back in his seat. An approaching truck second-guessed my intention, swerving to miss me—and still, I could not merge into traffic. We sat trapped in the turning lane for several minutes before I actually considered sliding over and letting him drive. But the move would've required getting out of the car—not an option—or sliding across Joel's lap. An option, but one I relinquished to the increasing daydreams I already hated myself for harboring, secretly.

I didn't know *why* I was having these fantasies, or when exactly they had begun. (Funny, I have a memory of tripping once when I went to hug him good-bye, and of throwing my hands forward to break my fall. Was it the force of that fall, my hands landing smack on his chest, that awoke something in me?) I loved Susan. And I was in a relationship myself, one that was physically and emotionally consuming, maybe even controlling. I had not yet learned how to dodge the line of fire—questions about where I'd been; who was with me; what I'd worn and said—let alone how to walk away for good, as I eventually did.

It was during this time that I went to a priest, though I had never stepped foot in his parish before. I had not made an appointment, and his schedule that day was *packed*—as his secretary indicated, clicking her tongue—but something in my response must've registered distress because the priest, stocky and gray-bearded, rose abruptly from his desk in the adjoining office, introduced himself, and offered me a seat across from his large mahogany desk. After listening to my choked confession, he unclasped his hands, leaned forward in his chair, and asked me why I thought I walked toward such unhealthy relationships in the first place. It was a fair question, I agreed. But at the time, I didn't see it this way—*a moth to the flame*; a *glutton for punishment*. His pat phrasings wedged me into a place of further shame and confusion. While he recited a parable, I pretended to concentrate, locking my eyes on the blinds that obscured the window behind him. Just beyond the edges of this church, I knew, lay the campus where Joel was teaching at that moment, probably pausing between points to run a hand through his hair, as I had seen him do so many times, smudging chalk on his temple. This priest was right—it was time I consider why I desired *the wrong men*. Was I depressed? Lost? Bored?

I was none of these, exactly, and yet, there *was* a bit of the self-saboteur in me, the one *laying the dynamite on the tracks* and the train *hurtling toward it*.

<hr />

At last, we pulled into the parking lot of Lake Laurel Lodge, the site of Joel's faculty picnic, a university clubhouse set on a fifteen-acre lake rumored to be full of water moccasins. I had delivered him safely. My legs were drum-tight with adrenaline and I wondered when it would go away and why all my consciousness was centered in my thighs at that moment.

"—you just need a little practice," Joel laughed, still imparting his lesson on merging. He gathered his briefcase and gear and removed the cup of coffee pinned precariously between his knees. "Can you pick me up at four?"

———•—•———

Susan was at the height of her career when we moved down South. The requests for interviews and readings came pouring in almost immediately after her first book of poems—a mosaic of Persian mysticism, imagery, and story—won a major national prize. Early into our second year in Georgia, she was asked to read her poetry during a museum's week-long exhibition, *Empire of the Sultans*, in honor of Ottoman art and Persian history. Susie needed someone to watch the boys the day of the reading, and again on the following day while she delivered talks. Joel had to teach; could *I* do it?

I quickly switched around some things I had scheduled, threw together a bag of travel board games, playing cards, and some assigned reading for class. I tossed my black bikini on top. I stared at it then—*I never swim at their place*—and took it out.

But with my hand on the front doorknob, I felt the impulse return. Running upstairs, I threw open the top drawer of my dresser and stuffed the swimsuit in the bag, then ran out the door, feeling it close behind me.

———•—•———

I arrived at Susie's place just as her ride to the museum pulled up. She pulled on her jacket, flinging her hair to one side, fanning me with perfume, and gathered her books. "I'm late," she mumbled, a piece of toast clamped squarely in her mouth. And then with one hand finally free, she removed the toast, smiled, "Boys are still asleep. Help yourself to coffee, anything." Adding over her shoulder, "Joel will be home at four."

———•—•———

At the lake's edge later that day, beneath a hazy white sky, Cyrus and Darius competed to gather the largest pile of sticks, with the older brother out-gathering the younger. Yet I remember peacefulness in their play, in the collaborative search for sticks that stayed sticks and not swords. The only drama developed when Darius planted a foot firmly atop a hill of fire ants, sounding a chorus of cries—first from Darius, then Cyrus, who danced around his little brother in total terror. I don't remember panicking, only a furious pumping of legs to the lake, charging the water with Darius on my hip and wading until we were both wet up to our chests.

"Hey, look who's in the water."

Joel's voice rang out from the back deck. He trudged down the hill, clutching his briefcase in one hand and unbuttoning his shirt with the other. With the front finally undone and untucked, I could see a bloom of blond chest hair peeking out through the top of his ribbed under-shirt, covering a set of pectoral muscles so defined, it was hard not to stare. And when I became aware of my own staring, something in me tightened. I had never seen this much of Joel before. And he obviously *wanted* me to look, had shed his shirt to make the point.

Joel stood on the dock, smiling at me. "Isn't it a little cold for swimming, Rach?"

I glanced down at the fine dark hairs standing up on my arms. My skin was still tan, still softened by the summer sun, but now a spread of goose bumps rippled across my forearms, making the swimming scene, its pretense, even more of a spectacle.

"Well, yes, but we're having fun."

We're having fun? I secretly willed Cyrus not to recount the rescue that had just taken place minutes before his father's arrival. Somehow he heard my prayer and redirected his dad's gaze to the proud pile of sticks he and Darius had spent all afternoon gathering and lining on the beach.

"That's impressive," Joel laughed, "but now we need to get you guys cleaned up and ready to go. Susie's reading in two hours."

You guys.

"What do you say, Rach? Come with us?"

"No, no," I stammered, "I don't think so." There were chapters I needed to read, a response paper due the next day. All I wanted to do was scamper out of the water, make a graceful exit for my car, and be absorbed by the speedy current down 441.

But an equal part of me was thrilled to be asked, which he seemed to sense. And the more Joel pressed, the harder he made it for me to resist, especially once the boys broke in with cheers of *come with us, come with us.* He must've read the question I was struggling to ask, because he insisted that Susie would be delighted to see me at the reading. And I had no doubt that was true; I knew that none of my peers were planning on going, with the museum an hour away.

But I also knew that it was one thing to show up on my own and surprise her, and quite another to accompany her family long after my babysitting duties had ended. Something about it felt wrong—and yet I eventually consented and hastened the boys, still jumping and tugging on my arms, up the hill and into the house.

Drawing their bath, I bent over the lip of the tub (still in my black bikini) in order to cradle Darius's head and rinse the shampoo from his dark curls. "I'll take over with that," Joel offered, climbing the stairs. "And you can use our shower." He added quickly, "To save time."

I shut the door of their master bathroom and stood for a minute staring at a counter lined with cosmetics and several kinds of perfume. Picking up a bottle of her body splash, the one with *Moonlight* in its name, I brought it to my nose, inhaling deeply. And then set it down carefully in its place, making sure the label faced the same way.

Only then did I look up at the mirror—*what are you doing?*—at a young woman I knew and didn't know, at her hair now longer and lighter, and her cheekbones, a little more pronounced than when I had left the Midwest. I flipped the lid of the toilet seat and sat down. In the garbage can nearby (did I really peer inside?) were wads of tissue paper, a few coils of floss, and something else that made me glance quickly away. Nothing that wasn't in my own wastebasket at home. But peeking inside this one, I could no longer deny I was the voyeur in this family theater, the one sweeping her eyes over this most private space, the one peering at their personal refuse—at what the body had touched, used up, and tossed out without so much as a thought that it might become material for study.

"Rachael?" A knock at the door. "I brought you a clean towel."

I shot to my feet. "Just a sec." In my hand was a clean towel I had taken from the cupboard beneath the sink. I dropped it in the corner, yanked on my suit, and opened the door.

"Sorry, I just thought—" He held out a white bundle. "Here."

I took the towel and we laughed a little, and in that second I felt each of us stalling, waiting—for what? What did I hope might happen in their bedroom, with their children a room away? Behind Joel's shoulder I could spot the boys' tiny, tanned bodies tearing down the hallway, naked, swinging their own towels in the air. Two little Prosperos, making the sea go wild and breaking the spell, all at once.

I often picked up Joel from work at 4:00, a repeated favor that I found myself looking forward to, without really analyzing why. I moved quickly through the days, busying myself with household chores, errands, sometimes exercise, always with the stereo or talk radio abuzz in the kitchen, in the bath, the car. I craved the company of another voice, yet I hardly ever called my parents or friends up north, and they felt and vocalized this distance. And I would reassure them I was doing fine— great, in fact, and I was not alone; Joel and Susie were down South with me—and the concerns would shift to talk of weather, family, school.

One afternoon, early in our second year in Georgia, Joel opened the car door and slid in. The weight of his body as it hit the seat told me he was tired. I joked that this time I was going to close my eyes and gun it on 441, so he'd better be ready. He smiled weakly. "Take your time."

Had he had a bad day? He kept running his hand through his hair, a habit I had long noted but finally understood was a gesture of self-comfort, after he launched into a story about his favorite baby blanket—the kind with the satin border that felt so good to him, growing up, that his mother cut it into smaller and smaller squares *until there was nothing left of it.* There were other stories like this, little jokes and anecdotes swapped between us, two Yankees homesick for the north, one for cornfields and the other for cranberry bogs, both for a Dunkin' Donuts and *my God, a real bagel.* But we had to admit, gas was cheap and so were the cigarettes, which somehow tasted better there because you didn't have to suck them down in the freezing cold—in fact, you didn't have to step outside at all in most of Milledgeville if you wanted to light up. And I did, often. In spite of my upbringing and better judgment, I took up the cliché of smoking in graduate school, a small transgression that Joel had once shared and missed, and we sometimes snuck outside for a quick drag during parties or receptions if Susie was deep at the center of a huddle. Which she was, often.

So, with very little effort and without much awareness, even to us, Joel and I became friends. Not through Susie but around her, on the fringes: sitting around the TV. On the benches at school. And of course, on drives to and from work.

What's more, our conversations had turned away from small talk to heavier subjects (his grandmother was dying and he couldn't visit her; he had considered going to seminary once but couldn't decide on a denomination). A closeness that felt good and for the same reason wrong, like a guilty pleasure. It was a point of confusion because while I didn't see the "sin" in my emotional intimacy with Joel, I never disclosed our conversations to Susie. And neither did he.

Still, I was not ready for what he said that afternoon, what he had never said to anyone: "I can't take it anymore—"

I shut the radio off, my signal for him to talk about whatever it was that had him so upset, usually a student's complaint about a grade, or the latest fight over the dress code at the military college where he taught the cadets how to write persuasively.

"—living this lie that everything's great, when it hasn't been, not for a long time." He was so tired of playing along, of pretending to be the golden couple for the whole world to see. Did I know how bad, how lonely that felt?

No. Yes. *What?* I was at once listening and spinning in thought, and he was talking so fast—if he would just slow down, maybe I could make sense of what he was saying to me: His marriage was in *trouble?*

They were unhappy, *the golden couple?* I turned the air conditioning fan to full blast.

"Rach," he reached over, turning it down a notch. "I just need for someone to know the truth."

Yet I needed for them to remain the way they'd always been. Untouchable. He was right; I didn't want to believe otherwise.

Didn't I? Already I was wrestling with another feeling in tension with resistance—one that had been there all along: the flattery of being the star student, favorite babysitter, family friend. And now chosen confidante. Not hers, but *his.*

He turned in his seat with a stare that searched for some recognition of truth, pleading for me to help pull him back from this awful precipice. Or to join him, it seemed. But I could only follow the double lines stretching before us—and with them, the gradual realization that I had merged onto *Suicide Stretch* without really thinking about it. Without really knowing what I was doing at all.

Tongues, Lust, and a Man from Indiana

Adriana Paramo

*I*almost didn't make it to the concert. Earlier that day, Tom had found a Florida scrub-jay nest in the dry woods behind our house in Lakeland. He snapped pictures from every angle, stopping only to feed me tidbits of information: this bird is endemic to Florida; he is sedentary, territorial, and highly monogamous. Tom crouched behind a tree. A cool breeze flapped his T-shirt against his solid back. The tree branches bent heavy with unfurled yarns of Spanish moss, which Tom says is neither Spanish nor moss. Everything around us burst with green, a big fat piñata of Florida Spring verdure. I stayed just for the sight of my husband: a 200-pound man with sturdy legs and muscular arms tiptoeing his way around a tiny bird. So sexy.

Above the nest, perched on a branch, was the sentinel scrub-jay.

"Lovely wee thing. Just lovely."

"I have to leave," I said.

"The noo?" he asked in his hushed Scottish voice.

"Yes, now."

"Sairy, darling. Ah canny stop looking at him." Tom took more pictures of the bird as he whispered the scrub-jay's unique features. No crest, the tip of their wings and tail feathers are pale blue, same color as the nape and *heeed*.

As we walked back to the house, the sun shone on my husband's goatee. It revealed a trimmed oval of white hair that used to be Celtic red. History, I thought as I looked at him: divorces, exes, three adult children living their own lives. We were free from the responsibilities of parenthood and still bonkers about each other after all these years. So much history, I thought again as I kissed him good-bye.

It was a long drive to Orlando. It would have been a lot more fun with Tom. We'd have listened to NPR for a while, commented on the news, looked for helicopters, cumulus clouds, and little wee things making nests atop light posts. But asking him to come to the concert would have been wrong. I was going to see Silvio Rodriguez: a guy with a guitar, singing in Spanish, a language that Tom hasn't mastered, a language whose quirks and bends elude him.

I made my way through an angry mob of Cuban exiles protesting outside the Amway Arena in Orlando. Rodriguez, a Cuban troubadour in his sixties, had supported Fidel Castro thirty years ago but had switched to a more neutral ground in the last decade. The exiles never forgave him for his past praise of the revolution or his tribute song to Che Guevara, which became the artist's hymn. The Cubans shouted anti-Castro slogans and waved banners that read "Death to the Tyrant" and "We Want Change" in Spanish.

"*Viva Cuba Libre!*" one of the Cubans shouted in my face as I walked away from the will-call window. I was supposed to yell back, "*Cuba Libre!*," shred my ticket in solidarity, and go back to my car. I didn't. My heart had no room for politics that day. It was full—of love for Silvio, the idol of my rebellious youth; of longing for the years past; of lust for the sounds of Spanish, my mother tongue, that rustle of dry bay leaves and prayer rosaries. The language of crowded kitchens, noisy dining tables, and mattresses sprawled around my grandparents' house.

In the lobby, I bought a shot of Bailey's on the rocks and made my way into the small, crowded venue. The theater was awash with nostalgia. I found my seat and scanned the audience of middle-aged Latinos. We were a bunch of romantic immigrants, far away from home. Silvio was here to remind us of younger, less cynical versions of ourselves.

———•·•———

I was about to take a sip of my overpriced Irish cream when the guy sitting next to me spoke.

"Didn't realize these Cubans don't like Silvio," he said. I nodded as I stirred the ice cubes with my left index finger, my wedding band in plain view. He continued.

"He is my favorite troubadour," he said. "So wonderful of him to come to Orlando."

He seemed to have a lot to say, and I let him, just for the sheer joy of hearing him speak to me in his American-accented yet impeccable Spanish.

"Where did you learn to speak Spanish like that?" I turned around to face him, to see the mouth delivering those incredibly sexy words. It occurred to me that a man this fluent in Spanish would have to have a curious tongue and a set of bossy lips that know how to get stuff done, when to suck and where to lick.

"Believe it or not, some boys make it out of Indiana," he said. He had left Indiana for Spain. Seven years and a master's degree in Spanish later, he made it back to the USA, not to Indiana but the Sunshine state. He was an ESL teacher at a local college in Central Florida.

"Not many gringos here tonight," he said in his effortless Spanish.

Tongue-tied, I uttered something that sounded like, *nuh-uh*.

I studied his face while he talked about Madrid and an ex-girlfriend, long story, who first introduced him to Silvio Rodriguez. With his face turned in a forty-five-degree angle I could see only his left profile, yet it felt as though I already knew the slick contours of his right half. He had the most splendid, deep blue left eye, and I immediately wondered what it would be like to see both of his eyes first thing in the morning. *Buenos días, mi amor.*

He had an ordinary nose, a forgettable mouth—so disappointing—and paper-thin eyelids, nothing remarkable about his eyelashes. *Just another thin-lipped white man,* I thought. *What's the matter with him, with me? He's so ordinary looking.* But then he spoke again. This time he said the singer's last name, and his tongue did some serious acrobatics with the "r" sounds of *Rrrod-rri-guez.*

I nearly lost my shit.

I wanted us to jump in his car and drive west to Clearwater. Beyond the condominiums I know of a talcum powder beach where bottleneck dolphins come to do nothing but whistle. We would dip our toes in the Gulf, saying fantastic words: *mar, arena, luna, promesa, secreto, caricia.*

He said something about a guitar. He wrote songs. He was working on a play. He flirted with poetry. He loved Edith Piaf and Carla Bruni. He gave it all to me in flawless, heart-beating Spanish. I wished I could fondle his words.

"*¿Y tu?*" he asked.

"Me?" I wanted to sound honest. To be honest. "I'm a writer," I said.

What I didn't say was: I'm a married writer. Out there, a man is waiting for me. A Scottish man with an irresistible brogue that makes my girlfriends sigh with something close to envy. We get drunk sometimes, laugh often, and love to dance after three shots of tequila because that's when we do our lame moonwalk, a decent robot, and the young kids have nothing on us when the DJ plays the dougie. We wake each other up in the middle of the night to make love. He knows my body by heart, he could recite the freckles on my back like a childhood poem, and his lips are in love with mine. We have volumes of private jokes and even a secret handshake. He makes excellent coffee, and he can fix just about anything.

But.

He.

Doesn't.

Know.

Silvio's.

Songs.

My man's Spanish is limited and choppy like a little boy's. He couldn't understand, for instance, that Silvio's song "Ojalá" (I Wish) is not about a scorned lover but about a Cuban deeply disappointed in Fidel Castro.

The man from Indiana looked at my drink and smiled. I think I caught him studying the Celtic knots carved on my wedding band.

"A writer?"

I nodded.

"*Ay, maravilloso,*" he said.

Here is the thing. He didn't say, *How wonderful,* or *Gee,* or *Wow,* or *Awesome!* He said, *Ay,* and that sound reduced my brain to ashes.

Ay, how much I missed making love in Spanish. *Ay,* to have a lover whisper *Mami, negrita* and whisper back *Mi negro, papi* in breathless patterns of pure devotion. *Ay,* to kiss in a lagoon of words spoken in language that sounds like a tango, the language of novenas and first communions, that tongue that smells of cumin and garlic, light and airy like a mosquito net on a summer day. *Ay,* to purr and whirr, to come and to make come, to sigh and to gag in the only tongue I knew when I was still a virgin, that hybrid between a tadpole and a woman.

Elope with me, man from Indiana. We'll take the Beachline Expressway and drive east to Merritt Island. Do you know that on moonless nights you can kayak Mosquito Lagoon with bioluminescent creatures leading the way? Do you know that mullet in Indian River love to be awakened in the middle of the night? Paddle away when July turns to August and you'll see hundreds of them, whole shoals jumping out of the water, tripping each other like African wildebeest, so many that you'll think it's raining mullet and you may even end up ashore with a few gilled stowaways.

The lights went out.

Silvio came onstage. He was not the scruffy rebel on the covers of my LPs back in the '70s and '80s. Now he was a balding man in his late sixties. He had a belly and moved slowly across the stage like he was just passing through. But he sat down in a low chair, strummed his guitar, and started to sing with the voice I remembered, the voice I loved, a voice untouched by time and aging revolutions.

Everything went to back to where I was in 1983, feathers in my head, no bra, only one earring, a pair of worn jeans, sandals made out of a recycled tire, a tangle of amulets around my neck. I was young and beautiful again. I caught myself trembling, or maybe it was this white guy next to me also trembling deep inside his Indiana-ness.

At some point, our arms touched in the dark. Neither of us moved away. I felt the hairs on his arm standing up along a line between my wrist and my elbow. The audience sang "Sueño con Serpientes" along with the troubadour.

"This is one of my favorites," he whispered in my direction. His breath smelled of mint and hay. *How many words do you know in my language, man from Indiana? Give me a bulk number. Say 44. Invent phrases containing the words* mujer, boca, leche, mano, piel. *Say something with the word* amor *in it. Right now, I'm so drunk on Silvio, on Spanish, on your left blue eye that if you tell me, te amo, I'll believe you.*

I looked for something to refocus my mind. I chose his hands. He had savvy-looking fingers, the sort that make a woman think of seaweed and azaleas. The type of hands that know how to drive a woman out of Merritt Island and down to Miami Beach. With his hands in mind, I outlined a perfect plan. We'd go to Mango's Café in South Beach, a nightclub where women don't dance, but quiver on the dance floor like mercury orbs. He'd hear that hodgepodge of Spanish dialects you hear only in Miami and say: *It sounds like music.* I'd show him the dancing devil I am. With his hands on my narrow hips, we'd traverse the dance floor to the beats of a raunchy mambo; I would welcome the slow crawl of his savvy fingers up my sides until his thumbs stopped at the base of my breasts, begging for a pass up north, not moving an inch further, just waiting, waiting. Then I would shudder.

Dance with me, man from Indiana. Let's lose ourselves, let's dance like whirling dervishes, naked and wild, wearing nothing but the moon. You should know that marriage has not killed the solar dust in my soul; my wedding band conceals creeks of desire, bamboo gardens, waterfalls roaring with lust. I am wild of heart, and my heart is a thing of sand, and the sand comes from a river without name. I know where to find the salt the oceans leave behind.

Indiana man tapped one of his feet to the music and the outer flank of his calf touched mine. An electrical surge zoomed through my right leg, fast and sharp, like a lost eel. I held my breath and stared at his knee. He noticed, and I didn't care. I forgot about the music. His jeans, I thought, would look wonderful in a corner of his apartment, the left leg thrust into the slit in my skirt. Preferably, the back slit, just because. *Go on, unstitch my every seam.* I imagined his place in perfect evening shadow: Leather couch . . . scratch that, suede love seat, gray suede; a substantial carpet that remembers bodies like a memory-foam mattress; and a wall-to-wall window with a grand view of Orlando's skyscrapers up in the horizon and Church Street down below, with its drunks, its women in miniskirts, and throngs of sunburned tourists.

I wanted to use the restroom and get another drink during the intermission, but Indiana man didn't move, so I stayed. With the lights back on, I revisited his face, the whole nowhere near as remarkable as the half I had seen in the dark. He looked to be in his 30s, a lot younger than my 44 years.

"*Mi nombre es Aaron,*" he said, offering me his right hand. I gave it a firm squeeze. His was a weak passionfruit juice, so much water and so little fruit, it didn't quite classify as a handshake. His four thin fingers went limp under my grip.

"*¿Cómo te llamas?*" he asked.

Oh, please don't be corny. I don't need to know your name. I don't want anything longer than this instant, anything more than the endless possibilities of my mind. That's all I can afford.

People moved around, *Hola, ¿Cómo estás?* kiss, kiss, hug, hug, *Long time no see.* I didn't tell him my name. We strained to hear each other over the general clatter. The couple sitting in the row in front of us started to make out. They licked each other's lips. We stared at their tongues as we chatted.

"That's what I love, *love*, about your culture," he said as if all Latinos sprung from the same little country. My initial impulse to correct him was surpassed by my desire to hear him say *cultura* again and again. Puckered lips, the roll of the damn "r." *Cultura. Cultura.*

———•—•———

The lights went out for a second time.

Silvio sang "A Woman with Hat." Man from Indiana sang along on the line about *amores cobardes*; that sonofabitch was on a quest to drive me mad. I mean, he sang my favorite line of my favorite song in my favorite language:

"Cowardly loves don't become Love or History; they just stay where they are . . ."

I cried and sang and clapped and hummed, but mostly I gave myself permission to imagine.

Let's take the turnpike on our way to South Beach. I know a Seminole guy named Bobby. He lives along the way and makes mean moonshine. If I let him know I'll be passing through, he'll make redneck caviar—a concoction of beans, peas, corn, tomatoes, onions, garlic, parsley flakes, and a killer secret dressing that his clan has kept a secret for over 100 years. And right where the highway intersects with SR-60 is Jackass Crossing. Well, it used to be called Jackass Crossing but now it's known as Jeehaw Junction. It's a piece of somewhere in the middle of nowhere. In this desolate intersection is the Desert Inn, a little run-down shack built in the 1800s, where we could stay. Look at the board hung on the door:

Open 8:30ish daily . . . maybe 9 on Sunday.

Always pass all health inspections.

Clean rooms and showers.

Truckers welcome.

Man from Indiana, won't you spend a night with me in Historic Cracker Cowboy Country?

Silvio bowed, smiled, and thanked all of us for our love and support through the years. We stood up, cheered, and hooted and asked him for an encore. *Otra, Otra, Otra.* On his feet, the man from Indiana wasn't much to look at. I've always liked men with meat on their bones. Like my husband. But this Spanish-speaking American did not fill the back of his jeans at all.

Silvio did three encores and called it a night.

"Do you live around here?" he asked when everybody started to leave.

"No," I said and smiled. I wished we could stop the pendulum of time mid-sway.

"Do you come often to Orlando?"

I shook my head. "No."

"Well, if you ever come this way, give me a call," he said, handing me his business card. "Maybe we can meet for coffee."

I smiled another dumb grin and took his business card, making the deliberate decision not to look at it, in case I miraculously memorized his telephone number.

"Do you have a business card?" he asked.

"A writer with a business card?"

We laughed nervously. We were now in the lobby, facing each other. A silence fell between us, so heavy and so real it felt as though the three of us were trying to say good-bye. He expected me to say something; I expected him to do something, pronto. He offered me a hug. I dove into his arms with closed eyes.

"*Adiós, amiga linda,*" he said on his way to me.

While you're there, man from Indiana, I want you to whisper sweet nonsense in my ear like a good Latin lover. Call me mami, mi cielo, mi vida. *Call my body parts by their names, the names that the nuns of my childhood made me wash my mouth with soap for uttering. Be choosy with your words. Give me only the little ones that count . . . así. ¿Te gusta? Mas,*

mas, aquí, que rico! *See? I'm not asking for poems or love songs. I don't have time for speeches.*

My lust for you is linguistic, not carnal.

———•·•———

We walked into the parking lot on Livingston Street. Under a live oak tree someone had parked a pickup that read "Juan the Handy Man." The words "Home Repairs Anywhere in Central Florida" were splashed with white blotches of bird shit.

"Damn birds," man from Indiana said in English. "Where is my gun when I need it, right?"

"What, you don't like birds?"

"Sure I do. All's I know is that they taste like chickin."

He could have been joking. Who knows? But without Silvio's music or the Spanish, this Hoosier was as memorable as the light posts in the parking lot. His twang made him sound ordinary and uncouth. It was only then that I became aware of my drunkenness. His English sobered me up. I had been intoxicated during the concert, not on the one shot of watery Bailey's, but with words, and with possibility.

"Got any plans for the rest of the evening?" he asked.

I was still sobering up, still in that limbo where your mind weaves in and out of right and wrong. Fifty-six miles east of Orlando is Daytona, one of the few places in the world where you can drive your car on the beach, on an 18-mile stretch of hard-packed sand. There, in Ponce de Leon Inlet is the tallest lighthouse in Florida. When you climb the 203 steps to the top, the view of the coastline, Ponce Inlet, and Halifax River is magnificent. A perfect place to end a perfect night; a place made for farewells. Then I remembered that it was spring break and that hordes of oversexed college students had taken Daytona Beach under siege.

Now I was utterly sober.

"I'm going home," I said, turned on my heels and set my mind on finding my car. Man from Indiana said something and then something else. I kept walking. I dropped his card in the first garbage can I found and didn't look back.

The thought of you is intoxicating; the reality of you isn't.

I drove west on I-4, the interstate that traverses the peninsula. I rolled down the window and let a mixture of night, spring, and Florida play with my hair. It felt good. Really good. I imagined man from Indiana driving home, checking his cell phone for missed calls, letting mile after mile between us turn this stretch of highway into an isthmus. I put my left hand out. The wind in front of the car hit the side of my hand, making it flap. The word *flap* gave me goose bumps. I know a thing or two about aerodynamics. I know that the wind doesn't actually come from in front of the car, it only seems to, and this is called relative wind, which is opposite to the direction of movement, and, combined with angle of attack, makes takeoffs and landings possible. I learned these things from my husband because he is a pilot and he likes everything that flies, living or not, and he is particularly fond of nests and wee birds, whether they shit on cars or not.

Yes, man from Indiana, I do have plans for the rest of the evening. I'm going to go home and make love in English as I have done for years. I'm going to moan in my second language of silent letters, soft vowels, and lilting questions. I'm going to hear my husband whisper nonsensical wee Scottish words in my ear. I'm going to toss his kilt atop my skirt and let him unstitch my every seam. Then we'll be light inside a crystal, transparent and unscratchable like diamonds. We will roll in the Saint Augustine grass in our backyard, look for shooting stars, and if we find none, we'll look at our lake, which used to be a phosphate mine but looks like the real deal, and think of the poor bastards in Indiana freezing their asses off while we're out here in the open, naked and free in a perfect Florida spring. And the next time I need a Spanish fix, we'll go to a little Cuban joint in Ybor City, Tampa's Latin Quarter, owned by a cigar-roller who refuses to learn English. We'll take the scenic route along SR-60 looking for birds. We'll stop whenever Tom spots a mockingbird and says, This is the loveliest wee thing I've ever seen—*and he'll say it again about the warbler and the waxwing, about the pipit, the robin and the kinglet, the Carolina Wren and the Brown Creeper. And he'll say it with his mouth that is pink, wet, and fleshy, just the way I like it, and he'll guide us west carrying the invisible sword he inherited from his Highland clan.*

Yes, man from Indiana. I have plans.

Trouble

Elyse Moody

*T*he trouble started with a simple request. Howard wanted back the things he had left at Ruth's place. Her house sat off Wilkerson Road, in the western part of Floyd County, Georgia, where people have to arrange their own trash pickup or burn it, where sad-looking ponies graze in scruffy fields next to double-wides. Sure, he'd probably been drinking when he appeared on her porch, but how often had she seen him sober? They had traveled together and stayed in hotels together. She had accompanied him to bingo and dances at Shanklin-Attaway Post Five, the local branch of the American Legion. Surely she knew Howard was always, always drunk.

And he was infatuated with her. Some people would say Ruth was the only person Howard ever really loved. He'd given her an engagement ring and lots of gold jewelry and fans to cool her house and a car. Now that they'd split up, he wanted those things back.

The minute Howard walked through Ruth's front door he lunged for her, knocking over her sixty-eight-year-old elder sister, Elizabeth, in the process. Elizabeth fell to the floor in a heap and stayed there.

Ruth's twenty-four-year-old son, Mark, entered the picture then, grabbing a claw hammer and starting to beat Howard with it. The two men scuffled and rushed out into the yard, a storm of swinging arms and swear words and that hammer.

All of a sudden, Ruth appeared on the porch with a thirty-eight-caliber pistol. She fired a single warning shot into the air. Mark then hollered one of two things: "Don't shoot, Mama!" or "Shoot him, shoot him!"—later, his testimonies contradicted each other. Except for the claw hammer, the men were unarmed. A second later, Ruth fired again. The bullet hit Howard's chest, and he was a goner.

At least that's how the local newspaper told the story. The front-page headline that ran in *The Rome News-Tribune* on August 14, 1986, screamed SLAIN: MAN SHOT TO DEATH IN FLOYD; EX-GIRLFRIEND CHARGED IN CASE. The man in question, Howard Phillips, was my maternal grandfather. The ex-girlfriend was Ruth Camp Burchett, a sixty-two-year-old woman seven years his senior who might have become his third wife. I was thirteen days shy of my first birthday when the story broke.

———•————

You might think that growing up in a city as small as Rome, Georgia (current population: 36,159), I'd have heard more about the murder, but I didn't. And anyway, my paternal grandfather more than made up for Howard's absence, being the kind of grandfather who gets up early to fix cornbread for Sunday lunch and who builds your first set of pine bookshelves, the kind who teaches you that the Georgia state bird is the brown thrasher and the state tree is the live oak and the state flower is the Cherokee rose. The kind of grandfather who invents a trick to help you memorize the names of the president and vice president ("there's a Quayle behind the Bush") and encourages you to have another Coke float to cool your belly. My younger brother, Adam, and I always called him by his first name: Hubert. Our Nannie (his wife, our grandmother) liked to say we started calling him that after we heard her yell out to him once—"Hu-*BERT!*" Probably sniping at him to stop smoking with the screen door to their green-turf stoop propped open. We spent much of our childhood at Nannie and Hubert's house, where I sewed doll clothes by hand and made crowns from the leaves of the magnolia tree in the backyard. Hubert was retired by then. He spent his mornings shooting the breeze with his Southern Bell buddies at the West Rome McDonald's; in the afternoons he'd take me with him to Hardee's, where he'd buy us vanilla soft-serve and meet his friend Bud Wooten for more old men's gossip.

I thought Nannie and Hubert's house was magic—nothing bad could happen to me there. But part of growing up is the way your world keeps getting bigger. I switched schools in seventh grade and suddenly everything was Friday night football games and dances, voice lessons and play rehearsals and ballet classes. College in the Shenandoah Valley eclipsed that as I left my family five hundred miles behind.

But when I came home after four years in Virginia, I realized how unfamiliar I was with the place—and my place in it. The summer after graduation I rode to Six Flags Over Georgia with my cousin Jenny and her daughter, Hannah. On the way there, Jenny, who's twelve years older than I, lifted a hand off the steering wheel of her platinum Honda CR-V and pointed to a skinny road off the Rockmart Highway. "That's where my granddaddy lived," she told Hannah. She meant Howard, the grandfather we share. It was the most specific detail I'd ever heard about him.

For the first time, I wondered about Howard. I knew vaguely that he'd gotten himself killed, but details of the matter—the where and why and when—had never come up. I'd never asked. But, I realized, I did want to learn about him and about what happened, as well as what he'd been like as a person, whether I was anything like him. As I moved to Washington, D.C., and on to New York City, farther and farther from home, the need pressed more urgently. How was it possible that I knew so little about my ancestry? On my father's side, there was my Irish-immigrant great-great-grandmother named Amanda, and talk of Cherokee blood; I knew even less about my mother's family. I especially wanted to know more about my long-dead grandfather so that I could better understand my mother. She was in her early twenties, a little younger than I am now, when her father was shot and killed by a woman whose name I had to look in the newspaper archives to find out, a name I'd never heard anyone say out loud. It was an astonishing feat of secrecy, really, in a town like ours.

———•—

You can see most of Rome, Georgia, from Clocktower Hill, the tallest point downtown. Just like its Italian namesake, the city sits in a valley formed by seven hills and is crisscrossed by two rivers that converge to form a third. A grid of 19th-century Victorians—dating back to the time when General William Tecumseh Sherman marched through, supposedly rode his horse up the staircase of a mansion that's now an elementary school, and burned almost every-thing—fans between the rivers. Historic storefronts of red brick line the section of Broad Street called the Cotton Block. At the north end of Broad, on the steps of the city auditorium, stands a bronze replica of the Capitoline Wolf, gifted to the city by Benito Mussolini himself. (The more conservative Georgians have at times, it is said, diapered nude little Romulus and Remus.)

Beyond downtown, Rome is a cluster of modern medical facili-ties; the brown-orange Floyd Hospital buildings dominate the skyline. The Etowah and Oostanaula rivers meet just south of the hospital to form the Coosa River. It flows southeast, shadowed by Horseleg Creek Road, with its lush-lawned homes that look across the riverbanks to the Coosa Country Club golf course. Then the strip malls begin, radi-ating Walmarts and fast food and subdivisions that used to be middle class and apartment buildings that have never quite held that status.

My parents and I lived in one such West Rome apartment build-ing, the Georgian Apartments, when the shooting happened. They rented the place while building the first of more than a dozen houses they built together, mostly by themselves; they finished number one, on Pine Bower Road, in the month between August 1 and Labor Day 1986 ("That's the God's honest truth," Mom said). That August was one of the hottest my mother and father can remember. One day, Mom came home from work to find me in my diaper and him in his under-wear, stretched out asleep on a mattress he'd dragged into the living room—the air conditioner had gone out. It was some kind of hot. August 13 was no exception.

"I'd gone to the washeteria to wash clothes, and on my way there, I got a really weird feeling," Mom said. "A yucky feeling came over me. But I put the clothes in, and when I got back to the apartment my mother had called."

Someone had called my grandmother to tell her they'd heard about the shooting on their police scanner—an ambulance with my grandfather onboard was headed for Floyd Hospital.

"He'd been in an altercation and I needed to call the hospital—that's what they said," Mom told me. "So I called and called and I couldn't get anybody to tell me anything. I kept telling them who I was, and they kept pushing me off to the next person, putting me off, until finally they told me that he wasn't all right, that he'd died."

Mom met two of her four sisters, Debbie and Terri, at the hospital. She remembered the mortician on staff lifting the sheet. Underneath, my grandfather's Marine-short hair and stocky body were unmistakable. He'd been about five nine, with a big beer belly. She glanced over his body for long enough to be sure, then looked away. She couldn't bear the sight of him. Minus the crew cut, it looked as if it were her oldest sister lying there. Janice had inherited their father's square face, his angular jaw, his bulldog cheeks, his deep-set blue eyes. Mom looked at Debbie and Terri. The three of them nodded. He was their father.

Afterward the girls came back to our apartment to call everyone else. Janice, who was at Disney World with her husband and two daughters, packed her bags and raced home. My dad and I had been asleep when they came in, but I woke up. While Mom and Terri and Debbie talked, they took turns holding my hands and leading me around the room. I was just learning to walk. Mom was just 22.

The graveside service took place the following Saturday, at East View Cemetery, off the Kingston Highway. The casket sat open, and, in spite of the undertaker's preparations, Howard Preston Phillips looked yellow. Cirrhosis of the liver, Mom thought. His drinking colored him even in death. And his fingers testified to the way Mark Burchett had beat him with the hammer. His nail beds were purpled with bruises.

It took a year for the case to come to trial. In the interim, Ruth Burchett lined up one of the hardest-hitting defense attorneys money can buy: Bobby Lee Cook, a Vanderbilt-educated lawyer who hails from Summerville, Georgia, about forty minutes northwest of Rome. Locally, Bobby Lee stirs up a mix of awe and revulsion. This is a man who has said that he keeps postponing retirement because he enjoys "waking up every morning and kicking somebody in the ass who needs it." In his 50-plus years of legal experience, he has crusaded for all manner of alleged criminals, from moonshiners to corrupt bankers to child-killers. He has defended more than three hundred people accused of murder and has won 80 percent of those cases. With his seersucker suits, soft brown billy-goat beard, and wire-rimmed granny glasses, he looks like a cross between Robert E. Lee and Colonel Sanders. He reportedly served as the basis for Andy Griffith's character on *Matlock*.

Bobby Lee told the *American Bar Association Journal* in 2009 that a defense attorney must prove two things to a jury to win a murder case:
  1) That the victim was a bad person who deserved to be killed, and
  2) That your client was just the man (or woman) for the job.

I grew up knowing just a handful of things about my grandfather: That he always smelled like beer; that he once burst into my grandmother's house on McDonald Street drunk, with a knife, prompting Janice to snatch my mother and book it out the back door. That alcohol armed him as if it were a weapon. Given his history of drunkenness, missed child-support checks, domestic abuse, arrests, and general meanness, the case must have looked open and shut to an expert like Bobby Lee Cook. It's easy to see how my grandfather fit his first criterion. If you asked my mother, she'd say, "They took what he'd done for the majority of his life and turned it around on him."

And Ruth Burchett, Bobby Lee argued, had a right to shoot my grandfather because "her home is her castle." In August 1978, after hearing three days of testimony, the jury took only an hour and 40 minutes to find her innocent by reason of self-defense.

Mom had found out a few months after the murder that she was pregnant with my brother. She kept getting up at six o'clock to feed me at seven and go to her job at Redmond Hospital in medical records at eight. She kept right on working until she had Adam in March, and she went right back to work after. When August came, she did not go to the trial.

But she did go to help clean out her daddy's house on Pleasant Hope Road, and something she found there surprised her. Tucked into the seam of a kitchen-cabinet door was a small photograph, a two-by-three of me, all three-pounds-and-change of tiny newborn me, born three months early, with a pink bow taped to my preemie head. What had he been thinking when he stuck that photo inside a cabinet he opened every morning? That made me wonder what he lived to regret—and what he died wishing he'd done different.

Matinee

Mendy Knott

The thermostat at my parents' house was set at a balmy 80 degrees. It was late June, in Arkansas. I would have been cooler sleeping outside on a cot. Instead, I teetered on a mattress, stretching to reach the ceiling fan. My parents stood in the doorway, saying good night. Dad had on a long-sleeved tee with his flannel pajama bottoms tucked into his socks. Mom stood next to him in her lace nightgown and a thick fluffy robe. She looked up at me. "It's not that hot in here, but I'll put another blanket on the bed and turn it down to 78." I knew I'd spend the rest of the night like a menopausal Pentecostal on a roll.

I was visiting my folks in Benton. Our plan was to drive to the PurpleHull Pea Festival and National Rotary Tiller Race down in Emerson, a town near the Louisiana line with a population of 359, except during the wildly popular festival. Mom and I had invented a new dish to enter in the purple hull recipe contest. If it was tasty enough, we might win some money as well as get published on the festival's cooking site, Purple Hull Reci-Peas. Dad and I planned to cheer on the competitors in the world's only garden tiller race. My partner, Leigh, had wisely declined this outing, opting for the relative cool of northwest Arkansas.

The Saturday of the festival arrived with record-high temperatures. I was afraid my 80-something-year-old parents would dry up and blow away like chaff in the triple-digit heat. We decided we'd be better off staying home in Benton. Dad was visibly relieved, but Mom and I were disappointed. We had a taste for adventure.

All I can say in my defense is that the ungodly heat, the fact that the thermostat could not be lowered during the day without Mom needing a sweater, and missing the Pea Festival took a toll on my rationality. I was desperate to find something—anything—to do. That's how I ended up taking my father, the minister, and his morally upright and socially correct wife to a gay porn movie. Well, not exactly porn, but close enough to count. Like hand grenades and horseshoes.

For years, I'd longed for a simple weekend with my folks, hanging out and talking, playing dominoes, making a trip to the purple hull pea festival. At nineteen, I had been partly pushed and had partly shoved my way from the family womb, and not through the kind of "born again" experience my father would have wanted. Dad was a Deep South minister, and my mother a model for preachers' wives everywhere.

On the day I sat at the breakfast table and told them, as calmly as I could, that I liked women instead of men, my dad stomped around, booming in his best hellfire-and-brimstone voice, "You have a choice, young lady. You can stay here and be saved by Billy Graham tonight, or you can leave and be damned! But if you leave, you will no longer be part of this family! You will not be a member of my church! You will be cut off forever. You choose."

With dogged defiance I answered, "I guess I'll be damned and go, then." I sat on the floor of my old room, shoving my belongings into a duffel bag: a couple of Bob Dylan albums, books by Richard Brautigan and Joan Didion, a few pairs of underwear, and a bra I wouldn't wear. I could hear Mom crying. She would never go against Dad in spiritual matters, but she was the boss of her family. I heard her demanding, "You *will* take her to the bus station and give her money for a ticket to Memphis." Then his angry, "No, I won't." And her stubborn, "Yes, you will."

When I dragged my flabby duffel into the den, Dad shoved two twenties in my face and growled, "Here's your inheritance. Now get in the car." We rode together in silence. I leaned my head on the window, tears smearing my view. I clutched the sweaty twenties in my pocket. Occasionally I'd try to talk to him. "Dad?" He wouldn't say a word until we passed the massive coliseum where Billy Graham would be preaching. "There, right there, you could be saved tonight. I can turn this car around and we can go home. It's never too late for salvation."

I shook my head and wiped snot on my flannel sleeve. He glared. "You're killing your mom. You know that?" At the bus station, I swung my bell-bottomed legs to the curb. I held the door open and bent to look in at him. "Look at me, Dad," I begged. "I'm sorry. I can't help who I am. I love you." Without turning his head, he said, "Shut the door." I did, and he drove out of my life.

After a couple of decades, Dad softened; by then he had wrestled a few angels of his own. But he was hard to trust. One minute he'd be all open arms and embrace, and the next he'd be warning me about the wages of sin. At least ambivalence was a step in the right direction. I kept showing up. I got sober. I was polite. Other family members liked me. I made it hard for him to condemn me. I settled into my graying gay ways and chose a life partner, which also helped. A union with one other person, even someone of the same sex, made me a more acceptable member of the family unit. At long last, my folks decided they actually enjoyed spending time with me, and they adored my smart, pretty, respectably employed spouse. Especially Dad.

Moving from North Carolina to Arkansas narrowed the gap from 700 miles to 170—a reasonable distance. I would be much closer to them as they entered their 80s. My siblings were ecstatic to see me show back up just about the time they were sending kids to college, making midlife career changes, and readying themselves for one more monetary push before retirement. They had less time than ever for the old folks at home, and the way they saw it, I had more time, and besides, I needed to catch up. This is how I became the gay child caring for her aging parents.

I visited regularly, and my folks and I began sharing the everyday events of our lives. Dad, officially retired, still worked as an interim pastor for small churches scattered around the River Valley, a modern-day circuit rider. Mom, as sharply dressed as ever, accompanied him to these outlying churches. At the time I visited for the pea festival, he was preaching in Prescott. While Dad sermonized, Mom observed the eccentricities of the 12 extended family members who made up the entire Prescott congregation. She watched the son, star of the high school football team, leave every 15 minutes to sneak a smoke, and smiled at the spoiled infant passed hand to hand as Dad did his best to prepare the clan for kingdom come. The one unrelated member, a poor soul suffering from Tourette's, spent the hour shouting out obscenities and "Praise the Lords!" Mom said, "Well, he can't help that. He's actually a really nice man."

They were also full of stories about their neighbors. Dad confided in me, "The fat guy next door is driving your mother crazy. She says he's putting a curse on her clematis." Dad raised his eyebrows, "I don't know about that, but he called us copycats the other day. See? He has a clematis growing by his mailbox, too." So did ten other neighbors. It was an idea whose time had come. Mom and Dad were victims only by virtue of proximity.

It was a long weekend, and by Monday we needed a distraction, an escape from the sordidness of suburban living. I suggested we go to the movies. I hardly cared what we saw as long as I could relax in the comfort of a matinee with air conditioning so cold it required sweaters and jackets to withstand the chill.

The paper rattled beneath the ceiling fan as I squinted at the tiny print of the movie listings. Dad advised, "Pick one a reasonable distance from the house." I took this to mean he didn't want to expend a lot of energy on the venture. Unfortunately, none of the films showing nearby looked like they were made for an audience over the age of twelve. "As for me," he continued, "I would be perfectly happy sitting on the porch." I wouldn't. I squinted harder, and groused until Dad generously expanded the boundaries to include the outskirts of Little Rock. He warned, "I don't like violence and bad endings. I'm not paying to be depressed." Mom piped in, "And I don't like animation or vulgar language." That left . . . what?

My eyes fell on *The Kids Are All Right*. I knew the film was about a lesbian family with kids. My friends Liz and Susan had taken their college-age daughter to see it, and liked it. They said, "It's good." Looking back, I blame them for not having given me more feedback, but I guess they never considered I'd take my parents to see it. Mom and I agreed we liked Annette Bening and Julianne Moore, and Mark Ruffalo was cute. It seemed like the best movie within Dad's allotted radius, and I thought it would meet their parameters: no violence, depressing content, or animation. And how bad could the language be if it was about kids?

Either I didn't look at the rating or it was too small to see without my glasses. Somehow I assumed it was PG.

I admit to one ulterior motive: I thought the movie might be good preparation for Leigh's and my upcoming 10th anniversary party. My parents had accepted their invitation enthusiastically, but I was still nervous about how they might handle the actual party. I hoped that when they saw the movie, they would see for themselves how lesbian families were like straight families. Then, if they saw same-sex affection at our party, they wouldn't be shocked.

Of course, they dressed. Mom fluffed her silver hair and put on makeup and tight jeans and a cute little jean jacket with lace down the front. Dad wore creased khakis, a collared shirt, and polished loafers. They looked great. No one but me would have guessed they were in their 80s.

The theater looked like something from the 1950s, with neon bulbs outlining the marquis. We pulled into the heat of a nearly empty blacktop lot. A pink Mary Kay Caddy pulled up a few spaces away. A woman my age exited the driver's side then helped what appeared to be her at-least-90-year-old mother out of the passenger side. They got in line ahead of us, and bought two tickets to *The Kids Are All Right*. I found this comforting.

The lady selling tickets paused before handing them their stubs. Her mouth pursed, but she said nothing. She never looked twice at our trio, though. If I saw someone like me, wearing cargo shorts, a man's shirt, and Crocs, taking two graying, well-dressed seniors to a lesbian flick, I would have pulled me aside and issued a parental warning.

Mom clapped a hand over her mouth when she saw the price of popcorn and Coke. "My Lord," she mumbled. I had told her before we left the house that I was treating. This would prevent her from sneaking a giant baggie of popcorn, homemade brownies, and three Sprites in her oversized purse. "Ma, these days they kick you out if you get caught with snacks in your bag." Her blue eyes widened at my ignorance. "You have to wait until the lights go out!" I shook my head, "I'm paying. We do it my way." She defiantly slipped a super-sized M&M's into her purse. "All right, but only because I don't want to embarrass you. No one can *make* me leave when I have a ticket."

Once we were standing in front of the concessions, Mom still felt compelled to comment, "I can't believe what they charge for this stuff." I agreed silently. Twenty dollars for a bag of corn and three drinks was highway robbery, but I didn't want to get kicked out of the theater. At least, at that point I didn't. Later on, I wished we had brought giant bags of Sun Chips in those noisy recyclable bags and pop-top Budweisers.

There weren't many moviegoers at a Monday matinee, and we got good seats on the second tier, front and center. Mom sat in the middle, embracing the giant tub of popcorn. "Don't drop a kernel. This stuff is worth its weight in gold," she reminded us. Inane movie star questions appeared on the screen. Dad read each question aloud: "What two famous stars were the leads in *Who's Afraid of Virginia Woolf?*" Mom jumped on the answer before the screen could change: "Elizabeth Taylor and Richard Burton!" She sniffed the air and looked around. The same olfactory superpowers that enabled her to smell a beer or cigarette on your breath at twenty paces were still intact. I smelled it, too, but employed my even stronger sense of denial to overcome any unpleasant odor in favor of air conditioning. She leaned over and sniffed toward the floor. "It smells like pee." I preferred to think it smelled like dirty socks.

When *The Kids Are All Right* finally began, I could tell within minutes that *one* kid, anyway—me—would not be all right. A vividly implied scene of oral sex between the two female stars spread across the screen. The camera panned back and forth between Annette Bening humping and bumping beneath the bedcovers and a gay male porn flick playing in the background, a Marlboro man putting it to the rear end of some guy whose face we blessedly couldn't see. My swallowing mechanism quit working. One of those expensive popcorn kernels stuck in my windpipe, and I hacked as quietly as I could, not wanting to draw my parents' attention. They seemed hypnotized by what they were seeing onscreen. Despite the chill, sweat popped out on my upper lip and brow. In my simple mind, "Oh my god. Oh my god. Oh my god" repeated on endless loop while giants continued to have sex on the huge screen, despite the horrified expressions of the two senior citizens sitting next to me.

I reached for the bucket of popcorn my mother gripped. She let go one finger at a time. I shoveled fistfuls in my mouth and guzzled Diet Coke. Later in the film, Julianne Moore and Mark Ruffalo get it on, and I felt some relief: at least this was straight sex, sort of. Dad suddenly asked, "Where's the popcorn?" Mom, staring straight ahead said, "Mendy has it." Dad grabbed the bucket like a life preserver and began stuffing himself, kernels snowing onto his lap and scattering on the floor.

My back cramped from sitting so straight in the sprung seat, and my neck sported a knotty crick. For two hours, or however long this movie lasted—twelve hours? Maybe longer?—my parents and I sat completely still and silent. My blood quit circulating. I was like a toad in winter. I took tiny, shallow breaths, just enough air to stay alive. Barely. I wanted to leave, but there was no place to go without having to walk past them. So I pretended I wasn't there. I was having a bad dream. I would wake up soon if I didn't in any way acknowledge their presence. Occasionally, I'd hear noises coming from my parents' direction— little clucks and gurgles, Dad crunching—but mostly they were silent and did not look at me either. We were still-life forms, statues that ate popcorn and scattered it at our feet.

I wanted to enjoy the movie, embrace it as my story, our story, a story about family and marriage. The acting was terrific, the characters believable, endearing, funny. An "Amen!" or two would not have seemed out of place had I been with friends. But I simply could not get away from the fact that my parents were old enough to pass away at any moment, and *this* would be the last thing we ever did together. I wondered how Dad would explain his final act to God when he arrived at the pearly gates: "My daughter made me do it."

When the credits rolled, we were out of there like a shot. I apologized to Mom and Dad as I herded them to the car. They murmured, "That's all right. You didn't know." I suggested that I never be the one to choose a movie again for the rest of our lives. Mom slid a sly look at me. "You probably would have enjoyed it if you hadn't been with your parents."

They talked about the movie in the manner of people who've gone to a fancy restaurant only to discover the food is mediocre but no one wants to admit the outing is a waste of time and money. "The acting was good." "The kids were cute." "I bet Leigh would have loved those beautiful gardens." The idea of Leigh sitting in misery at that movie with us was . . . well, I just couldn't think about that. Dad startled me from my reverie when he said, "I'm gonna need a long walk and a cold shower after that."

On the drive back to Benton, I stared out the car window in a stupor. Fingering the bills in my pocket, I experienced a moment of déjà vu. Would they still love me after seeing all that, after finally having the question, "What do they do in bed?" answered so very graphically? It occurred to me, too, that if they could sit through *The Kids Are All Right*, the anniversary party would be a cakewalk. What's a little kissy-face compared to what they'd just seen?

We didn't discuss the film when we got home. We played Scrabble.

I had to drive back to Fayetteville early the next day. We seemed to have agreed that our movie experience was best left in the dark. I was already behind the wheel, having said my good-byes at the door. I had the window rolled down, letting the truck cool before taking off. Dad followed me out and stood near the window. I thought maybe I'd forgotten something; he doesn't like you to leave anything behind. He leaned in, a serious look on his thin face. His brown eyes met mine, concerned. He kept his voice low. "Will Leigh get a chance to see that movie?"

"Probably so, Dad. We don't get to see our stories on the big screen very often." I didn't tell him I would like to see the movie again, since I had spent most of the first viewing with my inner Munch screaming at full volume. He nodded. "That's good. I'm glad she'll get to see it because there really was some important stuff in there."

My dad, still so completely unpredictable. I leaned out the window and kissed his cheek, my heart split between love and relief at leaving. I bumped out of the drive and headed home, wondering if they would cancel their trip to our anniversary party. They didn't. They came. They danced. They spent two nights in a cabin surrounded by our friends. Dad read a beautiful poem in front of a hundred members of our community, blessing the two of us in our union. Handsome women flirted with my pretty mother. We all had a great time. All of the attendees were impressed with the acceptance and respect my parents showed our love.

I had underestimated them. It's true. They were plenty tough enough for that movie. One thing, however, proved prophetic: I have never chosen another movie for my parents and me to see together.

Do I?

C. W. Kelly

lanning a wedding—as everyone knows—is difficult. Planning a wedding you're not sure you want to go through with is even harder. Unless you're 27, Southern Catholic, the oldest of three daughters, and afraid of being pitied at family reunions where upward of a hundred people show up and at least 40 of them say some variation of, "You'll find someone (eventually)." Then it's easy. Everyone wants to help, and you don't have to do anything except show up.

That's the hard part.

Jay and I met the first month I had moved to Arizona from Kentucky. At first sight, it was not love or lust, but a "Hmmm . . . Let's see how this goes." But he won me over with his silly sense of humor, independence, and what seemed like adoration. We were good on paper. Successful exec meets sweet Southern teacher. He was strong-willed and outspoken; I was quiet and placating. We followed the plan impeccably: dated two years, got engaged, and planned to get married a year later, somewhere near our third anniversary.

The fights started with the when, the where, and the how. We agreed from the start that we didn't want to get married in Kentucky since we both were uncomfortable being the center of attention and a Southern wedding has a 200-person minimum (and that's with hurting about 100–200 people's feelings and an additional 20–30 uninvited people showing up anyway). I wanted a small group of family and friends in a casual outdoor ceremony, an effortlessly crafted affair that would look like *Better Homes and Gardens* meets *Steel Magnolias* in Mexico. Jay waffled between wanting to elope and complete indifference, and the more I pushed him for help, the more he resisted.

"Hey . . . It's your day. Do what you want," he'd say, and leave for a business trip that I'd later find was not a business trip but a trip to a local hotel to get away from me.

Enter the helper. My mother. She stepped in when I called, crying, "Jay doesn't want anything to do with the wedding plans, and I can't do it all myself." I knew I was asking for it. I knew that once the wedding went to Kentucky, it was out of my hands, but I panicked. Besides, something about getting married in Bardstown sounded right. I wanted to go home.

I wanted to get married in my parents' backyard with strung Christmas lights and beers in giant steel tubs. This is not a traditional Southern wedding for middle-class girls, and accordingly my dream wedding was knocked down faster than Jimmy Robinson in his minute-and-a-half bout with Muhammad Ali in 1961.

Enter the contender, my father. He leads with a quick jab: "We don't have the space to host everyone at the house."

I bob and weave: "Well, we only want about 60 people."

Dad follows up with a left hook: "Our list is 150 family members and friends. How many people were you thinking of inviting?"

Mom tags in and attacks: "The Catholic Church doesn't allow outdoor weddings."

I cover up and counterattack: "Um . . . I haven't attended church regularly since high school and even then we skipped church most of the time, picked up a church bulletin on the way home, and pretended we heard the sermon. It was about sin and not doing it."

A low blow from Mom: "You have to have a Catholic ceremony. What would your grandmothers think?"

My knees start to buckle. I couldn't be responsible for killing Nanny or MeeMaw. They were the only grandparents I had left.

Sucker punch, Dad: "You're not going to make me look cheap," he said. "You're going to have a real reception."

Ironic when juxtaposed with his bullish tendency to negotiate every price down until the vendor stood cowed and defeated or infuriated and vowing never to do business with him again. (My parents still haven't gone back to the restaurant where we ended up having the reception.)

"Do you want help planning the wedding here or not?"

Knockout.

And the wedding train picked up speed. Bridesmaids: 0 to 7 in one week flat. Programs: Yes, please. Hometown DJ I'd never heard and who would play all the songs on our Do Not Play list: Why not? Wedding planner so Mom can take Valium: absolutely—pass me some. Entrées: a duo of steak and I-don't-remember.

I had stopped listening at the wedding meetings. At some point I started to have panic attacks. Little ones that felt like small seizures and dying.

At Nanz & Kraft Florists in Louisville, there was the most beautiful assortment of flowers. Gardenia, gladiola, lily, and hydrangea. Circus roses so vibrant yellow-orange-red and ringed so perfectly they looked hand-painted. Peonies, freesia, orchids. How could I choose?

"What are your cul-ars, honey?" asked the Paula Deen of floral arrangement. Well, they weren't "blush and bashful"—they were going to be black and a pain in my ass. I had let my bridesmaids pick their own black cocktail dresses so they'd have something they could afford and wear again. To the wedding circuit in the South that was sacrilege, the equivalent of saying, "I'm going to get divorced anyway, so who gives a fuck."

I knew I wanted Hypericum berries. Paula could work with that. She started pulling out photos and listing all the necessary arrangements: the bridal bouquet, the toss bouquet, bridesmaids' bouquets, boutonnières, corsages, church arrangements, pew markers, and on and on. I thought of Ophelia in *Hamlet* passing out pansies, daisies, violets, and rosemary, and the hysteria started the way it usually does—with laughter. The giggles tickled my throat and erupted into full-blown guffaws. My mother looked at me with a slow, uncomprehending grin, wondering what I found so funny. We had often shared a twisted sense of humor—trying to contain ourselves as the dermatologist who was taking a mole off my bottom kept robotically intoning, "Don't move now. Almost done," while his face hovered inches above my giggle-shaking butt cheek; or exploding into laughter at Christmas Mass when the foreign priest said "resurrection" but it sounded like "rots of erections."

Paula left the table while I covered my face, and I fought the urge to sob. My mom peered at me from across the table and said, "Are you going to get yourself together?"

"Yes." I think it's a Southern thing. We fight our demons in private so as not to disturb or inconvenience anyone.

After my breakdown at the florist's shop, I went back to Arizona and let my mom handle the rest. I taught my high school English classes on autopilot and barely talked to my fiancé. He was as absent from my life as he is from this narrative. We slept at different hours alone in our king-sized bed and rarely touched outside of it. And we were getting married.

My dress did not arrive in May as expected, which gave me a small hope for reprieve. *I can't get married naked. We'll have to postpone!* But when it arrived in late June, I went to my first dress fitting alone and saw myself in the simple sheath dress. I looked at myself in the mirror and thought, not for the first time, "I should be happier." I tried not to let my face crumple by breathing and looking at the lights. The seamstress said, "All brides cry," and nodded as if I had checked off another item on my bride to-do list. I stood perfectly still as she put 3,000 pins in the dress for "minor" alterations. I held myself in. No emotion. Someone looking in the store might have mistaken me for a mannequin. A complicated mannequin—smiling on the outside, but on the inside fighting the urge to rip every piece of Spanish lace off her I-starved-a-little-to-fit-into-this-dress body.

Three months before the big day, I went home to bridesmaid for one of my best friends, Haley. She had been the wild child of our group and the idea of her getting married sealed it for me. If *she* could settle down, so could I.

Two nights before her wedding, I met Haley at Porcini, a local restaurant with a nice wine selection and hot bartenders. We downed two large glasses of red wine and talked about our impending commitments. I told her I would help her escape if needed. I think I was hoping she would reciprocate. While I have never been an authority figure on "doing the right thing" or sanity, I genuinely tried to be good. Haley, on the other hand, thrived on chaos and a bit of scandal. She supported my choices whether they were bad or very bad. In her defense, I brought up Dan first. She just took it to the next level. *Want to call up that old boyfriend you've never gotten over three months before your wedding? Here's my cell. Call away.*

I had met Dan when I was 22. He was 38, tall, athletic, smart, entertaining, and sexy as hell. While I wouldn't call him a bad boy in the traditional sense, he definitely was a player who was content to have me when he wanted me and to see others as well. But I was addicted to him. I refer to the Dan era as "my sexual awakening." When other women deride trashy romance novels for the unrealistic passion, quivering thighs, rock-hard cocks, and orgasms in under five minutes, and sometimes every five minutes, I think, "You poor thing, you just haven't met your Dan." Dan and I had more sex in more ways, in more places during our on-again-off-again relationship than I had had BDE (Before Dan Era) and ADE (after) combined. Com-bined.

But despite the amazing, pulsating, we-may-have-broken-more-than-one-piece-of-furniture sex, in less than two years, Dan had broken my heart at least a dozen times. He would disappear for weeks, cancel plans only to show up at a restaurant with another woman, change the subject when I tried to tell him I loved him. I begged. I raged. I cried. He still couldn't—wouldn't—commit to me. The last straw was when he stood me up after I had made a big production to all of my friends about how he was coming to pick me up and had promised to come in and say hello. (*"Really, you're going to meet him this time!"*)

"I can't stay long. I'm only having this one drink," I said, waving my fourth bourbon and ginger ale at the door of Outlook Inn, where we had gone after Dan did not show up at Molly Malone's or O'Shea's. "Dan is picking me up anytime. I just texted him again."

And while I waited, Dan was actually picking up some other twenty-something. He accidentally brought her to the same bar where I was with Emily, Jess, Kaitlyn, and Meg. Jess told me later that when I saw him, I froze and just stared, my blue eyes large, childlike, and terrified. Dan came to say hello and I kept staring at him, not hearing anything, not responding to his questions. I vaguely remember throwing the glass.

Ninety-six percent of my decision to move to Arizona was to escape the drama of Dan. I knew that I wouldn't stay away from him if he were within 10 miles so I moved 1,750 miles away. But now that I was in town for Haley's wedding, he was again dangerously close. I dialed his number on Haley's new BlackBerry.

"Hey, stranger," he said when he heard my voice.

"Hey. Um . . . what are you doing?" I said while Haley grinned, cheered me on, and ordered more drinks.

"I'm at my house. How's Arizona?" he drawled, knowing the number on his cell was a local number.

"I'm not in Arizona. I want to see you. I'm with Haley at Porcini. Come hang out with us," I said. What I told myself I was thinking: *One drink. Minor flirting. No harm done.* What I was really thinking: *Please want me.*

"It's 10:00. There's plenty of alcohol at my house. I'm already on the couch. Come over," he said. I imagined him sprawled on the purple velvet couch I despised, watching a TV wider than my bedroom closet.

Haley gave me a shrug.

"Okay. We're coming."

"You always did." *Asshole.* "Remember how to get here?" he asked.

Frankfort Ave. Left on Zorn. Right on River Road. Drive over the plains of my heart. Avoid potholes. Cross over the bridge of memory. Don't look down. Sharp left, punch in the gate code, and straight to hell.

I will not have sex with Dan. I will not have sex with Dan. I will not have sex with Dan. I repeated it on the ride.

"What kind of sex are we talking?" Haley said. "Oral doesn't count, according to Presidential precedent."

We arrived at Dan's house. Massive, gray, cold stone modern architecture greeted us. Successful bachelor pad. He had left the front door open for me like he used to. We walked into the kitchen where he was already mixing margaritas, and the familiar smell of him nearly paralyzed me—clean linen and Cool Water cologne. Three years and nothing had changed except the blessed absence of the *Miami Vice* couch.

"I made these a little strong," Dan said as he passed us margaritas in 16-ounce glasses. Strong was an understatement. Within the hour, Haley and I were dancing to Kanye in the living room with Dan's CDs strewn across the living room floor and snapping photos with his Polaroid camera. Dan's dog, Jake, hid from our high-pitched squeals underneath the kitchen table, and Dan sat amused on the couch.

"I'm hungry," Haley slurred.

"Feel free to raid the fridge. I'm going to take Jake for a walk before bed," he said to Haley. Then he looked at me, "Want to come?"

Dan's private, gated community is eerily dark and quiet at night, but I felt exposed. And really drunk. We whispered, but it felt like the whole world could hear me. We trailed Jake through a patch of trees, but it felt like any moment someone would pop out from behind a bush and say, "You're engaged." And then Dan did.

"I'm happy to see you, Cute Girl, but why are you here? Trouble in paradise?" This is one thing I hated about Dan. He could comfort and mock in the same breath.

"Who are you fucking these days?" I hiccupped. "Still driving women crazy so your stock in mental health facilities will rise?"

"You don't have to get married," he said. "Call it off."

Could it have been that easy? Could I have had the balls to tell my parents that I had made a mistake, that the thousands of dollars in deposits would have to be forfeited, the $1,000 dress unworn? Could I send out letters proclaiming "False alarm!" and return the early-bird gifts with a note—"Thanks anyway"? Could I look Jay in the face and say, "I don't want to marry you"?

I was a coward. And an asshole. I smashed my face into Dan's. I felt his hands in my hair and suddenly everywhere. Familiar and warm. Interested and excited in exploring in a way that Jay hadn't touched me in months. This was the kiss that I thought I needed. One that erased me and left me not thinking at all.

We hurried back to the house and tried to sneak into the bedroom, but Haley shot up from the couch yelling, "I passed out! It's 3:00—my mother is picking us up at 8:00 in the morning! Vamos. Now." I had kept my promise to myself. I didn't have sex with Dan, but it wasn't on purpose.

Dan drove us home, guilt riding shotgun next to me. I started throwing up in Haley's bathroom about five minutes after we arrived and stopped sometime around 5:00 A.M. when I drunkenly crawled into bed with Haley and her fiancé. Later the special brunch her mother had arranged for the bridesmaids sat untouched in front of me as I vowed never to have an affair or another giant margarita again.

Dan called before Haley's rehearsal dinner. "Hello, my frisky little adulteress. Call the wedding off yet?" And just like that, I remembered all the fragments I had carried with me to Arizona. All the pieces of me that I had broken by chasing after Dan. I worried I would shatter. And again I started packing up for Arizona. I was ready for not perfect but stable. For a safe harbor away from someone who would have sex with me but never love me. Jay and I had problems, but he had chosen me, and we could make it work. My guilt over Dan fueled a frenzy of love for Jay and a devotion that can only be referred to as penance. I would be a good wife, starting now. I climbed back on the marriage train, waving bon voyage to the past.

The wedding photos cost more than a month of my teaching salary. I got the album in the divorce. Jay and I had decided two and half years of trying to pretend to be happily married was enough. It was only later, when my sister was getting married, that I pulled out the huge silver album and really sat down and looked through it picture by picture.

I looked for the signs of disaster—something I could point to confidently and say, "See! There's the proof." I saw my mother's arms encircling me after closing the clasp on my mother-of-pearl bracelet. My best friends, my bridesmaids lined up in black, holding vibrant lilies, gerberas, and roses. Jay smiling with his brothers, Hypericum boutonnières pinned in place. Wedding programs carefully glued into colorful fans to pass out at the church. A banquet hall with candles in hurricanes lighting the faces of 200 friends and family members, all cheerful and optimistic. Jay whispering in my ear and me with my head thrown back, laughing. We looked happy.

Nude Study

River Jordan

I'm a Southern girl, raised with certain sensibilities and more rights than wrongs. Taught from an early age to believe in Jesus, to take care of family, and to keep my clothes on. It was simple. There were two types of girls: good ones, and whores. They were easy to distinguish because whores took their clothes off.

I have a photo of my grandmother standing in the middle of a patch of sun-scorched earth. It was taken during a time of drought and dry cotton. She is tall and thin and has the look of a woman whom life has run through hard. Her back is bent and spent from years of picking cotton. Not a cheerful person, not given to whims or fancies, but a strong woman, full of truth and worry. When all is said and done, you can say of my grandmother that she was a good woman. A woman who kept her clothes on.

The two of us were close. It was common knowledge that I was the favored grandchild. The favor came from choices I made. Choices to sit at her feet coloring instead of playing outdoors with cousins. To stay by her side in the kitchen as she stirred chocolate into cakes.

To rock dreamily in her lap before the fire. And now, all these years since she is gone, some odd days I still sense her in the air, sense that she is watching me and that she knows. Everything. Including the times I have taken off my clothes.

———•◦•———

There is a road in Panama City that runs along the Bay waters of the Cove. It circles through in a lazy, residential way, shaded with old oaks dripping with moss, with magnolias and tall pines. A sleepy, salty place where families settle and raise their kids the right way. And it is here, in a hidden cove, that I first get naked.

It is at the urging of a new friend from seventh grade. I slept over and now we are walking the neighborhood in a meandering, seventh-grade way. Nothing but Saturday afternoon sunshine and time. We follow a road that dodges to the left, where the houses stop and the wildness of old Florida remains. A road that ends in dirt and sand and low palms and scrub pines. There on the other side of this undeveloped land lies a cove of water inland from the Bay.

"Let's get naked," Cee Cee says, kicking off her sandals.

"What?" I am a shy girl. Careful. Getting naked in broad daylight with someone I've known only a few weeks doesn't seem like a Momma-approved idea.

"Let's go skinny-dipping."

I look at her.

"Naked," she says, as if I am a bit slow. "Let's swim naked."

It is nowhere near sundown. No cover of darkness to hide my sin.

"We'll get caught," I say, stalling.

"Who's going to catch us?"

I look around. A bomber squad of low-flying pelicans are the only witnesses.

These hidden shores of the Cove lagoon will one day be developed, and showcase expensive houses of charming people, houses where years and years later I will gather at literary dinners and talk writing with best-selling authors. But right now it is still wild.

Cee Cee unzips her jeans, slides right out of them. I stay put, weighing the war within me. Do right. Do wrong. Then her T-shirt flies up, and she doesn't stop there. Her bra quickly follows, then her underwear.

She is buck-assed, as my Aunt Kate would say. Aunt Leaner says "naked as a jay bird." My Granny would just purse her lips and look the other way to not cast her eyes on do-wrong. Every whore has a beginning. I am pretty certain I don't want to be a whore.

Cee Cee swims backward, flips over, dives back into the blue water. I watch, envious now of her obvious lack of burden. She swims a few guiltless strokes farther out, and yells back, "C'mon!"

Do right? Do wrong? Hesitantly, I take off my shirt, look around, quickly unzip my jeans. I pull off all my clothes as if I am on fire.

I swim, dive, flip, backstroke, and feel the sun on my chest, thinking, surely a feeling this good just can't be bad. There is all this warm water and the sun and wind and a deliciousness that lulls me into an embryonic state. Still, there is this underlying sense that I am somehow being bad. That I have one wet foot over the county line to Hookerville.

Cee Cee and I never swim naked again. We try once but when we arrive there are boys on bikes riding the dirt road and kicking up sand, so it isn't the same. But that secret Saturday has baptized us into becoming inseparable, best friends for many lazy summers yet to come.

Much to my surprise, I do not become a whore. But where naked has been, naked comes again.

———•·•———

There's a road in North Florida known as 30A. It turns off of Highway 98 and runs the beach for 16 miles. Now, it has become famous for so many things—Seaside, Rosemary Beach, Sundog Books, Bud and Alley's Restaurant, Grayton Beach, Red Roof Bar, Criollas, Blue Mountain Beach. But on this night when I am 15, the beaches of North Florida have real sand dunes that curve around the warm Gulf Coast waters like white treasure. This is before the huge spring break clubs, before the condos that strip the beach and block the view.

At 15 I'm still a good girl. I do my homework, do my chores, make good grades, make my curfews. It's my birthday and to celebrate I pile into a VW van with friends and we head toward the beach and 30A. We are a motley group, clinging to the fringe of an old neighborhood getting older. Kids of pastors and sergeants, mill workers and sales-men. It is a time of Tolkien talk, of summers filled with lazy beaching to the sounds of AM radio. A time of Friday night concerts and Simon and Garfunkel. We are all in love with the we of us.

We have loaded down the van with coolers, Cokes and chips and blankets, and, in honor of my birthday, chocolate brownies. We must park the van on the side of the deserted road and carry our stuff high to keep it dry, wading the lagoon waters to the other side. We build a bonfire and tell stories under a night sky raging with stars.

Suddenly, with little discussion, we are peeling clothes off and we are laughing, running, diving into moonlit waves lazily rolling up on white sands. And of all nights, phosphorus fills the water so that as we swim we are moving light, a reflection of those stars above us. Someday we will die. By accident, by illness, by suicide, and by simply growing old to gone. But on this night we are so young, we are immortal.

———•·•———

There is a road that runs due south from North Florida to South Flor-ida. It takes you through groves laden with oranges to a place filled with money where the homes of the wealthy are cradled by their ocean view. It is a different country, where the winds turn warmer and the palms grow five stories high.

My only bona fide vacation has been to Tennessee, to see Rock City in third grade. But now my mother has received a bonus and surprised me and my cousin, Deb, and my Aunt Margie with a week in West Palm. Alone, Deb and I are pretty good girls. Even at 17 we manage to steer clear of trouble. But together? Together we are notorious. Trouble and a litany of stories, of shenanigans, will follow us through life.

At 15, we stole our cousin's convertible in a small town down by the river. She ran after us on foot until we were out of sight, driving the country back-roads just for the thrill, the top down, laughing all the way. We jumped from high trees into raging waters and almost drowned. We got lost and found and did things we will never confess. Through a host of lies and alibis, we never got caught—except for that time my dad caught us sneaking in at daylight.

In West Palm Beach, Florida, the palms grow taller than any we have ever seen. A different palm tree than we ever knew existed. We are on a real vacation for the first time, not just a drive to visit all our southern relatives. A vacation made sweeter by the fact that it's February, and in our hometown our friends back home are in school. Somehow, my mother has managed to convince the school to let us go for seven school days. We feel giddy, jailbroke. We check into a seven-story Holiday Inn with an ocean view where we will eat seafood and laze our days away by the pool, turning a glorious winter brown that we will carry back to school to the envy of our friends. We wear the scent of privilege. West Palm Beach is rich, foreign. It's our Paris. And on one particular night in this rich, south Florida town, someone dares someone to get naked. And so we do. On an eight-lane landscaped boulevard that runs between the hotel and the water, a boulevard filled with rich people driving rich cars. On the hotel grounds below our room, in a grove of blooming azaleas, we shuck our clothes.

"So here's the plan," Deb says.

My cousin Deb is a God-blessed, natural-born athlete. She has spent summers riding me on the handlebars of a bike. She has walked 500 steps on her hands every day in the summer just for something to do. She can dive, swim, run, and jump, and whip a man at tennis. And now she is telling me, her bookworm-buddy cousin, to take off my clothes and run for the bushes. I am not beyond a dare. I don't look competitive, but occasionally something rises up in me that will surprise someone. Even me. This is one of those times.

I strip down to nothing and clutch my clothes in my hand. Bare naked, and this time, there is no warm water waiting to embrace me. Just the sound of the traffic next to us and those palms slapping in the wind high above, and we say, "One, two, three, go!"

I am running out of the trees when it dawns on me: I am naked.

In public. On an eight-lane boulevard. I can't say shame overcomes me because it isn't shame. It's modesty. Suddenly I am overcome with a sense of modesty, which is hard to pull off when you are running naked. So the modesty is replaced by a great sense of panic.

I run like Jane in the land of Tarzan. The sounds of the cars passing, the palm trees slapping, the distant waves, an occasional horn, have all been surpassed by the sound of my cousin the Olympian laughing at the site of my rear end streaking for a group of azaleas a football-field length away. She is laughing so hard she has forgotten she is naked, and cannot run. She is doubled over somewhere behind me. I make it to the bushes and am clothed again before she can catch up to me.

Being bad with a relative seems like less of a sin, as if we have taken naked and divided it by two. I am guilty at half weight, relieved at the feel of my clothes on my back, and laughing too hard to feel shame.

Some roads are unseen by the naked eye but you must learn to navigate them just the same. There are saltwater roads that run deep between Shell Island off the coast of Florida and the land-locked beach. The high tides that run through them are strong enough to lead you out into the deep and eventually connect you to the Gulf Stream.

Once upon a time, in a life before this life I now live, there was an island and on it a solitary house that faced out toward the waves. A place of luck and lore. A place of story.

We reach Shell Island by boat and are dropped in the breaking waves, on the beach before the house. My sons are still boys. There is just us and the island and one lone, perfectly primitive house.

Pelicans fly in low every day, skimming the water. We count 27 once, the largest squadron we see, the same as my age. A pelican for every year.

For days we play cards and checkers. We watch thunderheads roll in, and lightning streak across the water. We wander the sand searching for shells. Bones of fish. Bottles washed ashore. We collect these treasures. We live without power, lighting candles to eat dinner. The sun rises and we wake. The sun sleeps and we rest. We become naturally human.

After days we wash our naked bodies in the Gulf to save our drinking water. I stand at a small distance from the boys—washing quickly, storm coming. They are little boys but not babies. Yet, there I am, naked, if only for minutes. And right at this moment, this one naked moment, a photo is taken.

I didn't realize it until after, until the film was developed and then there it was: proof that I was—well, naked. From a distance, mind you. A pretty good distance. It would be so easy to discard. It's not digital. Not Facebooked. An old photo, now yellowed with time. I've started to throw it away a dozen times, but I cannot. I put it behind photographs of other photographs and keep it hidden there. Hidden—and protected. This wild photo on an island, storm clouds circling, Gulf waves lapping at our bodies.

I save it because we are each innocent and as young as we will ever be.

———•———

There's a stretch of road in the American West where you could wander waterless for days, until the sun burned the clothes from your body, till you were nothing but white bone. Depending on your direction this road delivers you to the swampy air and salt waters, or to high deserts full of sky, a place of wonder where you can see the shadows of clouds sailing across the landscape. There is an aloneness in this place that can eat you or set you free. It called to me once and found me. It calls to me still. But in this moment I am returning only to leave it for good.

My daddy's dying. It's a slow death, a time that will tick by without a definite end in sight. But we know that it's coming. Seven days ago I took the boys to visit. But it didn't take long to see the truth coming. My sister took a good look at Daddy and agreed. It was time to come home. To stay close by so I wouldn't have a thousand miles of blacktop stretched out between us. So the little moments, the daily moments, won't be missed. For the sake of speed, I leave the boys there with Nana and Pawpaw in northwest Florida and make a dash back to New Mexico to get our clothes, our books, a few good pots, a box of favorite toys and come back to live—and wait.

New Mexico—Taos, especially—gives me something no other place can. Orange neon sunsets to stop a clock. The air full of places I haven't been. Flat rocks, and cold streams, and the gorge that stunned me silent when I first laid eyes on it. The rawness of the earth split open, exposing ancient mysteries. And then, of course, there is the light. Over a hundred years ago artists were traveling through Taos when their wagon broke down. So a few stayed with their supplies while one man went for a new axle, but by the time he returned all they could say was—the light. Then they never left. And it's how those of a lighter persuasion came to settle in this place of native light and shadow.

It takes 23 hours and 17 minutes to drive from Panama City to Taos. A little over 24, stopping for gas and coffee. I hit Tucumcari at midnight, the smell of sage on the air. There's more room in this country than you can fathom. I pull the top off the thermos filled up at the last truck stop on I-40. It's one o'clock as I take a right turn, head up State Road 84.

I'm 21 hours in, and if I manage to hang on for a few more hours, if I can just stay awake, and not fall asleep at the wheel, I'll be there, grab our things, load the car. I've used the miles to clear the clutter in my mind.

The lightning intensifies, the dark sky now spitting fire. The horizon is cluttered with clouds. Lightning rips on the horizon across that blackness, illuminating nothing but the flat-top mesas stretching out for miles and miles—and me.

There are many kinds of alone but there is only one that is the alone of driving through the high desert at 2:00 A.M. Fighting the beast of sleep, I unbutton my shirt, shift hands on the wheel, shuck my clothes one arm, one shoulder at a time until I am bare-chested. Just jeans and boots, driving into the storm. I roll the windows down, stick my arm out into the electric air.

I ride alone on this planet riddled with light and dark, full of shifting shadows. I am the first life and the last life. I am Eve in the wilderness of God's creation. My foot on the pedal, pushing to dawn, to deliverance, to destiny.

And I am not ashamed.

A Country Where You Once Lived*

Sheryl St. Germain

I
t starts when you're thirteen, and those tight shorts make your crotch wet when you ride your bike on the levees surrounding Lake Pontchartrain. You like these shorts, the way they make you feel this new way: sexy. You fall asleep at night thinking about sex. You listen to songs that encourage you to think about sex. And of course, New Orleans is the original Sin City. You know, even as a child, that the strippers you can see through the swinging doors on Bourbon Street are sinful, but you lust for the power they have over the men who walk into their dens. The fact that you want sex so much and think about it so much, and that you know it is a sin, just spices things up a bit; it's like adding a bit of cayenne to your gumbo or jambalaya. It hurts, but also wakes you up.

But you are Catholic, too, and attend Catholic school. And although you discover you can even think about sex at church and in the classroom at St. Lawrence the Martyr without anyone knowing, if you keep a certain demeanor and cross your legs a certain way, the nuns have convinced you that even partial sex, like letting your boyfriend touch your breasts, or touching his penis through his jeans, is

---

*Names have been changed to protect the privacy of those mentioned in this essay

a sin, which is why you confess to Father Schutten every few weeks that you've had another petting session with your boyfriend and you're really sorry. You say your penance, three Hail Marys and one Our Father, and go out to sin some more.

Eventually you graduate from high school, and you start *having* almost as much sex as you used to think about. By the time you are in your 20s you are picking up men in bars and bringing them home with you, so many you can't keep track of them all, so many you don't remember all their names today, but you still keep fantasizing about the sex you're not having and reminiscing about what you've had, remembering the exact details: the dimensions of the lips, the shape of the tongue and how it first entered your mouth, the precise smell of the shoulders and neck, each lover's body, as poet Jack Gilbert writes, a country in which you lived for a time.

All your life, you think, you'll want it. You think the wanting will be a constant companion, like a faithful dog. You think you'll always be up for it, through sickness and health. Oh, sure, as you get older, in your 30s, say, there are times when you feel less like having sex, or times when you get bored with your lover, or depressed, but then you just find a new partner, and there's desire again. You're sure it will never go away. You know this because movies and TV and advertisements for Viagra tell you that old people have sex too, that it is not strange to have sex after you get old, and you know because you see old people, including your father and mother, dressed up all sexy-like during Mardi Gras. You are fairly certain your parents still have sex even though they are in their 50s. You will be an old woman who still has sex, you tell your mother one evening as she is applying plum-colored lipstick and more Chanel No. 5 perfume to her wrists. You will have sex until you die, you tell your father as he dons your mother's blonde wig and caftan for yet another Mardi Gras where he will dress as a sexy pregnant woman. Maybe, in fact, you will have sex on your deathbed, you say to no one in particular. You will die a well-fucked woman.

You are so determined to keep on having sex that, when you find yourself in a long relationship in middle age, it's difficult to acknowledge that your desire for sex is starting to wane. You explore sex toys and read books about how to spice up your sex life. Since you are in a committed relationship, sex with your partner is no longer a sin, or so you tell yourself, and you worry that this is the beginning of a slide to a boring and sinless life without sexual desire. There begins to be a kind of desperation in your search for ways to make yourself want sex the way you once did. Sometimes you feel like a nonbeliever who continues to go to church because she can't admit she's lost faith.

Your sex-toy strategies seem to work for a while. Then you break up with your partner, and you figure out that if you keep changing partners, or having long-distance relationships where the sex is only every other weekend, everything will be fine. After many years of this behavior, though, you marry late in life, and you don't want to change partners, and all of a sudden (or so it seems) you can't keep up with your husband's desire, and you are mortified. It's like a terrible secret: you feel not yourself, freakish, and, worst of all, boring. You have learned from your mother that the absolute worst thing anyone can be is boring. Women, especially, you have intuited from her, must always be beautiful, always seductive, always sinfully wild.

You're able to talk yourself into sex for the sake of your marriage and out of love for your husband for awhile, but it's not pleasant because, although you don't want to admit it at first, penetration has started to hurt. No longer do you welcome that once-sacred entering. It's as if your whole body cringes when he tries, and sometimes—and now we're getting to the part that no one prepares you for, not mothers or aunts or even kindly physicians—sometimes you bleed when you have sex because, as a male doctor explains to you later, your vagina has "atrophied." Your body, the doctor says, is experiencing penetration as physical trauma.

How can this be? You are still a young—or youngish—woman. But when you get home and phone your mother, who is now in her late 70s, she says the same thing happened to her at the same time, in her early 50s. (*Why didn't you tell me this before now?* you think, as if you could have somehow prepared for this moment.)

"I haven't had sex in 24 years," she adds in a cheerful way—a fact that is really not at all helpful at this point. "And really, Sheryl, don't you think you've had enough sex by now?"

All of a sudden you begin to notice that there are an awful lot of men your age who are with significantly younger women, and you are starting to understand why. Your vagina has shrunk—there's no other word for it—and every act of sex is as painful as the first, maybe more so. You think the inside of your vagina must look like a shrunken morel. You examine it in a mirror to see if it looks any different on the outside, but it doesn't. You look at your face, too, in the mirror, and think you are still beautiful in a deep, older-woman kind of way, but you feel awful. You wish the word *atrophied* did not exist.

The male gynecologist you consult says atrophy is common in women your age, and gives you a prescription for some hormonal cream—much safer than orally administered hormones, he assures you. He recommends an over-the-counter vaginal lubricant and tells you to be patient.

"If you were 75," he says patronizingly, "this wouldn't be a problem."

You want to hit him.

"It's the lowered estrogen levels," he continues, "that cause dryness of the vagina, which can cause severe burning, discharge, and dyspareunia," [dis-puh-ROO-ne-uh], the clinical term for painful sex. Though you wish he would speak to you in a way that acknowledges you are a suffering patient and not a medical student, you're grateful for the information.

You go online to learn more, careful to visit only sites such as the Mayo Clinic and Medscape, where the comments are written by physicians and make reference to clinical trials and papers. One doctor writes that chronic and progressive vaginal atrophy is *the* twenty-first-century health issue affecting quality of life for women. Researchers estimate that 50 to 60 percent of postmenopausal women experience it, although it's difficult to get accurate numbers because many are too embarrassed or ashamed to talk about it.

The Mayo Clinic confirms that thinning, shrinkage, and inflammation of the vaginal walls are due to a decline in estrogen levels as women age. Both sites suggest hormone-replacement therapy, creams, and gels. Ads pop up that promise relief. One shows an attractive older woman with gray hair smiling and blowing bubbles. You hope that the cream will work for you and that you will soon be blowing bubbles, because the latest study shows that women on hormone-replacement therapy are more susceptible to heart disease, breast cancer, stroke, and blood clots.

You try the hormone cream and the lubricating gel for a few months, but they don't seem to help much. Your vagina just doesn't want to open the way it once did, and the pain remains. You keep trying, though, hoping that continued intercourse will force it to stay open. Finally you decide it's time to find a new gynecologist. A friend recommends a woman doctor she's been seeing for some time: "She'll be more understanding," your friend says.

Dr. D'Aquin looks to be in her late 50s. She has a head of curly locks, full lips, and an intense, seemingly genuine interest in you. After she performs the exam, she peels off her plastic gloves and says, "You can still have sex. I can get two fingers in you. Some women with atrophied vaginas, I can't even get one finger in. But if you don't keep having sex, you'll eventually lose the ability to be entered at all."

You discuss the pros and cons of hormone therapy with her, and decide it's worth the health risks to give it a try. She prescribes a stronger hormone cream and a special vaginal ring that exudes hormones over a period of three months. The ring looks like a doughnut.

"The same thing happened to me," Dr. D'Aquin says as she's writing out your prescriptions. "I married in my 50s, too, and couldn't keep up with my husband. The cream, the rings, and the hormones will help with the physical pain."

"What about desire?" you ask.

"It differs with each woman."

"How long did you stay on hormone therapy?" you ask.

"Three years," she says. You are afraid to ask what she did after that.

So you start taking hormones, and you use the stronger cream and the ring faithfully, and you and your husband wait for things to improve. But each time you try to have what your husband calls "regular" sex, it still hurts. A typical encounter goes something like this:

He asks ahead of time if you might want to have sex that evening or the next morning, so that you can be prepared. You agree, although knowing ahead of time takes most of the fun, the *sin* out of it. It is more like homework than sinning. At the prescribed time, though, you go through with it: he lights candles, draws the blinds, gets out all the various lubricants and gels you will need. He starts with a back rub, kisses you sweetly, touches your breasts, tries to excite you with words. You try to get into it, but all you can think about is that at some point he will enter you, and it will be painful. You use your yoga training to focus on the moment and the pleasure he's attempting to give you, but all your legs want to do is clamp shut. You open them, though, remembering that you must have intercourse if you want to remain able to have it. Finally you're as ready as you will ever be. He climbs on top and tries to enter you, gently, just a bit.

"Does it hurt?" he asks, excited but concerned.

"A little," you say. "But it's OK. Just go slow, not too deep."

You close your eyes and try not to cry out as he moves in and out, slowly and not too deeply. There are tears in your eyes, but you don't let him see. Finally, after five minutes that seem like an hour, he's finished. You are quiet for a while, hurting but happy to be in his arms. A few minutes later you excuse yourself to go to the bathroom, where you clean yourself, wiping off the bright-red blood.

You report this failure to Dr. D'Aquin, but she still insists that you try to have sex once a week. "Think of it as your homework," she says, brightly, and you don't have the heart to tell her that you already do.

You try to adapt. You and your husband joke about doing your "homework." You tell him you think you might try to write about the whole matter, that it might make you feel better, and would he mind if you got something published?

He thinks for a few seconds and says, "No, as long as you say that I have a big penis."

You smile and are happy for a moment. If you didn't both have a sense of humor about all of this, it would be much worse. The truth is, he does have a large penis, and you have sometimes wondered if sex might not hurt so much if his penis were smaller. You used to love his penis, the way it filled you. And he is a handsome man—one of your friends even called him "drop-dead gorgeous." A tall, strikingly dark Frisian man with a full head of thick black hair and the most intense and haunting eyes you have ever had the pleasure of engaging.

Your husband tries to spice up the homework, putting up red curtains, transforming the spare bedroom into a room that could be straight out of Storyville. He brings bottles of wine and plays music: soft jazz, blues, and, inexplicably, Gregorian chants. Sometimes he spins out fantasies to whet your interest: he pretends he's a sailor returned from a long voyage, and you are his beloved. Sometimes the fantasies make the sex seem a little bit more like sinning.

When penetration still hurts, you take to having sex without it. You feel guilty, though. You know that's not what he wants, even though he tells you it doesn't matter that much. You tell him it would be OK with you if he wanted to have an affair, although you are not really sure how you would feel about that. He does not want to have an affair, though, or so he says. He loves you, he says.

At some point you wonder if it is just that you no longer want your husband, but as soon as you wonder it, you know that this is not the case. There is no one else you want. You don't even want yourself. You don't even have those sinful moments of masturbating that you used to enjoy, when the only pleasure you thought of was your own.

You have begun to think about not having sex almost as much as you used to think about having it, and while you are trying to be patient and wait for the hormones to make a difference, you slowly begin to bring up the subject of waning desire with women who are around your age, and you learn—surprise!—that you aren't alone.

You visit a Louisiana couple you've known for about 25 years. They seem to have a happy marriage. Recovering Catholics, they are gardeners, collectors of art and music. Antoine, the husband, has recently recovered from prostate cancer and told you, when he was going through treatment, "If I can't fuck anymore, I'm going to be really pissed off." Caroline, his wife, had a hysterectomy a few years ago and has been on hormone-replacement therapy since then.

You are sitting with them in the backyard of their home in the Garden District of New Orleans, surrounded by oaks, bamboo, dark-leaved tropical plants, and a dizzying number of large-belled, sweet-smelling flowers. It feels like the Garden of Eden. After Caroline had the hysterectomy, she tells you, it induced early menopause, and she lost the desire for sex.

"It felt like my whole body was drying out. I only worried about the risks of hormone therapy for about two minutes, though." She smiles and takes a sip of her iced tea. "There was no way I was spending the rest of my life like that. Sex or Death!"

"So it worked?" you ask.

"Oh, yeah, honey, it worked. But I had to get on the natural hormones, and it took a while to get the right dose. A few years."

"I'm fine, too," Antoine says, smiling. "Viagra is a lifesaver."

When Caroline reveals the huge dose of hormones she's taking, you're shocked, but you can't argue with success. You are happy for them, but leave feeling somewhat lonely.

About six months after this conversation, Caroline tells you that she has developed some life-threatening health issues that her doctor thinks are related to the hormone therapy, and she is considering lowering or even stopping the dose. You wonder about the kind of mind-set that values sexual activity over health. Is it worth it, you wonder, to maintain the delicious sinfulness of lusty sex if it shortens your life span? The scary fact is, you're not sure yet you can say *no* to anything that might improve your sex life, and you imagine that there are many other women out there like you.

You begin to wonder why there are so many Viagra commercials on TV and nothing for women that seems to works like Viagra. What does it matter if a man can get it up if the woman can't take the up-ness into her? You guess that is where the younger women come in.

Other older friends admit to waning desire. One successful editor friend says she's told her husband he always has to be the one to initiate sex, that she'll comply, but he can't expect that she'll ever really want it again. Another has given her partner permission to have sex with anyone he'd like, as long as it's not her. A former rock-musician friend says simply, "It will never be what it was. We'll never have that feeling again. Never."

You don't ask them for specifics because it seems too private (*So, do you have an atrophied vagina?*), but you can't help but wonder how many of them have the same problem as you. Some talk about just living with their partner's unhappiness until something happens to him—prostate cancer, say—and then sex becomes a nonissue, at least for a while.

These are vibrant, smart, beautiful women in their 50s and early 60s. They are strong, they are healthy, and you always thought of them as lusty, too. They lead meaningful and interesting lives, but they don't feel like having sex much anymore.

Of course there are exceptions. You meet a friend for lunch one day, an energetic woman around your age. You both eat spicy lamb curry and dal and chat about your personal lives.

"Bill and I never have sex anymore," she says. Bill, her husband, was treated for prostate cancer a few years earlier. "He just can't do it."

"Do you still want it?" you ask.

"Wow, yes, but I can satisfy myself with a vibrator if need be. I just wish he still wanted me." She goes on to tell you how she's thinking about having an affair. She can hardly stop talking, between bites of curry, about how much she still wants sex and how sad it makes her that her husband doesn't.

You can't bring yourself to tell her about your problems.

You find a forum online devoted to vaginal atrophy with many stories like your own: women confused about the pain and trying the hormones and creams, mostly without success. Some recommend other ways to boost desire: vitamin E, testosterone, caffeine (yes, caffeine!).

One post, however, breaks your heart:

> *I feel like a failure. I would be quite happy to never have sex again, and my husband just can't under-stand that. Why isn't there some sort of surgical intervention, a vaginal transplant or replacement, like for burned skin or something? I really feel alone and miserable. Doctors don't seem to want to talk about this, and everyone just seems to sigh and expect me to live with it. I could, but what about my husband? Please, can anyone out there give me hope for a happy ending to this story?*

A happy ending. Some of your single-women acquaintances do talk about living without men, happy with their female friends in a world of dinners and movies and book clubs. This is the route your mother, whose husband died some years ago, has taken. Still others take the hopeful pills that don't always make much of a difference and go on living their full and busy lives, carrying this small sadness within them, this wish that they could again love something they once did.

You wonder if longing for the strong libido and the supple sex organ you had as a younger woman makes you too much like those women you hate who keep having face- and breast-lifts. Is it possible for you to accept the waning of sexual desire as a rite of passage to a quieter, more reflective time, a time in which the blinders of sex and sin are gone and you can focus on other things? Perhaps this waning is your body's way of suggesting there are more important matters to which you might pay attention in this last third of your life. You're a little embarrassed to remember how much time you wasted as a young woman thinking about sex.

Eventually you stop the hormones and decide to try to live with the fact of diminished desire. Maybe you've just lost the will to try to recapture the longings of your youth. Your husband says he understands.

It sometimes seems that aging is only about loss: not only does our desire diminish, but hearing and eyesight weaken, memory becomes a struggle, and the physical body in general loses tone and elasticity, no matter how much you exercise. It's hard to imagine being happy about this, but maybe you can be present in it, accept it, interrogate it, meditate on it, learn from it the way you have learned from other losses all your life.

When sex is mostly out of the equation, you're surprised to find that there is this gift: the irrefutable proof that you can love someone without sex as the primary driver of the relationship. There's a depth to the affection you have for your husband now that feels rich and complex, more nuanced than when you first met and spent almost every night having sex. And you learn there are more mature ways of sinning: going against established rules and laws or working as a bit of an outlaw in academia to build support for ideas, programs, people you believe in, for example. You start hanging out in jails and prisons, halfway houses, teaching creative writing to those whose sinning has landed them there. If you have trouble mustering up the energy to commit sexual sins yourself, you can at least help others to reflect on their own transgressions.

Happy ending? Not if the only thing that would make you happy is the return of the libido and body you had 15 or 20 years ago.

But if happy can mean contented, at ease, appreciative, then maybe this is a happy ending, one in which you find eroticism outside yourself, in small things you hadn't noticed before: the careful way a bee enters a foxglove's flower; the feel of a heavy, ripe tomato when you pick it from the vine; the dark beauty of your son's new mustache; the breathtaking intelligence of your daughter; the vibrant, angry tattoos on your female students' skin; the precise tea-brown color of the Atchafalaya Swamp in Louisiana; the sweetness and patience of your husband as he works at his desk, or paints the basement, or walks the dog, and tries to understand the haunted sadness you carry, this memory of a country where you once lived, whose language you seem to have forgotten.

Porn Star

Elane Johnson

I t's been a long-held goal of mine not to become a porn star. I was
raised in the First Baptist Church of Thomaston, Georgia, and
while the only things of substance I recall are miniature glasses
of grape juice, squares of saltines, and a permeating scent of Play-Doh,
I'm certain the congregation frowns upon pornography to this day.
And yet, against my most fervent wishes, I find myself to be nearly 50
and a reluctant porn star.

My mother would have been so proud. Really.

My mother, whose physical beauty did not help my fragile self-
esteem one bit, taught me important lessons growing up: how to sit
still, goddammit, on a torturously rigid pew while waiting an eternity
for the grape juice and saltines; how to apply Revlon foundation without unsightly streaks; how to pin a hairpiece onto a nearly hairless
three-year-old scalp (mine) with minimal scarring and only moderate
pain; how to make a superb egg salad and an incredible sour cream
pound cake; how to surprise one's lover by sneaking out the back door

in nothing but a fur coat and then, the moment said lover answered the front doorbell, dropping the fur. Things like that.

Mother met me for lunch one day when I was still in high school. During the second half of my egg salad sandwich (Mother, who grew up on a chicken farm in Butler, was irrationally averse to eggs not prepared by her own hands, and she insisted that the waiter verify—twice—it was freshly made), I indignantly brought up my recent discovery of a couple of affairs she'd had while married to my father.

"You'll understand after you have your first affair," she said. And damned if I didn't!

To say I'm relieved that Mother didn't live to see the day her darling daughter joined the tainted world of pornography would be a pointless lie. She would have been proud, in her "everything reflects back on me" way, and not a little jealous. Perhaps she's somewhere glowing with pride right this second. Or maybe the glow is from eternal flames. Whichever. Let's not quibble.

What happened is this: I inherited my father's muscular legs. I've grown accustomed to the countless comments from students as I've stood at blackboards that turned into green chalkboards that turned into whiteboards. "You have huge calves!" "Do you know that your left leg is bigger than your right leg?" "Do you work out?" The last one is my favorite, and if you could see my under-chin and belly rolls, you'd understand why I reply the way I do.

"Does it look like I work out?" I exclaim, grabbing two or three rolls for emphasis. It's exhausting, having to account for the extremely bulgy and defined legs that do not match the rest of me. Especially when I'm trying to save the benighted masses from the eternal damnation of split infinitives and misplaced modifiers. Concentrate, people!

Recently, I was leaving one of those mail-your-package places when a very beautiful, slight, and soft-spoken woman approached and asked to speak with me outside. She didn't look panhandle-y or anything, but I had my counter-spiel ready if she launched into any "Have you accepted Jesus Christ as your Lord and Savior" shenanigans. So I put on the super-wide grin I generally reserve for times when I can't hear a single word the speaker is saying, but want to appear that I do, and accompanied her to the sidewalk. She fumbled a couple of times before blurting, "I noticed that you have very muscular calves." This again!

I mumbled something apologetic, and we both blushed like preteens moving in for a first kiss in the sacristy. Then, somewhere in the haze of the conversation, I caught the phrase "50 dollars an hour" and immediately turned up my hearing aids. (Did I mention that I'm deaf? I'm probably the world's first deaf porn star. Bonus!)

The woman's boyfriend is in the fetish business, which, I've since learned, is a big-dollar industry. Oh, the myriad ways that people find sexual satisfaction! And some of those people are probably damned good Baptists.

With the advent of the Internet, almost anyone can get immediate gratification with just a few keystrokes and twenty bucks. So I agreed to have my muscular calves photographed for display on the World Wide Web. No one will ever know whose calves they are because I'm masked by my "fantasy" name. My mother—rest her soul—might be able to pick them out in a pinch. But for all intents and purposes, dear reader, only you know what I've become.

I tore through my closet to prepare for the photo shoot that would take place that very evening, hunting for any short skirts that still fit my middle and stuffing all my sexiest heels in a Kroger bag. I'd succumbed, a few months prior, to the craze for perilous and tawdry platforms, snatching up deals on shoes I could wear approximately never. Except to a porn shoot. It's almost like I knew.

I arrived at the photographer's business address a little after suppertime. He fretted constantly over the waning daylight as he assessed my calves—by which I mean he measured their circumferences and murmured things like "spectacular" and "fabulous"—while I attempted unsuccessfully to appear charming and as if I did this sort of thing every day. God knows I didn't want to look like a virgin or anything. To begin, he filmed me sensually oiling my legs; it was extra hard not to snigger. Of course, the artiste selected the highest shoes, and he coerced me into behaviors that might have made even my mother blush—though come to think of it, she once described in great detail the "pencil pubes" of some gorgeous dancers at the Gold Club in Atlanta. So, probably not.

Two straight hours of wearing high heels and tensing one's calves in various positions isn't as easy as you'd think. I sashayed in front of the building, in front of Main Street traffic whizzing by, in front of townsfolk who craned to see why the hell some guy was filming a fat woman on tiptoe as she caressed an office window on a globally warmed summer evening. By this point, I was perspiring in a most unladylike fashion. And then my photographer needed seven good, strong minutes of my pumping up and down on a stair-climbing machine, still in the heels, still on my toes. I stopped occasionally for cramps, but I tried to be a trouper. I worried that my photographer, in his ever-increasing appreciation for my *gastrocnemii*—made evident by his combination wink-whispers—might show signs of arousal. I furtively checked, from time to time, and was relieved beyond measure to spot no goings-on in his khakis.

I choose not to think what might accompany any future viewings of my photos or videos. After all, what people do behind closed doors is their business. And if I've helped another soul achieve liftoff—well, so be it. Perhaps when that happens, somewhere my mother gets her wings.

The truth is, I'm not exactly young and trim, and it felt kind of luxurious to be adored for a couple of hours, if only for my massive calves. I left the photographer's office a hundred dollars richer, sweaty as a farmhand, and with a shiny new résumé item. Lapsed Baptist. Teacher. Writer. *Porn Star.*

The Search for the Perfect Sidecar

Kendra Hamilton

I first encountered the sidecar—and I mean the beverage, not the wheeled buggy attached to a motorcycle—when I lived in Houston, Texas. Ground zero for that life-altering encounter was a smoky little bar downtown on Travis Street named Warren's.

Warren's had this turn-back-the-hands-of-time appeal that drew an odd, but oddly stimulating, cross section of Houston's bibulous classes. Step through the door at happy hour and you'd find downtown business types loosening their Gucci ties and stretching their legs after a long, hard day in the cubicles; reporter types from the newspaper building one block away, slightly scruffier, full of embellished tales of the "real" Houston; beauty-parlor blondes with perfectly square nails and rose-lipped smiles.

By around nine, the yuppie mating ritual would have concluded, and the hipster artists would have crowded in. You'd know them by the mantle of cool they wore like cowtown royalty plus the uniform: the paint-spattered jeans and stained Chuck Taylors, the vintage cowboy boots, or, if they were Urban Animals, the skates.

Closer to closing time, you'd find the pressmen from the paper—men who really *were* the real Houston, who looked like they remembered the days when a bottle and a gun were stashed in every copy editor's desk, who looked like they might have kept similar items stashed in their lockers.

The fellas'd tip their baseball caps at me and Janelle (mostly at Janelle) and sit at the bar trading beer and shots of amber-colored fluid with buddies who were, in fact, wearing guns because they were, occasionally, off-duty cops but, more often, well . . . bounty hunters.

Warren's, with its leatherette seats and ancient barkeeps and waiters—all male at that time, not a perky waitron to be found in the joint—yes, Warren's attracted them all and kept them all coming back for more by sticking to a simple formula: Warren's was a drinker's bar. You could get anything in Warren's—anything at all, from absinthe to a Pimm's Cup to a Rusty Nail. And you'd get a whole lot of it, too. A review I read recently described Warren's as a place where the singles were like doubles and the doubles were like a whole fifth. A bit of an exaggeration, but the bar has earned its legend.

I had, of course, done some drinking at Warren's before I met Janelle, but it wasn't until we bonded over headlines and page proofs at the newspaper that the full potential for a girl like me—or like I was then—in a place like Warren's—as it was then and as it apparently will be forever—could be fully realized.

Janelle and I moved through that dimly lit and masculine milieu as all women in their 20s who know themselves to be hot have moved for time out of mind: as if floated through the door on a cloud of their own exquisite scent. We made a striking pair and we knew it: Janelle with her masses of ruler-straight blonde hair, her swimming-pool eyes, and Vargas Girl figure; me, with my dancer's build, short black curls, honey-almond skin, and legs and an ass I'd been told to my face were the best in the newsroom.

I'd come to Houston just a few months before as a pending divorcée, a late-'80s true confession headlined: "My husband dumped me for a crackhead!" My life had unfolded into the kind of low-life-imitates-art tawdriness that lands a hard right hook to a girl's self-esteem. In times of crisis we need a story to tell ourselves. Mine was, "following a dream, a sheltered Southern girl slogging obits and breaking news at the Miss South Carolina pageant gets a chance at the big show" kind of dream—I'd moved 1,500 miles west to a real paper, a big paper, to forget him, to *show* him, to show *everybody* . . .

. . . Only to find myself floundering in the big city.

It wasn't loneliness precisely—though I didn't know a soul the first time I rolled over the Sabine River Pass into Texas in my brand-new GM car. What I was feeling was more like . . . a dawning awareness that I could move across the country—hell, I could move to the moon—but there was one thing I couldn't leave behind, and that was my face in the mirror . . .

The face of a woman whose husband had left her for a crackhead . . .

The face of a woman who had picked a man who would leave her for a crackhead . . .

There were days when looking at that woman's face in the mirror—and those cute cowboy boots she had cleverly accessorized with the vintage Mexican swing skirt and the Betsey Johnson bodysuit—made me want to go out and tear up the dance floor, somewhere, anywhere. Or go out and find a mall so that I could put together an even cuter outfit. Or find a man—'cause all this shopping, of course, had to have a higher purpose.

Of course, there were those other times, when the face in the mirror made me simply, suddenly, desperately afraid.

I can't remember now if they were the same times.

It sounds crazy to say this now, but I didn't know when I was married to him that my husband was an alcoholic. Months before I met Janelle, a kind woman at the reproductive health clinic had given me a smile of wondering pity after my initial interview and questionnaire. She was a black woman with features of the kind we call "Indian" and a sprinkling of freckles on her nose. She'd sighed and stood up, fetched a brochure from a plastic shelving unit on the wall, and placed it in my hand. It was a listing of the Al-Anon meeting schedule at the hospital.

Apparently, all I needed was a taste. In short order, I was freely shopping à la carte from a Twelve-Step menu that included Adult

Children of Alcoholics, Codependents Anonymous, Romance Addicts Anonymous, Co–Sex Addicts Anonymous, and a few more I can't even remember. In between the moments of exquisite boredom at the Twelve-Step buffet, in between the banal or the blood-curdling life histories, there were also glimpses . . . hazy glimpses of creepie crawlies in the midden heap of my psyche. Big. Hairy. So I did what most folks do. I found not just a diversion, I found a perfect storm of a distraction, the woman who was to become my BFF, my ace boon coon, my other self: Janelle.

What kind of girlfriend was Janelle? The kind who had slumber parties. Grown-up slumber parties for grown-up girls. She'd design the invitations in between page proofs at the paper. We'd be required to wear lingerie. To drink martinis. To play Mystery Date™. To watch old movies like *Gilda*, *I'll Cry Tomorrow*, and *Butterfield 8*. Dialing crushes while drunk was optional. Playing Frank Sinatra loud and lip-syncing to the words? A rule.

What kind of girlfriend was Janelle? She was a contradiction. I've mentioned the body, but I haven't described the walk, that simultaneously haughty, seductive, fearless walk. The proud carriage masking a shyness so crippling that she'd had to drop out of college her freshman year. She suffered mightily from shyness even when I first knew her—simply dreaded getting into the elevator with work colleagues she'd known for years.

Yet she refused to give in to it. She'd worked broadcast journalism for a while. She was a party-thrower, a scheme-for-world-domination hatcher. "Let's do a spoof of the performance-art scene and invite all those snooty artists we hate."

That was a classic Janelle plan.

I was, of course, a willing accessory before the fact—became, in fact, her chief aider and abettor. Partly because I was having so much fun. And not just big fun. Epic fun. And partly because . . . well, what had I been doing B.J.—Before Janelle, that is? Sitting in school gyms with circles of other women, trying desperately to observe a "no-cross-talk" rule while listening to chilling tales of ritual sexual abuse by Satanic cults. These were tales that I wasn't sure I believed, tales that I was desperate *not* to believe. What, indeed, had I been doing B.J.? Just looking in the mirror and getting scared.

At least with Janelle at my side, when I looked into a mirror, it was for one reason and one reason only: to check my makeup.

And there was another reason, as or more compelling. Janelle had many passions—for art, fashion, food, and an artist named Puck—but above all she loved music and loved to dance. These were passions on which we could agree. My dad was a jazz musician, so I was literally a jazz baby. Attending high school in the '70s meant, almost by default, that I was a disco queen. But at Janelle's side, I discovered live music in genres I'd never heard, and some I'd never heard of. The blues I'd heard of, of course, but rockabilly? Zydeco?

I learned to jitterbug at Club Hey Hey. I remember the night as if I'd scrapbooked it. The band was the Wild Cards, a Latin rock quartet that anticipated Los Lonely Boys' sound by about a decade. My teacher was tall, lean, blue-eyed, a looker with a job that was so odd I've never forgotten it: prison dentist.

He showed me the basic step. I followed so effortlessly it was more like remembering than learning. After one song, he gave me a smile of pure reckless devilment and we blistered that dance floor until closing. Did not exchange numbers. (He had a girlfriend who, sadly, couldn't dance). But I was off to the races. One partner dance down, many to go.

I learned the Texas two-step and the cotton-eyed Joe at a series of black cowboy bars on the south side of town. These were places where, if a woman pulled out a cigarette, some broad-shouldered hunka-hunka-burning-boytoy in skin-tight jeans would leap across three tables to light it. Heady stuff for a recovering shy girl who'd had precisely one date in high school.

I learned to zydeco at the Continental Zydeco Ballroom, a dive in a northeast neighborhood so gritty I have no idea how Janelle found it. She wore her "milkmaid-meets-biker-girl" outfit—sky blue vintage cowboy boots, tight mini, eyelet corset, denim jacket. I wore a circle skirt, ballet flats, spandex, and chunky jewelry. We took Juan—the reason the top Latina reporter at the paper hated my guts—and a bottle of Maker's Mark to go with our order of setups. The guy who showed me the steps was a *creole negre* named Gervais, about sixty, but handsome, courtly as all hell, and light on his feet. That circle skirt whipped like a flag in a gale as we stormed up and down the dance floor, and I got my first-ever nickname: Queen of the Zydeco Ballroom.

Hey, I told you. Fun. Epic fun.

One thing I loved about Janelle. If it was a question of music or food or even just a new experience, she did not care if she was the only white face. We'd venture to the Heights for Mexican beats then, at closing, drive all the way to scarf greasy, cheesy chicken enchiladas at the Triangle Café (where if anyone spoke English, they sure didn't bother to speak it to us). When George Clinton played a cavernous disco off Westheimer—a decade, mind you, before the hip white people in Houston admitted to having heard of "the Mothership"—Janelle put on her black mini and knee-high suede boots to check the scene out. I returned the favor, venturing with her to explore cheap beer, honky-tonk music, and men in tight jeans at "icehouses"—a thing I've only seen in Texas: roadside, open-air bars with cases upon cases upon cases of beer on ice.

If this sounds like a lot of partying, believe me, it was. We worked a weekend shift of "four tens" that ended around midnight, allowing us—all but daring us—to dance all night. Our days off were Tuesday through Thursday, so theoretically we could repeat the ritual up to five nights a week. Sometimes we pushed for seven.

Tuesdays we celebrated girls' night out—we'd go out to dinner then hit Lola's for the dollar rail drinks. Janelle swore the bartender had a crush on me, and it was true that our drinks—served in plastic cups and gulped down on a patio jammed with Houston's tragically hip— seemed extra strong. Wednesdays it was two-stepping or jitterbugging the night away at Club Hey Hey. Ladies night. No cover. Thursday to Saturday would be anything from headbanging at Rockefeller's to margaritas at Local Charm as we caromed among the music venues with bouncers or doormen who would let us in free. Sunday and Monday nights, nights of relative rest, we knocked off work around midnight, walked the three blocks from Texas Avenue to Travis, and settled in to chill and chat, over sidecars, at Warren's.

Yes, sidecars. You knew eventually I'd get there.

Believe it or not, even though I'd been married to an alcoholic, I never spent much time thinking about what form of alcohol I used to pickle my liver before that first sidecar at Warren's. My ex's tastes were . . . shall we say, catholic. Pot, cocaine, acid, mushrooms. Basically, whatever assortment of drugs he could scrounge from his coterie of much-more-successful former classmates from Duke. When drugs weren't available, drinking tequila down to the worm was something he liked to do, though beer would do the trick if he started early enough . . . like at 8:00 A.M. when he dragged ass out of bed. As for me, I was a wino. Liked the good stuff but I'd settle for the house swill if I was out bar-hopping—and what I really liked, embarrassing though it is to admit it, was cheap cava from Spain.

I was probably settling for house swill the first time I saw Janelle order a sidecar. Handing over our drinks as we chatted and scoped out that night's male talent was the lugubrious waiter who always served us on Mondays.

"Thank you," Janelle cooed in her oh-so-proper Louisiana-meets-network-news accent. "I just adore sidecars, and Warren's makes the best in town." She looked avidly down into her glass—one of those cute little martini glasses bars used in the days before they started charging $11 to serve a drink "up"—and took a sip.

"Mmmm," she said, and beamed.

I looked at her drink again, my interest in my glass of wine starting to flag. It was a lovely peachy amber color with a thin line of what I assumed to be salt on the rim.

"What's in it?" I asked.

"Brandy, lemon, cointreau—or really any orange liqueur."

"With salt on the rim! Sounds . . . nasty."

"Silly! It's sugar!" she said with her tinkling laugh. "Here, try it."

How to describe the delicate balancing of brandy, citrus tartness, that hint of sweetness on the back of the tongue and the lips? My breath caught. I looked down at the glass and then at her.

Again, the tinkling laugh. "I love sidecars," she cooed, flipping her buttercup hair. "It's like an old Hollywood glamour drink. Rita

Hayworth with a full-length mink slung over one shoulder dragging the floor. Nick and Nora Charles dancing the night away . . . Mystery and danger and romance." She took another sip.

Mystery? Danger? Romance? And a lovely fruit-scented taste with a kick like a Texas mule at the back end? I waved the sad-eyed waiter over. Forget the house wine. I was having a sidecar.

That was the beginning of a love affair that's lasted, like my friendship with Janelle, for nearly 20 years. Our lives, of course, have changed. For the better? I guess so.

Janelle found "true love" 15 years ago, married her man, and moved with him to New Mexico. They dance the tango, the foxtrot, and the waltz a few nights a week, cheek to cheek, in a ballroom dance community they joined there. Neither one of them has touched a drop of alcohol in over a decade. But then the drinking in Houston, like the fun, *was* epic.

As for me, I get my live music fix these days singing in my church choir.

Umm-hmm, that's right. I've turned into a church lady—at least the cradle Episcopalian version of that: Altar Guild and home communion, Domestic Violence Teach-Ins, pet blessings. That kind of thing.

I still love to dance, but it mostly happens at the odd house party or, ahem, gala. I'm less of a drinker these days. But I still love the color and the taste and the smell of a well-made sidecar.

My party-hearty days were so far in the past that I had frankly forgotten all about the sidecar. What reminded me was the "martini bar" craze that swept the Southern college town I now call home. You recall the martini bar craze, don't you? Perhaps your town is still in the grips of one? In mine, the craze involved heavy cardstock, prices that in other times would have bought an entrée with salad, and shall we be kind and call them *whimsical* combinations of flavors. My epiphany came as I was nibbling Asian-fusion tapas and pondering the martini menu at a hipster hangout called Bang.

Now Bang has its charm. The walls are a fiery red, the heavy wooden furnishings stained nearly black, and the aforementioned Asian tapas may be oxymoronic, but they've got plenty of bang. What did not bang, what landed with a leaden thud for me, were the flavor combinations on the martini menu: ginger-lemon, cucumber-kiwi, cranberry-curacao.

A word rose up from the depths of my guts, traveled on a puff of air to the tip of my tongue. I spoke it, clearly and aloud: "Bullshit!"

As if I'd conjured her, I saw Janelle, swinging that heavy sheaf of blonde hair. She pursed her lips, cooed "sidecar." And just like that, I remembered. The word called to me, promising relief from frou-frou fruit infusions: a perfect balance of orange and lemon essences, brandied heat, just a breath of sweetness at the back of the tongue and on the lips . . .

Of course, the bartender at Bang, a child with a nose piercing and blue highlights in her dishwater blonde hair, had never heard of the drink.

She did try . . . and served up a disaster for which I dutifully paid. But perhaps if I'd known that this storyline—bartenders trying, and failing, to make a drinkable sidecar—would become the news crawl underlying the next two years my life, I'd've gotten a beer.

That's correct. For two full years, no matter what the top story was—dating X, breaking up with Y, working for Z, quitting work to finish my long-delayed degree—the ticker at the bottom of the screen would be telling off plot points in my quixotic quest to find "the perfect sidecar." During which I learned a fact as startling in its implications as it was annoying and expensive to endure: that there was not a single bartender in the entire town of hip, New South sophisticates in which I lived capable of making a sidecar that met the rigorous standard established by Warren's.

Not at Bang or C&O, Blue Light or Rapture, Fellini's or Blue Moon could I find one. Not at Ten. Not even at Boheme—which for a brief, glorious time had a Sunday brunch that, for overall quality, consistency, creative use of local ingredients, and price, surpassed anything I've tasted in the borders of the continental United States. No day, no how, nowhere was I able to find even an adequate sidecar.

I lost my pride. I sunk so low that, once, dining way out in the county at a (shudder) chain restaurant, I rolled the dice—what the hey!—and received for my daring a surprise: a drink that was peachily amber, frosty, with both smoothness and a bit of a bite. I asked Wellington, the scornful redhead who served it (verily, a prince, a strutting stud among bartenders!) for his secret. Knowing I could never duplicate his feat, he smiled indulgently and told me.

Champagne.

And OK, I'll admit it. Even though I was wearing a shapeless Flax dress and shoes with arch support and carrying a "sensible" purse, I had a Houston flashback—complete with strobe lighting, a thumping bass beat, and the unshakable conviction that the night would be mine.

I asked Wellington for his schedule, made a date to come back for another sidecar. But by the time I made my way back up to his side of town, my stud bartender had quit the job. (Working for a chain was so clearly beneath him). And in that way of fabulous service people, the true pros who brighten your life briefly and then disappear, I never saw him again.

After Wellington, the whole thing began to seem faintly ridiculous. And then just plain ridiculous. It had been nearly two decades, after all, since anyone had called me the Queen of the Zydeco Ballroom. What need did a woman like the one I'd become—a woman whose idea of a good day was six solid hours spent writing in flannel pajamas—have for a signature cocktail?

I decided to take an oath to officially forget the word once again. Staring into the mirror and looking serious, I even raised my right hand: "I will never, ever order a sidecar again," I said, looking like I meant business.

Because I did mean business.

And I was firm in my resolve for two whole days—until that crisp October day when Tonia took me out to lunch to introduce the idea of cocktail hour at her "gay college homecoming."

Tonia is one of the people in my life who helps me to measure the distance I've come since those frantic years in Houston. She's Newark, not New Orleans. Remembers the old Times Square. Once managed to navigate the subway tunnels from Penn to Grand Central Station without ever emerging into the winter cold. Tonia loves Daily Kos and tinkering with something called CSS. She loves music—but her refusal to dance is adamantine and her lack of interest in fashion . . . well, for someone like me, it's simply breathtaking to observe. Tonia wears jeans almost every day. For dress-up, she wears black jeans. She confesses readily and without shame that her mother picks out all her "good" clothes.

So back to the gay college homecoming. Tonia is a "Serp," a member of the Serpentine Society—a not-so-secret society of gay alumni of the University of Virginia named for Thomas Jefferson's famed serpentine walls. A small group of Serps was breaking off from the main group to meet for cocktails downtown, and there was someone I just *had* to meet: a former classmate who was now editing a literary journal with a venerable "Southern letters" pedigree. The guy, she swore, would adore me, publish my work, change my life . . .

I understood perfectly, of course: She wanted to go, but didn't want to roll in without a date, and I would do in a pinch. I gave a bit of thought to the question of what the well-dressed straight-woman-passing-for-a-lesbian might wear to such an affair—then said, "Sure. Why not?"

We stepped into Escafé a little after 8:00 P.M. the following evening, a Friday. The joint was absolutely jammed with people, the throbbing house music so loud that the aquatic walls actually seemed to vibrate.

Tonia quickly found her friends, but the table was full, so after making myself pleasant for a few moments I moseyed over to the bar to order . . . and I got a tingle up the back of my neck. Tonight could be the night, I found myself musing. I could actually get lucky.

I ran an assessing eye over the blond bartender. He could have been the twin—or actually, the son—of the skinny blond painter Janelle had worshiped from afar almost twenty years ago. There was a wispy zydeco dot below his pouting lower lip. It made him look even younger . . . I hesitated.

"Can you make a sidecar?" I yelled over the pulsating music. I had to yell it twice before he heard.

"Sure," he said, and went to work. He didn't look quizzical, ask for instructions, or secretly consult a book under the bar. He just whipped out the brandy and Cointreau and started pouring.

I turned to check on Tonia—a few more preppie, fortyish guys had arrived. Chairs were being lifted over heads, tables shoved together. I observed idly that the girls' team must've opted for a bar with pool tables. When I looked back over my shoulder at the baby bartender, the drink had arrived.

I found myself holding my breath. The drink was the right color. It had sugar on the rim of the glass—I hadn't told him about that. The kid . . . might actually have game. I took a sip . . .

. . . and the flavors pooled on my tongue, detonating wave after wave of remembrance. Janelle whipping around town in her sporty red hatchback. Power walking with our dogs along Buffalo Bayou. Playing Ella Fitzgerald, Bob Marley, and Al Green—the same three songs, over and over again—on that legendary jukebox at La Carafe . . .

I wanted to laugh. My eyes flooded with quick tears. Because there's one detail I left out. Janelle, my beautiful, gay Janelle, has M.S. She's had it, actually, for nearly two years. And more recently, she's been seriously ill, suffering from a neuralgia so painful that she has no will to write, to tend her beautiful roses, or even to eat. She'll drag herself out of bed to dance on Friday nights—and rest for three days afterward. Talking on the phone tires her. Sitting at the computer and writing emails tires her. I began counting the months since I'd heard her voice as I stood there. Had it really been so many?

I set the drink down and gave myself over to the thought: *I miss Janelle.*

I realized I've been missing her, quite a lot, without fully allowing myself to own the feeling, for many, many years. And this bumbling down blind alleys in search of the perfect sidecar had, in effect, been a search for her.

"How is it?" I looked up to see a faint line of worry between the baby bartender's eyes. Tears are probably not the reaction he's accustomed to evoking—at least not at the first sip of the first drink.

I glanced back over my shoulder at Tonia, then back into his eyes. Sidecars, I was thinking, are meant to be drunk in twos.

I gave him a smile as big as Texas.

"It's fantastic, the best I've had in years!" I shouted. "And I'll have one more—without sugar this time—for my friend Tonia."

And tomorrow, by God, I told myself: I was calling Janelle.

———•◦•———

The Goddess of Gumbo's Sidecar Recipe
4 measures of brandy
2 measures of Cointreau or other orange-flavored liqueur
Juice of two lemons
Splash of simple sugar to taste

Chill two martini glasses. Swipe the rims with lemon and roll in sugar if desired. Pour liquids into a shaker full of ice and shake well. Adjust flavors to taste. Strain into the martini glasses, and enjoy with a friend.

Rahab's Thread

Katie Burgess

As a child, I loved the names of biblical whores: Jezebel, Delilah, Salome. The name "Mary" looked so blah without a "Magdalene" attached to it. In Sunday school we learned about the virtuous woman of Proverbs 31, the one who "seeketh wool, and flax, and worketh willingly with her hands," who "riseth also while it is yet night, and giveth meat to her household," who "layeth her hands to the spindle." The illustrations on our classroom posters, though, sent a different message. In those pictures, the good women like Martha and Ruth generally wore plain, bulky brown robes and seemed to spend most of their time holding up jugs, while the bad women always had chic red tunics, fabulous jewelry, and come-hither stares. How could anyone look at them and still giveth a crap about wool and flax and spindles?

My favorite was Rahab, the streetwalker who helped hide two Israelite spies—she was sort of an Old Testament Bond girl. Because of her courage, her house, marked by a red thread, was spared during the Battle of Jericho. I didn't understand what Rahab did for a living. I thought "streetwalker" meant that she exercised. It was the '80s, and everyone was power walking. I used to read and reread her story and think how if I ever had a daughter, I would name her Rahab.

I didn't plan on having children, though. My future, as I saw it, involved owning ten cats and becoming a famous artist—the end. When I heard stories about women screaming in delivery rooms, I'd think, *No thanks*. I understood that the pain of childbirth was womankind's punishment for Eve eating of the tree of knowledge. I didn't question the justice of such a punishment. I simply figured I'd beat the system by never getting married, which, as far as I knew, meant that I couldn't be impregnated.

I didn't know where babies came from, but I thought I did. I thought that getting married was how you let God know you were ready for a baby. Then *boom*, it appeared inside you. In the case of the Virgin Mary, I supposed that God was in a hurry for her to have Jesus, and so he didn't wait for her to marry Joseph. Why Joseph would be so freaked out about it, I had no idea. I didn't know what "virgin" meant; I assumed it was some kind of Christmas-y nonsense word, like "wassailing" or "figgy pudding." She might as well have been the Fa La La La La Mary, as far as I was concerned. I had no idea that there was more to conception, or that men had anything to do with it. I saw fathers as a mere formality—nice enough to have, but not strictly necessary. I did notice that there were lots of jokes on TV about kids asking their parents where babies came from and the parents getting uncomfortable, but this still didn't make me wonder if there was something more I didn't know. I attributed such jokes to the fact that most sitcom families were non-Christian—you never saw them praying or going to church—and so they were afraid to tell their children that babies came from God.

I never tried to verify these assumptions with my parents. I was sure I was correct, so why would I? I'd also learned at an early age that it was useless to ask them for information. The simplest questions—like "What's breastfeeding?"—tended to make my mother go all weird and quiet on me, while my father would give me unhelpful non-answers. I remember asking him once why Scooby-Doo had spots. He looked up from his magazine, shrugged, and said, "I guess that's the way God made him."

One afternoon I saw a public service announcement about teen pregnancy. "I didn't think it could happen to me," the voice-over said as a tiny adolescent girl rubbed her abdomen. Here was a whole new thing to worry about. Apparently God, for whatever infinitely wise reasons, might sometimes choose to make you pregnant, even if you were unmarried and still a kid. *Pregnancy could come at you out of nowhere.* If the girl in the ad wasn't safe, neither was I. I began monitoring my belly constantly, certain that little Rahab was already on her way. Every night I prayed about it.

"Dear God," I would say, "please, please, please don't let me be pregnant. I'm only in the second grade. I mean, Thy will be done." I knew I was always supposed to add that part. "But really, please, can I not have a baby right now?"

"I can't promise you that," God would answer in a voice that I felt deep down. "My ways are mysterious. If I start making promises about what will or won't happen, my ways won't be mysterious anymore. They'll be—not mysterious."

"Can You at least promise that I won't have a baby this year?"

"Nope. You're going to have to wait and see what happens. You're going to be so totally surprised!"

I did, however, know about sex. Or rather, I knew the mechanics of it without knowing what it was exactly. Summer*, one of my neighborhood friends, was older and knew things. She was sophisticated, already wearing makeup and pantyhose in fourth grade. The scenarios she came up with for Ken and Barbie were downright disturbing. Summer explained everything to me, but she didn't have words for everything she described. She talked about boys having a "ding-dong," which was confusing, since that was also her cat's name. My mother grew suspicious of my friend's influence. "Did you learn that from Summer?" was her inevitable question whenever I said something that, unbeknownst to me, was inappropriate.

I tried inviting Summer to church with us, thinking that would placate my parents. She showed up to children's Bible study with teased

---

* Name has been changed to protect privacy.

hair, blue eye shadow, and a jean jacket covered in Bon Jovi buttons. She seemed unimpressed as we sang "Father Abraham" and colored in maps of Israel. When I invited her to come back, she politely declined.

One afternoon we had a fight. I don't know exactly what it was about, only that it involved her failing to follow the rules to a game that I was making up as we went along. Summer began to cry. "I don't know how to act," I remember her saying, over and over. "I don't know how to act." We were at my house, on the porch. My blue plastic kiddie pool was propped against a chair to dry; the cats had peed in it that morning, and my mother had just scrubbed it clean. Summer climbed under the pool and motioned for me to follow, so I did.

The sun shone through the plastic, making everything look blue. There, in that blue glowing world, Summer began telling me about the things she did with her stepfather. As she spoke, I pictured her as Salome, dancing before King Herod. Summer, too, was glamorous.

"And that's why. That's why I don't know how to act," she said. "You have to promise not to tell anyone, though."

I nodded. I knew that these were awful things she had told me, but I also knew I would get in trouble for talking about those parts of the body.

Soon after that, Summer and her family moved across town, and we lost touch. I didn't see her again until we ended up in the same middle school. She looked older by then, much older than thirteen. Sometimes we exchanged shy smiles in the hallway, but we never resumed our friendship. She got placed in the at-risk program and hung around with eighth-grade boys who could drive themselves to school, while I was an honors student and band nerd. I started to avoid her, seeing her as one of the bad kids—I who, of all people, knew better.

———————

Middle school also meant sex ed, for all of us except the two Mormon kids whose parents wouldn't sign the permission forms. I wasn't sure about my parents, but they signed gladly, probably relieved that some other adult would give me the talk. The class was taught by a matronly science teacher who made putting a condom on a banana seem as wholesome as baking a casserole. So many things finally started to become clear; for instance, I now understood many of the jokes on *The Golden Girls*. It was kind of a dirty show, as it turned out. But my grandmother loved it—maybe she didn't get the jokes.

We learned about reproduction, and while I still considered myself a good Baptist girl, now I was a good Baptist girl who didn't go to bed every night begging God not to get her pregnant. I didn't intend to have sex until I was grown up and married to Jonathan Knight from New Kids on the Block, but I found myself forming contingency plans. On the off chance it ever happened, I decided, I would use a condom *and* birth control pills *and* a diaphragm *and* a sponge *and* spermicide; I would gather up all the contraception I could find and fashion it into a type of body armor. Not that it would ever happen. But if it did happen, I would be ready. But it wouldn't happen.

A few years later, our church hired a new youth minister, who started a Bible-based sex ed program of his own to counteract all the public-school brainwashing. The class met on Wednesday nights in the church gymnasium and included pizza, roller skating, and door prizes. One week I won a tape by the Christian rap group DC Talk. Another week I got a T-shirt with Jesus's name inside the Ford logo, with the slogan "Have you considered the Lord lately?" Our school sex ed classes may have been more science-based, but church had them beat in the free stuff department.

We learned that, contrary to what we heard in school, condoms were full of tiny holes and utterly useless in protecting against anything. I couldn't figure out why our teachers would have lied to us like that, unless maybe they were in league with the devil. And yet they *seemed* like decent people. I knew one of them was Presbyterian, which wasn't as godly as being Baptist, but it was respectable.

Even more troubling was finding out how, if we gave into temptation before marriage, we would one day have to go through the humiliation of explaining to our future spouses that we hadn't waited for them. They would be devastated, of course. They would never look at us quite the same way again. Sure, they might forgive us, these noble, long-suffering future spouses, and choose to stay with us, but that would be purely out of a sense of duty. The marriage would pretty much be a sham.

Our basic guideline came from Matthew 5:28: "Whosoever looketh on a woman to lust after her hath committed adultery with her already in his heart." Or, as one of my Sunday school teachers put it, "If holding hands makes you think of going further, then you shouldn't even be doing that." Thankfully, no boys wanted to hold hands with me in high school, so I was safe for the time being. I did develop a habit of silently praying for forgiveness every time I so much as thought about the concept of sex.

"Sorry, God—I am so, so, sorry. Please don't let my impure thoughts ruin my future relationship with Jonathan Knight from New Kids on the Block."

"I have plans for you, my child. Before you came forth out of the womb, I ordained that you should marry Jonathan Knight. But now you would jeopardize those plans?"

"No, God, I think they're awesome plans. I won't think anything dirty ever again. Promise."

"You're thinking of something dirty right now."

"Sorry, Lord—I am so, so, sorry . . ."

———·—·———

When I was in high school, the youth group went to Columbia for a state-wide abstinence rally. It began with the same kinds of warm-up cheers we did at every youth function: "We love Jesus, yes we do! We love Jesus, how 'bout YOU?" A former Miss South Carolina finalist gave the invocation, praying, "Father God, just be here and just guide these beautiful young people, and just help them to keep their clothes on, we just pray." There were skits and Bible readings, and a Christian jam band performed in between presentations.

Most speakers followed a pattern—they would start by saying something about how great sex was, eliciting cheers and giggles. Married speakers came out and said, "I love sex!" or "I have an *amazing* sex life!" The single ones, presumably having no frame of reference, had to resort to reading from Song of Songs, something about how the beloved's body was like a tree or the Tower of Lebanon or a flock of goats. After getting their teenage audience all hot and bothered, it was time to segue into how if we had sex before marriage, a) our future spouses, as we already knew, would love us less, b) we would become so desensitized that, before long, normal, healthy sex wouldn't be enough to satisfy us, and we would become depraved porn addicts, or worse, *homosexuals*, and c) every time we sinned, it would make Jesus relive the agony of his crucifixion. Also, we would get pregnant and contract many terrifying diseases.

At this point in my life, I was going to church a minimum of three times a week. I listened exclusively to Christian music, having recently decided that the New Kids were too edgy. I prayed for forgiveness every time I overheard someone else use a swear word. Yet even I thought the abstinence rally was perhaps a little silly. I knew I wasn't ever going to have premarital sex, so why did I need to sing about it for three hours? I slipped out and spent the afternoon wandering around, looking at all the True Love Waits merchandise for sale: T-shirts, CDs, gold-plated promise rings. The lobby of the Columbia Civic Center looked like the money changers in the temple, only Jesus wasn't there to get upset over it. On the bus ride home, I felt strange but didn't know why.

⸻⸱•⸱⸻

I made it to college without ever facing the temptation of holding hands with a boy. I declared a major in art and joined the Baptist Student Union, then found that I didn't quite fit in either world. My fellow art students wore tongue rings, did drugs, and were openly bisexual. They made pornographic ceramic teapots and shot Super 8 films of naked ladies on stilts. I was scared to death of them. The BSU kids, on the other hand, wore khakis and polos as if we had a uniform, and no one seemed to want to do anything but gather round and sing "Awesome God" three thousand times in a row. At meetings, whenever I mentioned that I was an art major, the first question would be, "So, y'all paint from nude models?" That was all anyone seemed to know about the art department, that we took classes on how to gawk at naked people. "It's only to learn anatomy," I would tell them. "There's nothing weird about it." I hoped I was right; I hadn't taken any figure drawing classes yet.

One night I overheard two BSUers discussing a classmate who "acted gay." Right away one khaki-clad chick said, "I swear, I hate gay people." Point blank, like she was auditioning for the role of Bigoted Townsperson Number Two. I looked around, waiting for someone to respond. My own feelings about homosexuality were conflicted. Growing up, I had learned that we should pray for gays to be cured, but I had also recently seen *Priscilla, Queen of the Desert* and loved it, so now I didn't know. No one contradicted the girl, and the conversation transitioned from there to the upcoming Baptist ski trip. I eventually quit going to meetings.

I gradually became more at home around the art students. Once I did take a nude drawing class, it was no big deal. As I stood face-to-face with my first naked man, I felt a twinge of embarrassment, but my brain immediately moved on to other thoughts, like "Why can't he sit still?" and "Why is the human foot so ridiculously hard to draw?" Adam and Eve must have seen each other like this before the Fall: pure, innocent, boring. It took Satan to make them see their bodies as evil. In art history, we were studying Masaccio's *Expulsion from Paradise*. Our professor asked, in the baby voice she used when she felt like we needed things dumbed down, "You all realize that the original sin was sex, right?" I was confused. I'd always thought that the original sin was knowledge. Although, come to think of it, why was that a sin?

I also discovered soon enough that my still being a virgin didn't stem from any sort of special willpower, but from lack of opportunity. Maybe our youth minister was right to warn against hand holding— or maybe it's that, if you've waited for it long enough, holding hands can become an intensely erotic experience. Whatever it was, I did find myself immediately thinking of going further. I started sleeping—at this point it was *only* sleeping—with my first boyfriend, a nineteen-year-old poet who claimed to be in love after having known me for a few days. Of course this filled me with guilt, but I also hoped that we would get married soon, which would square everything away.

"Dear God," I prayed, "I know I shouldn't keep doing this, but we're probably going to get married after finals week. Plus, I would like to point out that he hasn't technically put it in yet."

"Do you ever wonder," God said, "if what you think is my voice is actually a combination of what other people have told you and what you want to hear?"

"Um . . . what?"

One night my boyfriend and I were watching Pink Floyd's *The Wall* and sipping frozen wine coolers that an older coworker had purchased for him. In such a cliché-packed situation, how could we not end up having sex? This was it. I didn't exactly want to, but I also felt that it was my fault, that I'd led him on by being in his room in the first place. I was afraid it would be rude to say *stop*, and so I never did. During it, I kept thinking that I could see Satan standing over us, watching approvingly. The whole thing was terrible, which was sort of a relief—surely it couldn't count as a sin if I didn't enjoy it? When it was over, my boyfriend apologized, and I realized that I was crying. We broke up soon afterward.

Over the next several months, all I could think about was death and hell and HPV. I was sure I was already pregnant and had every disease, that I would drop dead any day now and then burn for all eternity. Worst of all, my parents would find out that I had had sex.

"Such a tragedy," people would say at my funeral, which would have to be closed casket because of how disfigured all the STDs would have made me by then.

"Yes," my parents would say. "She was so young."

"Of course, she deserved it," people would then say. "After all, she had sex."

"Yes," my parents would sigh and agree. "She deserved it."

After graduation, I spent a year working at the campus bookstore. There was a free-speech platform facing the store, used mainly by traveling preachers. They came every week to denounce such evils as evolution, Hollywood, and women who wore pants. One morning, I was walking to work and stopped to watch one of them. He had attracted a small crowd already—mainly hipsters who enjoyed the spectacle ironically—and he was lambasting them all for their promiscuity. His wife stood behind him. Docile and serene, she wore an ankle-length denim jumper and had angelic blonde curls down past her hips. She was wearing a sandwich board that listed various sexual sins in all caps: "MASTURBATION! ADULTERY! PORNOGRAPHY! ABORTION! SODOMY!" She nodded silently at everything he said and didn't seem to mind having the word "MASTURBATION" right under her face. I listened to the man's ranting for a minute or two and then headed for the bookstore.

"Whore!" the man yelled.

I wasn't sure if he meant me, but I turned and looked back. He was pointing in my direction. It hit me how in another time and place a man like him might have stoned me or burned me at the stake. Now all he could do was wave a sign around and call me names. My heart swelled with love for the 21st century.

"Whore!" he yelled again, right at me.

I considered what the word "whore" meant for him and concluded that I did fit his definition. I remembered my childhood heroes, Jezebel and Rahab. And Eve. Why was he targeting students in the first place, but because knowledge was the original sin?

I smiled and waved, deciding to take the compliment.

ABOUT THE CONTRIBUTORS

Dorothy Allison was born in Greenville, South Carolina, and makes her home in Northern California with her partner Alix and their son, Wolf Michael. She is the author of *Bastard Out of Carolina*, a finalist for the 1992 National Book Award; *Cavedweller*, a national bestseller and a *New York Times* Notable Book of the Year; the memoir *Two or Three Things I Know for Sure*; and the poetry chapbook *The Women Who Hate Me*. She also has a collection of short fiction, *Trash*.

Louella Bryant is the author of *While in Darkness There Is Light: Idealism and Tragedy on an Australian Commune* and *Full Bloom: Short Stories*. Her essays, stories, and poems have won awards and have appeared in *WomenArts Quarterly Journal*, *Hunger Mountain*, and elsewhere. She teaches in the MFA in Writing Program at Spalding University and the New England Young Writers' Conference at the Bread Loaf campus in Vermont.

Katie Burgess lives in South Carolina with her husband, mother-in-law, and various cats. She holds a PhD in creative writing from Florida State University.

Sarah Cheshire is a radical debutante, poet, satirical writer, and collector of postcards and ghost stories. She has been awarded the Academy of American Poets Stuart Friebert Poetry Prize, and her poetry and nonfiction have been published in the *News & Observer* and the *Plum Creek Review*, as well as on PBS.org. Three years ago, she moved from central North Carolina to northeast Ohio, where she studies creative writing and gender studies at Oberlin College. She recently traded in her high heels for a pair of neon-orange Doc Martens.

Sarah Einstein is a PhD candidate in creative nonfiction at Ohio University. Her work has appeared in journals such as *Ninth Letter*, *PANK*, and *Fringe*, and has been awarded a Pushcart Prize. She is also the managing editor of *Brevity*.

Beth Ann Fennelly directs the MFA Program at Ole Miss, where she was named the 2011 Outstanding Liberal Arts Teacher of the Year. She's won grants from the NEA and United States Artists and a Fulbright to Brazil. Fennelly has published three books of poetry and one of nonfiction, all with W. W. Norton. *The Tilted World*, a novel she co-authored with her husband, Tom Franklin, was published by HarperCollins in October 2013. They live in Oxford with their three children.

Sarah Gilbert is a writer, photographer, original mommy blogger, and sometime investment banker living in Portland, Oregon. She is editor in chief of *Stealing Time*, a literary magazine for parents. Sarah received a "notable" mention in *Best American Essays 2012*, and her essay "Veteran's Day" was nominated for a Pushcart Prize; she is currently working on a memoir about life as an army wife, told through the prism of mythical archetypes.

Gail Griffin is the author of three books of nonfiction, most recently *"The Events of October": Murder-Suicide on a Small Campus*. She is also a widely published poet who recently won *Folio* magazine's annual poetry contest, judged by Martha Collins. She lives and writes in Michigan.

Lee Gutkind is founder and editor of *Creative Nonfiction* magazine and has written and edited books about baseball, health care, robots, and creative writing. He is currently Distinguished Writer in Residence at the Consortium for Science, Policy and Outcomes and a professor in the Hugh Downs School of Human Communication, both at Arizona State University.

Aaron Gwyn was raised on a cattle ranch in rural Oklahoma. He is the author of a story collection, *Dog on the Cross* (Algonquin Books, 2004)—a finalist for the New York Public Library Young Lions Fiction Award—and two novels: *The World Beneath* (W. W. Norton, 2009) and *Last of the Cowboys* (Houghton Mifflin Harcourt, 2014). His short stories and creative nonfiction have appeared in *Esquire, McSweeney's, Glimmer Train, The Missouri Review, The Gettysburg Review,* and other magazines, and have been anthologized in *New Stories from the South* and *Best of the West*. He lives in Charlotte, North Carolina, and contributes book reviews, articles, and narrative nonfiction to *Esquire* magazine and Esquire.com.

Ellen Hagan is a writer, performer, and educator. She has received grants from the Kentucky Foundation for Women and held residencies at Hopscotch House and Louisiana ArtWorks. A proud Kentucky writer, she is a member of the Affrilachian Poets and Conjwomen, and a co-founder of the girlstory collective. Her debut collection of poems, *Crowned,* was published by Sawyer House Press in 2010.

Kendra Hamilton's poetry and essays have appeared in *Callaloo,* the *Southern Review, River Styx, Obsidian III,* and others, as well as in the anthologies *Bum Rush the Page: A Def Poetry Jam; The Ringing Ear: Black Poets Lean South;* and the forthcoming *Defining Moments: Reflections of 25 African-American Women Writers*. She is a Cave Canem and a Rockefeller Foundation/Bellagio fellow.

Elane Johnson's nonfiction has appeared in *Brevity, Superstition Review, Sonora Review,* and the *Indianapolis Star,* among other publications. Her award-winning essay "Aftermath" is featured in creative writing programs across the country. She is married to the writer Stephen Ulrich.

River Jordan is the critically acclaimed author of four Southern literary novels filled with mystery and mystical suspense. Her most recent work is a nonfiction bestseller, *Praying for Strangers: An Adventure of the Human Spirit*. She is a regular contributor to *Psychology Today*'s "Spirituality" blog, and the host and producer of the literary radio program *Clearstory*, which airs from Nashville, where she makes her home. She is currently at work on a novel, *The City of Truth*, and a nonfiction book about labyrinths.

C. W. Kelly is a Kentucky native and holds an MA in English from the University of Louisville. She teaches high school and university courses in literature, composition, and critical thinking.

Mendy Knott lives in Fayetteville, Arkansas. Her work reflects her experiences as a former police officer, military veteran, and Southern preacher's kid. She is an award-winning screenplay writer and poet. Her book of poetry, *A Little Lazarus*, was published by Half Acre Press in 2010.

Molly Langmuir is a reporter in New York. She has written for *New York* magazine, the *Village Voice*, *Salon*, and *The Hairpin*.

Sonja Livingston's first book, *Ghostbread*, won the AWP Award for Creative Nonfiction and has been honored with awards from the Barbara Deming Memorial Fund, *The Iowa Review*, and the New York Foundation for the Arts. Essays from her latest collection-in-progress have received Pushcart nominations and an *Arts & Letters* nonfiction prize, and have appeared or are forthcoming in *Fourth Genre*, *Seneca Review*, *South Loop Review*, *River Teeth*, and *Arts & Letters*. Sonja teaches in the MFA program at the University of Memphis.

Georgia native **Elyse Moody** has written about books, travel, and culture for *Elle*, Elle.com, *The Daily Beast*, *BBC Travel*, *Publishers Weekly*, *Kirkus Reviews*, and *Shenandoah*, among other outlets. She holds a BA in English and journalism from Washington and Lee University and an MA in writing from Johns Hopkins University, and currently works as a copy editor and contributor at *Elle*. She lives and writes in Brooklyn.

Adriana Paramo is a cultural anthropologist and writer of women's issues. Her book *Looking for Esperanza*, winner of the 2011 Social Justice and Equity Award, was listed among the top ten best books by Latino authors in 2012. She is also the author of *My Mother's Funeral*, a memoir set in Colombia.

Rachael Peckham is the author of *Muck Fire* (Spring Garden Press) and the recipient of the 2010 Robert Watson Poetry Award. Her essays have been nominated for a Pushcart Prize and received a "notable" mention in *Best American Essays 2012*. Most recently, her work has appeared in *Hotel Amerika* and *Under the Sun*. She currently teaches creative nonfiction at Marshall University in Huntington, West Virginia.

Sheila Raeschild has a PhD in American literature from Tulane University and has had postdoc fellowships from the University of London (twentieth century British literature) and Johns Hopkins University (autobiography as a genre). Her publications include three novels and a volume of poetry. She lives in Santa Fe.

Chelsea Rathburn is the author of two poetry collections, *A Raft of Grief*, recently released by Autumn House Press, and *The Shifting Line*. Her work has appeared in *The Atlantic*, *Ploughshares*, *New England Review*, and other journals. A native of Miami, she is currently at work on a collection of essays that examine her Florida childhood and surviving Hurricane Andrew.

Suzanne Roberts is the author of the memoir *Almost Somewhere* (winner of the 2012 National Outdoor Book Award), as well as four collections of poetry. She was named "The Next Great Travel Writer" by *National Geographic Traveler*, and her work has been published in many literary journals and anthologies, including *The Pacific Crest Trailside Reader* and *Best Women's Travel Writing 2013*. She teaches at Lake Tahoe Community College and for the low-residency MFA program at Sierra Nevada College.

A native New Orleanian, **Sheryl St. Germain** has published ten books of poetry and prose, the latest of which is *Navigating Disaster: Sixteen Essays of Love and a Poem of Despair*. She's won numerous awards for her work, including two NEA awards and the William Faulkner Award for the Personal Essay. She directs the MFA in Creative Writing program at Chatham University in Pittsburgh.

Amy Thigpen is a native New Orleanian whose work has appeared in *The Best Travelers' Tales 2004*; *Hot Flashes: Sexy Little Stories and Poems*, the *San Francisco Chronicle Magazine*; and in online publications including *The Huffington Post*. "The On-Ramp" is part of a memoir-in-progress about the cemeteries and street corners where the author's life and that of her one-hundred-year-old Maw Maw finally intersect. She lives with her husband in Berkeley and New Orleans.

Katie Burgess's "Rahab's Thread" first appeared in *Pembroke Magazine*, Number 45. Reprinted with the author's permission.

Sarah Einstein's "Fat" first appeared in *PANK* 5.10/October 2010. Reprinted with the author's permission.

Kendra Hamilton's "The Search for the Perfect Sidecar" first appeared in *Callaloo* Vol. 32.1/Winter 2009. Reprinted with the author's permission.

A previous version of Sheryl St. Germain's "A Country Where You Once Lived" was published in *The Sun*, Issue 443/January 2012. Reprinted with the author's permission.

Sonja Livingston's "Mad Love: The Ballad of Fred and Allie," Chelsea Rathburn's "The Renters," and Amy Thigpen's "The On-Ramp" first appeared in *Creative Nonfiction* #48/Spring 2013.